SCOTLAND 101

An Introduction to

the National Team SCOTLAND 101

Tom Brogan

pitch

First published by Pitch Publishing, 2023

Pitch Publishing
9 Donnington Park,
85 Birdham Road,
Chichester,
West Sussex,
PO20 7AJ
www.pitchpublishing.co.uk
info@pitchpublishing.co.uk

A CIP catalogue record is available for this book from the British Library.

ISBN 978 1 80150 496 6

Typesetting and origination by Pitch Publishing

Printed and bound in India by Thomson Press

Contents

Acknowledgements 11
Introduction 12
1. Scotland 0 England 0 – 1872 13
2. The First Hampden Park – 1873 17
3. Andrew Watson 19
4. Archibald Primrose, 5th Earl of Rosebery 22
5. Robert Smyth McColl 24
6. Robert Cumming Hamilton 27
7. Scotland 4 England 1 – 1900 29
8. The Ibrox Disaster – 1902 31
9. The Game That Changed the Offside Law – 1906 . . 35
10. Alan Morton 37
11. England 1 Scotland 5 – 1928 40
12. Hughie Gallacher Scores Five – 1929 44
13. Norway 3 Scotland 7 – 1929 47
14. The Hampden Roar 49
15. Scotland 2 Austria 2 – 1933 52
16. Tommy Walker 55
17. Scotland 2 Germany 0 – 1936 57
18. Scotland 3 England 1 – 1937 62
19. Scotland XI 5 England 4 – 1942 65
20. Billy Liddell 68
21. George Young 71
22. Jimmy Cowan 74
23. Lawrie Reilly 77
24. The SFA Refuse to Accept Scotland's Place at the 1950 World Cup 80
25. Bobby Collins 83
26. The Scotland Badge – 1953 86
27. Uruguay 7 Scotland 0 – 1954 88

28. Scotland 2 Hungary 4 – 1954. 91
29. Sir George Graham. 95
30. Scotland 4 Spain 2 – 1957 97
31. Matt Busby as Scotland Manager – 1958 100
32. France 2 Scotland 1 – 1958 105
33. Scotland Under-23s 4 England Under-23s 4 – 1960 . 108
34. England 9 Scotland 3 – 1961 111
35. Czechoslovakia 4 Scotland 2 (AET) – 1961 117
36. Denis Law Scores Three Hat-Tricks in a Year and a Day – 1962/63 121
37. Mr Baxter Goes to Wembley – 1963 125
38. Spain 2 Scotland 6 – 1963 128
39. John White 131
40. Alan Gilzean 133
41. Austria Abandoned – 1963 135
42. Scotland 1 Italy 0 – 1965 139
43. Pelé Comes to Glasgow – 1966. 143
44. England 2 Scotland 3 – 1967 147
45. Tommy Gemmell Boots Helmut Haller – 1969 . . . 156
46. Peter Lorimer. 159
47. Edna Neillis 161
48. Scotland 2 Czechoslovakia 1 – 1973 165
49. Jimmy Johnstone Goes to Sea – 1974. 169
50. The Copenhagen Five – 1975 172
51. Scotland Under-23s 2 Netherlands Under-23s 0 (AET; Netherlands Win 4-3 On Penalties) – 1976 . 176
52. Scotland win the Cannes Youth Tournament – 1976 179
53. Bruce Rioch. 182
54. The Wembley Invasion – 1977 185
55. Santiago – 1977. 190
56. Anfield – 1977 195
57. Ally's Tartan Army – 1978 200

58. The Hampden Send-Off – 1978 202
59. Teófilo Cubillas. 205
60. Archie Gemmill's Goal Against the Netherlands – 1978 209
61. Maradona Comes to Glasgow – 1979 212
62. First to Have Names on Shirts – 1979 216
63. The Tories vs Hampden Park 218
64. Scotland Win the European Under-18 Championship – 1982 222
65. Scotland the Brave 225
66. The Toepoke – 1982 228
67. Scotland 3 Spain 1 – 1984 231
68. The Death of Jock Stein – 1985 235
69. Only a Game? – 1986. 252
70. Only an Excuse? – 1986 254
71. Uruguay 0 Scotland 0 – 1986. 257
72. Andy Roxburgh. 262
73. Arthur Montford 265
74. The U16 World Championship Final – 1989 268
75. Flower of Scotland 272
76. Juan Cayasso – 1990 276
77. Ally McCoist 279
78. Scotland Under-21s 4 Germany Under-21s 3 – 1992. 283
79. The Gentleman's Agreement – 1992. 286
80. Portugal 5 Scotland 0 – 1993. 288
81. The SFA vs Duncan Ferguson – 1994 292
82. Gary McAllister's Penalty Miss – 1996 296
83. Estonia Fail to Arrive – 1996. 299
84. Julie Fleeting 302
85. Hugh McIlvanney 304
86. Tom Boyd. 307
87. Jim Leighton 309

88. Berti Vogts 312
89. Scotland 1 Netherlands 0 – 2003 316
90. James McFadden from 35 Yards – 2007 319
91. Scotland 1 Italy 2 – 2007 322
92. Boozegate – 2009 325
93. 4-6-0 – 2010 329
94. Professor Stewart Hillis 332
95. Scotland 2 England 2 – 2017 335
96. Women's World Cup – 2019 338
97. Andy Robertson 341
98. John McGinn 344
99. Serbia 1 Scotland 1 (AET; Scotland Win 5-4 on Penalties) – 2020 347
100. 'Yes Sir, I Can Boogie' 351
101. Scotland 2 Spain 0 – 2023 353

Bibliography 357

For my dad Jim (1928–1997), who originally told me about many of the players and the games mentioned in this book, and my mum Cathy (1935–2022), who never stopped supporting me.

Acknowledgements

THIS BOOK would have been so much harder to write without the number of people who ensure that Scottish football history is kept alive online. In particular, my friend Andy Smith who runs the @ScotsFootyCards Twitter page; Miles McClagan, who scans a multitude of programmes for his Flickr account, The Sky Strikers; and Londonhearts.com for the large database of Scottish international facts and figures.

Also, thanks are due to everyone who contributes to and maintains the scottishleague.net forum, which has been a valuable source for information on all aspects of Scottish football history for many years, and David and Robert, who run the Scotland Epistles website/Facebook/Twitter and produce the *Scotland Forever! Football Magazine*.

I'd like to thank Jane at Pitch Publishing for the opportunities provided to me, and thanks to Duncan Olner for the excellent cover design.

A big thank you to everyone who bought and said nice things about my first book, *We Made Them Angry*. Thanks to my brother Chic and my cousin Jan for their support and encouragement. Thanks to Andy Bollen for his advice. Thanks to Megan Stamper and the staff of the Scottish Football Museum at Hampden Park.

Introduction

THE SCOTTISH national team has offered several highs and lows over the years and created many heroes and villains. This book aims to capture a few of them and provide an introduction to some of the bright spots and lowlights the national team has provided since its formation.

In these pages, you will meet some of the talents that lit up the game, encounter some of the bureaucracy that, for some reason, Scottish football does so well, and read about the games, events, feats, songs and goals that linger in the memory as well as the matches that fans may rather forget. I also look at some of the people outside the game who have contributed to what Scottish football means to all that follow it.

Willie Allan, who was the Scottish Football Association secretary from 1957 until 1977, once said, 'Us Scots do not behave in spite of failures but because of them. Because we have never reached the top, we can allow ourselves to feel that we are always about to do so. It's precisely because we have no past standard to live up to that we travel with great hope that this may be the day.' Since he said that, Scottish teams have established standards to live up to but also to live down. The hope lives eternal.

1

Scotland 0 England 0 – 1872

30 November 1872
West of Scotland Cricket Ground, Glasgow
Attendance: 2,500

Scotland: Gardner [C] (Queen's Park), Kerr (Granville and Queen's Park), Taylor (Queen's Park), Thomson (Queen's Park), J. Smith (South Norwood and Queen's Park), R. Smith (South Norwood and Queen's Park), Weir (Queen's Park), Leckie (Queen's Park), Rhind (Queen's Park), Mackinnon (Queen's Park), Wotherspoon (Queen's Park)

England: Barker (Hertfordshire Rangers and Wanderers), Greenhalgh (Notts Club), Welch (Harrow Chequers and Wanderers), Chappell (Oxford University), Ottaway [C] (Oxford University), Smith (Oxford University), Chenery (Crystal Palace), Clegg (Sheffield), Brockbank (Cambridge University), Maynard (1st Surrey Rifles), Morice (Barnes and Harrow Chequers)

Referee: William Keay (honorary treasurer, Queen's Park)

THERE HAD been five unofficial matches played between Scotland and England sides before this date; the first, in March 1870 at Kennington Oval, resulted in a 1-1 draw. The most recent encounter had been in February 1872, again at the Oval, when a Scotland team lost 1-0.

In March of 1872, Glasgow's Queen's Park played against Wanderers of London in the semi-final of the FA Cup. The game finished goalless, but Queen's Park could not afford to travel again to London for the replay, so scratched from the competition.

Charlie Alcock, England's captain in all five unofficial internationals, wrote in his 1906 book *Football The Association Game*[1] that this fixture 'was, beyond a doubt, mainly responsible for the institution of an international match between England and Scotland on a strict basis'.

Alcock felt that the previous games were not representative of football in Scotland as the players selected for Scotland were all habitants of southern England of Scottish extraction, adding 'And in some cases perhaps of even less substantial qualifications.' Alcock felt that the Wanderers-Queen's Park game could be called a bona fide international as the Queen's Park players were all Scots based in Scotland.

He issued a challenge in a Glasgow newspaper for England to play 11 Scots. His plan was to authenticate football in Scotland, which was at the time a poor relation to rugby. There had been a Scotland-England rugby international in Edinburgh in 1871, followed by a return in London a year later.

A letter signed by representatives of the leading rugby clubs appeared in *The Scotsman*, pointing out the absurdity of Scotland taking part in an international match played with rules that the majority of Scottish footballers, who played rugby, were unfamiliar with. 'There was, of course, a good deal of sense in the objection,' Alcock wrote, 'but as was only to be expected, it did not have any effect in checking the advance of the Association game.'

No organised body existed in Scotland, so Queen's Park agreed to host the match in Glasgow and took on responsibility for all the arrangements and for selecting the Scotland team. Their secretary Archibald Rae put out a call for players in the press.

Queen's Park had no ground of their own at the time. Glasgow Academical Rugby Club offered their Burnbank home free of charge. However, it was not enclosed so admission couldn't be charged. The West of Scotland Cricket Club's ground in Hamilton Crescent, Partick met that criteria, and the club

---

1 Republished in 2014 as *The Classic Guide to Football*

received £20 for its hire. As well as cricket, the ground regularly hosted rugby matches.

Trial matches had been played, and various possible players had been looked at, but the Queen's Park committee opted to draw the Scottish team exclusively from their members.

The Scotland team wore the Queen's Park strip of dark-blue shirts with a red, single-lion crest, white knickerbockers, with blue-and-white-striped socks (Queen's Park's now-famous black-and-white one-inch stripes only came into being in late 1873).

The crowd was estimated at 2,500. They paid one shilling entry each. Ladies were admitted free. There had been rain over the past few days and fog the previous evening. The rain in the morning had relented, and by the time the teams came out, the sun was just about shining.

The game kicked off 15 minutes later than the advertised time of 2pm. 'The Scotchmen won the toss, and the strangers kicked off at a quarter past two,' wrote the *Glasgow Herald*.

Scotland played in a 2-2-6 formation, while England lined up in a 1-2-7 shape. There was a contrast in style between the two teams. It was noted by the *Glasgow Herald* that England 'had all the advantage of weight, their average being about two stones heavier than the Scotchmen'. England played a style which relied on individual dribbling and playing the ball forward, while the Scottish team played a passing game.

At half-time, goalkeeper Robert Gardner swapped places with forward Robert Smith. England did similar, with Barker going outfield and Maynard taking his place in goal.

The Scotsman summed the game up, 'The match, after an hour and a half's play, ended in a draw, Scotland having the best of it in the first half of the game, England in the second.'

The English weekly sporting paper, *Bell's Life*, reported that the match was 'one of the jolliest, one of the most spirited and most pleasant matches that have ever been played'.

In February 1873, Archibald Rae wrote to Scottish clubs playing the association rules to recommend the formation of the Scottish Football Association (SFA) and set up Scotland's own cup competition. The founding meeting of the SFA was held at

Dewar's Hotel on 13 March 1873, just five days after Scotland had lost a return match at the Oval 4-2 to England.

Association football had now become firmly established in Scotland.

2

The First Hampden Park – 1873

THE PROFIT made from the match at Hamilton Crescent in 1872 amounted to £33. The committee at Queen's Park, who couldn't charge for admission as they didn't have an enclosed ground, began to think of establishing a ground of their own where they could charge spectators to see them play.

An application was made by W. Ker, J.J. Thomson and R. Leckie to the Corporation of Glasgow, who gave Queen's Park a corner of ground flanked by Hampden Terrace.

The row of houses gave the ground its name. The houses were erected by Glasgow builder George Eadie, who named them after John Hampden, an English parliamentary leader who died at the Battle of Chalgrove Field in 1643.

The ground was originally let from October 1873 to 1 May 1874, when the rental was £20. This was later increased to £100 annually. A sum of £21 was spent on the original clubhouse, which was replaced in 1878 when the pavilion of the defunct Caledonian Cricket Club was bought, transported and re-erected at Hampden.

The ground opened with a Scottish Cup tie between Queen's Park and Dumbreck on 25 October 1873. Queen's Park also used this occasion to debut their new black-and-white-hooped shirts.

The first international played there was Scotland's ninth game overall, a 7-2 win over England, where John McDougall became the first player to score a hat-trick for Scotland. 'Scotland sent a very formidable 11 into the field, and as they were lighter and passed the ball better than the Southerners, the result was an easy victory,' reported *The Times*. It was the first time England had played in a purpose-built venue.

On Saturday, 11 March 1882, England visited once more. Scotland were 2-1 up at half-time. *The Times* wrote, 'The second half, however, proved disastrous to the Englishmen, who seemed to have shot their bolt in defending their goal in the first half, because they did not play so well and could not retain the ball when they did get possession.' Scotland won 5-1.

The last international there was a 5-0 win over Wales in March 1882.

Queen's Park were forced to move in 1884 due to the building of the Cathcart Circle railway line. The second Hampden Park was not far from the original site and opened on 18 October 1884.

Having to vacate that location for building work in 1899, the Queen's Park committee began work on what is the present-day Hampden Park. Queen's Park bought 12 and a half acres of land south of Mount Florida and fronting Somerville Drive for the sum of £10,000. The first match at the new ground was Queen's Park's league game with Celtic on 31 October 1903. The first time Scotland played there was in April 1906 in a 2-1 win over England.

The exact location of the first Hampden had been lost over the years but, in 2017 Graeme Brown, Hampden Bowling Club secretary, made it his mission to find the location. His search took him through Queen's Park's history, the National Library of Scotland's maps, and the National Record of Scotland logs until he discovered a railway map proving the first Hampden Park was on the site where Hampden Bowling Club now sits.

In 2019 artist Ashley Rawson created a mural depicting Scotland's victory over England in 1882, on the pavilion's rear wall. It depicts Andrew Watson and Charles Campbell and can be seen from the trains that travel into Hampden from Glasgow Central.

3

Andrew Watson

3 caps (1881/82)

WITH ONLY three caps to his name in 1881/82, Andrew Watson made a big imprint on Scottish football in a short period, although it took many years for his legacy to be widely acknowledged. He was a largely forgotten figure of the Scottish game until 1992 when Ged O'Brien, the director of the Scottish Football Museum, and his staff saw that Watson was awarded his rightful place as a trailblazer.

O'Brien found a book on Queen's Park players in which he noticed a black player, although there had been nothing up until then to acknowledge any black footballers playing in Scotland in the 19th century. He was then given SFA annuals by the Scottish Football Association. Inside there were pictures of teams who played against England, Wales and Ireland. There, O'Brien noticed the same player. 'We were able to start our serious search to find out who this man was,' he said. O'Brien's focus was not only that Watson was the first black Scottish player but also on how influential he was to the game.

Watson was born on 25 May 1856 in Demerara, in what was then known as British Guyana. His mother, Anna or Hannah Rose, was from Guyana, and his father was Peter Miller Watson, a sugar planter and former slave owner born in Kiltearn, near Dingwall.

At the age of five or six, Andrew and his sister Annetta joined their father for a new life in Britain, where he was educated in the English public school system. When his father passed away in

1869, Andrew inherited enough money to keep him comfortable for the rest of his life, and indeed he used some of his wealth to forward the game in Scotland.

Watson's footballing talent was discovered while a student at King's College School in London. In 1875 he attended the University of Glasgow, where he studied engineering. He played football for local sides Maxwell FC and Parkgrove. At Parkgrove, based in Govan, Watson put some of his money into the club, finding them a ground to play at.

Queen's Park, the biggest name in Scottish football of the era, spotted the stylish full-back, and not only did he play for them, but he was also the match secretary.

His debut for the national team came on 12 March 1881 at the Oval against England, where he became the first black international footballer. Watson captained the Scottish team, who won 6-1. It remains England's record home defeat. The game also saw the first international own goal when England's Edgar Field scored Scotland's fourth. Watson's second cap was two days later in a 5-1 win over Wales. On 9 April, he won his first Scottish Cup with Queen's Park, the club's fifth.

A profile in the *Scottish Referee* in 1902 noted, 'Andrew Watson's bearing was that of a gentleman both on and off the field of play. If he charged an opponent, he did not, after the manner of some modern boorish backs, glory in the act, for he was ready with a kindly, "Beg your pardon, are you hurt?"'

His final cap came in March 1882 as a 25-year-old at Hampden Park in a 5-1 win over England.

After Queen's Park's 1882 Scottish Cup win, Watson moved back to London to continue his engineering career. The move ended his international career as the Scottish Football Association would only select players based in Scotland to play for the country.

Down south, he continued his football career, although still an amateur, playing for London Swifts, where he became the first black man to play in the FA Cup. He also played for the prestigious amateur team Corinthian FC.

His wealth allowed him to make frequent trips north of the border, and he returned to Queen's Park to win a third Scottish

Cup in 1886. As he was not a permanent resident of Scotland, the SFA still wouldn't select him.

Moving to Merseyside, where he worked as a maritime engineer, he also played for Bootle FC. Watson is listed as a crew member on many ships leaving Liverpool for the Americas.

Watson died aged 64 on 8 March 1921 in Kew. He was inducted into the Scottish Football Hall of Fame in 2012.

It would be 2004 before another black player earned a full cap for Scotland when Portsmouth's Nigel Quashie started a friendly against Estonia.

4

Archibald Primrose, 5th Earl of Rosebery

Honorary president of the SFA

BORN IN May 1847 into a family of Scottish landowners, Archibald's father died when he was three. After attending a boarding school in Hertfordshire, he went to Eton between 1860 and 1865. In 1866 he entered Christ Church, Oxford but left in 1869 without taking a degree when university authorities gave him a choice of giving up either his studies or his racehorse Ladas.

On the death of his grandfather, the 4th Earl of Rosebery, on 3 March 1868, Archibald Primrose, at 19 years of age, became the 5th Earl of Rosebery, inheriting a fortune and a seat in the House of Lords.

Lord Rosebery first became a public figure when he managed William Ewart Gladstone's successful Midlothian campaign in 1879. On his public appearances, he and his wife were regularly met by crowds, attaining celebrity status.

His political career within the Liberal Party led him to reluctantly become Gladstone's successor as prime minister in March 1894. His government lasted only until June 1895. He resigned as Liberal leader the following year. He was much more successful as a racehorse owner. His horses won the Epsom Derby three times; Ladas in 1894, Sir Visto in 1895 and Cicero in 1905.

Roseberry's love of football was unusual for aristocrats of his time. He served as honorary president not only of the Scottish Football Association but also of Heart of Midlothian.

At the 1900 Scotland-England international at Celtic Park, Rosebery was noted by the press to 'wave his hat at every Scottish success, with all the abandon of an Aberdeen tripper in the shilling enclosure'.

Scotland wore Lord Rosebery's racing colours of primrose and rose for the first time in 1881. They were worn on a further ten occasions in his lifetime – in 1900, 1901, 1905, 1906, 1907, 1908 and 1909. They were revived in 1949 and also used in a 1-0 win over France in 1951. The *Glasgow Herald* reported that Scotland wore the Roseberry colours for what would have been the last time in a 3-1 win over Finland in Helsinki in May 1954.

Lord Rosebery's colours made a comeback in the 2014 to 2015 Scotland away kit. It was worn in a 6-0 European Championship qualifier win over Gibraltar in Faro in October 2015.

Literature was also a great love of Lord Rosebery's life, and he wrote many political biographies. He was also chairman of the Royal Fine Arts Commission for Scotland and chairman of the Scottish Tourist Board.

He died in 1929, requesting to hear 'Eton Boating Song' before he passed away.

5

Robert Smyth McColl

13 caps, 13 goals (1896–1908)

ROBERT SMYTH McColl began his career with Queen's Park as an amateur at the age of 18 in 1894. Playing as a forward, McColl made his Scotland debut against Wales on 21 March 1896 in a 4-0 win. A week later, McColl scored two in a 3-3 draw away to Ireland.

McColl's 13 caps came against Wales, Ireland and England. He scored three hat-tricks for Scotland. The first was on 18 March 1899 in a 6-0 win over Wales, the second a week later in a 9-1 win over Ireland, with the third arriving in April 1900 in the 4-1 win over England. It was around that time that the readers of *Scottish Referee* voted him the country's most popular player, receiving three times more votes than the runner-up, Rangers' Alec Smith.

In 1901, McColl was looking to turn professional. The Liverpool manager Tom Watson told the *Sheffield Independent* in 1919 that he received a telephone call from McColl saying he was at the North Western Hotel in Liverpool and 'open for a professional engagement'.

'In a very short time I had laid the matter before my directors,' Watson said, 'but greatly to my chagrin I found that McColl's terms were too much for us. He would not relinquish his amateur status unless he benefitted considerably, and the situation for which he stipulated was beyond the power of the Liverpool club to guarantee.' Watson called his brother-in-law Jack Oliver, a director at Newcastle United. The St James' Park side paid Queen's Park

£600 to sign McColl. McColl used part of his signing-on fee to set up the newsagent chain RS McColl alongside his brother, Tom. This gave him his nickname of 'Toffee Bob'.

The author and journalist Jonathan Wilson credits McColl for beginning a philosophy of possession play that grew in England, stretched across Europe and lives on today through coaches such as Pep Guardiola.

In *The Guardian* in 2013, Wilson wrote of the early days of football's passing philosophy, 'Passing slowly spread, but Queen's Park remained its epicentre, its players schooled in pass-and-move. Then, in 1901, the forward RS McColl took the philosophy to Newcastle United as he turned professional. Newcastle, at the time, were a direct side, but McColl soon persuaded them of the advantages of holding possession. One of the keenest converts was the wing-half Peter McWilliam who, in 1912, was appointed manager of Tottenham.'

At White Hart Lane, McWilliam's players would go on to manage clubs including Tottenham Hotspur, West Bromwich Albion, Ajax and Barcelona, passing on the playing philosophy initially spread by McColl.

McColl returned to Scotland with Rangers in 1904. In 1906 *Scottish Referee* reported on interest in McColl from teams down south. 'He is not disposed now to consider these,' the newspaper wrote, 'largely because his personal nature is not suited to the bustle and rustle of English Leagueism. Our quieter and easier Scottish methods are more in keeping with his modest, sensitive, and rather shy nature.'

Instead of going south, he returned to the amateur ranks and signed once again for Queen's Park. There was, *Scottish Referee* suggested, some consternation among the directors there over re-signing McColl. It seems that some on the board had issues with McColl exporting the Queen's Park way of playing football down south. 'The barrier to RS McColl's re-appearance at Hampden,' the newspaper wrote, 'is caused it is said by a difference of opinion in the directorate, some of whom have retentive memories and are loth to forget the way in which the ex-centre took his *coals* and goals to Newcastle.'

McColl's 13th and final cap for Scotland came almost six years after his 12th, in March 1908. As an amateur, McColl received a gold badge, valued at £2, while the professionals in the team were paid £5. Prior to that match, amateurs received nothing while professionals were paid £3 3s. Scotland won 5-0, with Jimmy Quinn scoring four.

Retiring from the game at the age of 34 in 1910, in 1916 he enlisted in the armed forces, serving in a Mechanical Transport company of the Army Service Corps, attaining the rank of sergeant.

McColl died in 1958 and was inducted into the Scottish Football Hall of Fame in 2011.

6

Robert Cumming Hamilton

11 caps, 15 goals (1899–1911)

BORN IN Elgin, Robert Cumming Hamilton began his career with Elgin City before moving to Glasgow to study at the University of Glasgow. He signed for Queen's Park around 1896, turning professional with Rangers in June 1897.

On the morning before playing in Rangers' 2-0 Scottish Cup Final win over Kilmarnock in 1898, Hamilton sat a three-hour exam at university. He graduated with an MA to qualify as a schoolteacher and eventually became a schoolmaster.

R.C. Hamilton, as he was commonly known, was the top scorer for Rangers in each of their four-in-a-row championship seasons between 1898/99 and 1901/02, combining brilliantly with Alec Smith. He was Rangers' top scorer nine times and Scotland's top scorer six times.

Making his Scotland debut in the 6-0 win over Wales in March 1899, Hamilton scored his first international goals the following week against Ireland in a 9-1 win, netting twice.

Hamilton scored four in an 11-0 win over Ireland in February 1901. A year later, he notched a hat-trick in a 5-1 win in Belfast.

His tenth cap came in a 1-1 draw with Ireland in March 1904, when he scored the Scotland goal. His 11th and final cap came almost seven years later, in 1911. By this time, Hamilton, now 34, was a Dundee player and was a late call-up to the team. He scored two equalisers in a 2-2 draw with Wales.

After his football career, he was involved in local politics, serving on Elgin Town Council between 1914 and 1937 and, for the last six years of this period, he held the position of Lord Provost. Hamilton also carried on the family business of net manufacturing right up until he passed away in May 1948, aged 71.

7

Scotland 4 England 1 – 1900

7 April 1900
Celtic Park, Glasgow
British Home Championship
Attendance: 63,000

Scotland: Rennie (Hearts), Smith (Rangers), Drummond (Rangers),Gibson (Rangers), Raisbeck (Liverpool), Robertson [C] (Rangers), Bell (Celtic), Walker (Hearts), McColl (Queen's Park), Campbell (Celtic), Smith (Rangers)

England: Robinson (Southampton), Oakley (Corinthians), Crabtree (Aston Villa), Johnson (Sheffield United), Chadwick (Southampton), Needham (Sheffield United), Athersmith (Aston Villa), Bloomer (Derby County), Smith [C] (Corinthian FC), Wilson (Corinthians), Plant (Bury)

Referee: James Torrans (Ireland)

Goals:
Scotland – McColl (1, 25, 44), Bell (6)
England – Bloomer (35)

BEFORE THIS date, Scotland had never defeated England by more than one goal. The Scotland team lined up in Lord Rosebery's racing colours of primrose-and-rose hoops. Lord Rosebery watched the match from the balcony of the pavilion, which was also decorated in his colours, while the crowd sang 'For he's a jolly good fellow' in his honour. His son Lord Dalmeny was also present along with Lord Kinnaird of the Football Association.

The official attendance of 63,000 was a new world record for an official international match. The ground struggled to contain the crowd, with several spectators bursting out of the terraces and on to the running track.

Scotland went ahead in the first minute when Robert McColl picked up the ball from a throw-in, beat a defender and shot past John Robinson. It was 2-0 after six minutes when Jack Bell dribbled and scored.

McColl scored his second with 25 minutes gone with a shot that 'whizzed past Robinson at a pace which no one could have stopped'. England's then record goalscorer Steve Bloomer pulled a goal back before McColl completed his hat-trick just before half-time, with a goal that was the 100th England had conceded.

At the end of the match, a crowd converged under the pavilion and shouted to Lord Rosebery for a speech. He dutifully obliged, 'I am pleased to have been present to see Scotland win such a glorious victory over England today. We all hope that no worse civil war will ever occur between us. Football is a grand game for developing courage, pluck, determination, and resistance. While we have seen Scotland win, we must admire the plucky fight made by England. I am very proud that Scotland played in my colours today. I consider it a great compliment and would have gone away disappointed had she not won.'

Match reports were universal in their praise for the Scottish team. 'The Englishmen were quite outclassed,' the *Manchester Guardian* wrote. 'No Scottish 11 ever played better football,' began the match report in *The Scotsman*.

The result gave Scotland the British Home Championship for the eighth time outright, also having two shared titles with England. With 29 contests between the two nations, Scotland had now won 14, England nine, with six draws.

8

The Ibrox Disaster – 1902

THE VENUE for the 31st international between Scotland and England, on 5 April 1902, was decided between two candidates – Ibrox or Celtic Park. Ibrox, which had been redeveloped in 1900, was decided upon by only one vote. Ibrox had hosted Scotland internationals three times previously – twice versus Ireland, in 1889 and 1897, and once against England, in April 1892 when there were 21,000 in attendance. The last international against Wales in March had been played at Cappielow in Greenock.

When Rangers took a lease of Ibrox Park, all the old erections were demolished, and new stands were put up under the supervision of Archibald Leitch and his partner Henry S. Davies. Mr Holmes, the burgh surveyor for Govan, inspected the stands when complete and passed the ground as perfectly safe for large crowds.

The ground was built to accommodate 80,000, and John Kevan McDowall, the secretary of the Scottish Football Association, would later say in court that he had a letter confirming that figure. Prior to the day of the game, the largest crowd the ground had held was around 38,000 to 40,000.

The match, the first time in the fixture's history that both teams were entirely professional, kicked off at 3.30pm, with 68,114 in attendance. Only a few minutes had been played when tragedy struck.

The Scotsman reported the disaster by writing, 'The game had not been long in progress when shortly before four o'clock a portion of the terracing, packed with a seething crowd of humanity, gave way under the unwanted pressure, and between two and three hundred of the spectators were precipitated to the ground from a height of forty or fifty feet.'

A portion of the west terracing, estimated to be around 70ft long by 11ft wide, had given way. The stand, directly behind the English goal, consisted of sloping wooden flooring resting on steel beams supported by steel columns on a concrete foundation. The highest height of the furthest-back columns was 36ft from the ground.

Leitch examined the stand after the accident, and he felt that the wood was not of the finest quality. Instead of the red pine required, it was what was known in the trade as 'bastard yellow pine'.

The game was halted for around 20 minutes before resuming. The majority of the crowd was unaware of the magnitude of the disaster.

The injured were initially taken to the Western Infirmary, but when that became full, cases were dispatched to the Victoria Infirmary. When they also couldn't take any more, the injured were transported to the Royal Infirmary. *The Scotsman* summed up the horror, 'The moans of the injured mingled with the cheers of the unknowing thousands in other parts of the field who were still intent upon the game, and so terrible were the wounds from which many of the victims were suffering that even hardened ambulancemen turned sick at the sight.'

Crowds of women formed outside the ground, hospitals and Govan police station, desperate for news. Among the doctors who attended on the day were Sir Hector Cameron, Dr George Beatson and Dr James H. Nicoll.

The game was played to a conclusion, finishing as a 1-1 draw. Twenty-five spectators died and 587 were injured.

Perversely, blame became attached to one of the Scotland players. Bobby Templeton, then a regular in the number 11 shirt at Aston Villa, was making his debut for Scotland that day. It was alleged that the stand broke under the weight of spectators leaning forward to watch him dribbling around the England defence.

One of the spectators present wrote his account of the accident in the *Dundee Evening Telegraph* many years later, 'Scotland were pressing. The crowd was swaying on the terracing when suddenly part of it collapsed about ten yards from where I stood. Hundreds were pitched forward in a great struggling heap.'

The match was declared void by both the SFA and the English Football Association. The teams replayed in Birmingham the following month in what was primarily a fundraiser for the disaster appeal. The England players handed over half of their three guineas match fee. The £990 gate receipts and money in coins showered down by fans to collectors at the interval also went to the Ibrox Disaster Fund.

Alexander McDougall, the contractor, went on trial at Glasgow High Court in July of 1902, charged with culpable homicide. The prosecution alleged that the defendant failed to erect the stand in a substantial manner – substituting in the yellow pine for red pine. Yellow pine was noted as being greatly inferior in strength, costing around 50 per cent less than red pine. It was also alleged that he did not place the joists in a 'broken banded' fashion, or alternatively long and short. The prosecution presented 88 witnesses. Thomas Shaw KC was the leading counsel for the defence.

One of the prosecution witnesses was John Muir, a steward at the stand. He said that while the terracing had never previously been put to such a severe strain as on that day, it was the case that the part which gave way was the least densely crowded of the whole. One of those injured, Daniel Scott, also stated that the part of the terracing that gave way was not overcrowded. Witnesses would say that they hadn't observed overcrowding but that they did see swaying.

Carl Bonn, a civil engineer who had charge of the structural part of the Glasgow Exhibition, said he thought the stand gave way through a lack of joistings. A structure such as Ibrox, he said, would have a life of from ten to 12 years. If these joists had been made of good yellow pine, they could not, in his opinion, have fallen or broken under the maximum load to which they had been subjected. It was known that these joists had before been overstrained with heavy loads, and they would be reduced in strength with every strain.

The jury, after half an hour's deliberation, returned a unanimous verdict of not guilty. The accident ended the practice of supporting wooden terracing on steel frames.

9

The Game That Changed the Offside Law – 1906

THE 35TH match between Scotland and England had the result of leading to a change in the offside law due to the tactics employed by the English.

Hampden Park was newly redeveloped and a vast open bowl. 'Banked up to a great height, the new ground of the famous Queen's Park Club affords accommodation it is claimed for a hundred thousand people,' the press wrote. The crowd numbered 102,741, at the time a new world-record attendance. Several thousand more were locked out.

The Scotland team turned out in Lord Rosebery's racing colours of primrose-and-rose-hooped shirts and white shorts, or knickers as they would have been known at the time.

With no substitutes available, England went down to ten men from very early on when left-half Harry Makepeace went off injured in a challenge for the ball with Alex Menzies.

There were five minutes to go before half-time when Crompton handled, giving Scotland a free kick. Liverpool's Billy Dunlop, playing his only game for Scotland, played the ball into James Howie, who shot from close range. Ashcroft saved but was adjudged to be standing over the line, and a goal was awarded.

Eleven minutes into the second half, Scotland were two ahead when Smith's cross found Howie, who scored with his right foot.

Instead of what would happen in the modern game, a forward being sacrificed to shore up the defence, England's captain

Stanley Harris opted to push forward the left-back Herbert Burgess to play in midfield. Right-back Robert Compton sat in deep. The rest of the side played around 20 to 25 yards from the Scottish goal in what would be known in the modern era as a pressing game.

At the time, the offside rule was such that a forward needed three players ahead of him and the ball. Both sides, at times, played the 'one-back game' where protection was offered by having one defender hang back. But the law that came into focus this day was that players could be offside anywhere on the pitch.

The result of England's tactics was that Scotland's players were repeatedly caught offside 25 yards from their own goal.

Alex Shepherd scored direct from a free kick for England's consolation.

Criticism would be levelled at Harris and England for the tactics, although they were perfectly legal. It would be the last time the 24-year-old Harris played for his country.

At a meeting of the International Football Board held in Oban in June 1907, Law 6 was amended so that a player could not be offside in his own half of the pitch.

'The score was totally misleading,' wrote *Lloyd's Weekly Newspaper*, 'for in the unfortunate absence of Makepeace, the visitors were overplayed to a ridiculous extent.'

Jimmy Conlin, who won his only cap for England that day, was born in County Durham but began his career in Scotland playing for Hibernian, Falkirk and Albion Rovers. At the outbreak of the Great War he enlisted in Coatbridge with the Highland Light Infantry and was killed in action before the Battle of Passchendaele.

10

Alan Morton

31 caps, 5 goals (1920–1932)

MORTON BEGAN his career with Queen's Park in 1914. The son of a coal master, he qualified as a mining engineer and continued this profession in Airdrie throughout his playing career. As a youngster Morton practised with a small ball, hitting it against a coal cellar door. Morton later described the attributes required to become a top player. 'The three essentials are balance, ball control and quickness off the mark,' he said.

A natural right-footer who played at outside-left, Morton made his international debut for Scotland on 26 February 1920 against Wales while still a Queen's Park player, winning his second cap against Ireland the following month.

At 27, Morton moved from Queen's Park to Rangers in 1920, becoming Bill Struth's first signing. Despite Morton being part-time, Rangers made him the highest-paid player in Scottish football. Morton often trained alone, having to make the time in the evenings after his shifts down the mine. It wasn't unusual for him to work on a Saturday morning before a match.

In total, Morton played 11 times against England. Alongside Bobby Walker, who also played the same number, it's the most any Scot has played against the Auld Enemy.

The 1924 British Home Championship match was the first England-Scotland game to be played at Wembley. Morton would win his 11th cap in the 1-1 draw.

The following year, Morton was part of an all-Scotland-based 11 that took on England at Hampden Park. He set up the first goal for Hughie Gallacher in a 2-0 win. *The Times* wrote that England were 'outmanoeuvred and outplayed'. Charged with stopping Morton was West Bromwich Albion's Tommy Magee. Being similarly small, the thought was that he would take a firmer grip of Morton. Magee said of the experience, 'I could catch him all right. Except that I never knew which way he was going.'

Morton's nickname of the 'Wee Blue Devil' came from a frustrated England fan at Wembley in 1928 during the famous Wembley Wizards match. Journalist Ivan Sharpe overheard, and once in print, the nickname stuck.

Sir Frederick Wall, the secretary of the English FA from 1895 to 1934, once wrote about Morton, 'His brain was quick to see a situation, and his feet swiftly adept in working it out. I cannot recall an English back who mastered this little, quiet, modest man.'

On the occasion of his 30th cap in April 1932 at Wembley in the game against England, Morton broke the Scottish caps record of Bobby Walker, set in 1905. Morton's 31 Scottish caps stood as a record until broken by George Young in 1952.

All his caps came in the British Home Championship bar his final appearance in May 1932, where he played in a friendly against France. With this appearance, Morton became the second-oldest player to play for Scotland at the age of 39 years and 14 days. Jimmy McMenemy had been 39 years, six months and 19 days when he played against Ireland in March 1920. Scotland defeated France 3-1, with Third Lanark's Neil Dewar getting a hat-trick.

Speaking later that month, Hughie Gallacher said, 'Alan Morton was, and is, in a class by himself. The daisies never grow under his feet. He crosses a ball with the accuracy of a mathematician. His passes are such that a man need not be a gazelle or a giraffe to accept. He has every trick of the footballer's trade at his toes. I saw him play for Scotland in Paris. I said then, and I repeat now, that Alan Morton never got one cap too many.'

Morton was noted for his dribbling ability, but more importantly, he knew when to release the ball, and his accuracy with crosses provided great service for his team-mates. Like many great players, Morton mystified and enchanted the spectators who looked on expectantly, wishing and hoping for flashes of brilliance. Morton delivered in the form of his 'floating lob'. Spectators swore that he had the ability to make the ball sit up in mid-air. He was once asked to explain it. 'I cannot,' he replied, 'but I always noticed that the lob came off when I crossed the ball at speed … it was a thing I never tried to do. It was almost as if the ball was showing me a thing or two.'

Bob McPhail played alongside Morton for both Rangers and Scotland, and said of his colleague, 'He was simply in a class by himself. The wee man was simply a magician. He would never beat his opponent the same way twice. Outside, inside or through his legs he would torment the life out of full-backs. He took all his corner kicks with his right foot to get that peculiar inswinging hanging lob of his. You could see keepers hesitating as the famous Morton lob seemed to hang in the air.'

On Morton's death in 1971 at the age of 78, Shearer Borthwick wrote in the *Evening Times*, 'Alan Morton was perhaps the greatest winger of all time – certainly in his time. He was small, wiry, and had a brilliant swerving motion that caused full backs great trouble.'

Former international team-mate Jimmy McGrory commented, 'As his record proves he was one of the finest outside-lefts ever to grace a football field.'

11

England 1 Scotland 5 – 1928

31 March 1928
Wembley Stadium, London
British Home Championship
Attendance: 80,868

Scotland: Harkness (Queen's Park), Nelson (Cardiff City), Law (Chelsea), Gibson (Aston Villa), Bradshaw (Bury), McMullan (Manchester City), Jackson (Huddersfield Town), Dunn (Hibernian), Gallacher (Newcastle United), James (Preston North End), Morton (Rangers)

England: Hufton (West Ham United), Goodall (Huddersfield Town), Jones (Blackburn Rovers), Willis (Leeds United), Wilson (Huddersfield Town), Healless (Blackburn Rovers), Hulme (Arsenal), Kelly (Huddersfield Town), Dean (Everton), Bradford (Birmingham), Smith (Huddersfield Town)

Referee: William Bell (Scotland)

Goals:
Scotland – Jackson (3, 65, 86), James (44, 67)
England – Kelly (89)

THE RESULT gave birth to the first Scottish team to establish itself as legendary, becoming known as the 'Wembley Wizards'. Going into the match, however, Scotland's chances of winning the British Home Championship for the fourth year in a row had gone after drawing with Wales 2-2 in October 1927 and losing to Ireland 1-0 in February.

England, too, had forfeited their chance of winning the tournament by losing to Ireland 2-0 in October 1927 and to Wales 2-1 at Turf Moor in November.

Wales had secured the championship, so this game in a wet and dreary London was to avoid the wooden spoon. England had never lost all of their matches in the tournament before.

This was only the second England-Scotland game to be played at Wembley. The attendance was a record for England at the stadium.

The selection committee regularly put their faith in the Scottish League versus English League game to select their 11 for the annual Auld Enemy fixture. The Scottish League lost 6-2, leading the committee to drop eight players. Jack Harkness in goal and forwards Alan Morton and James Dunn were the only players to survive the cull.

The new Scottish forward line averaged five feet six inches in height. Dunn was 5ft 6in, Hughie Gallacher 5ft 5in, Alex James 5ft 6.5in, Morton 5ft 4.5in and Alec Jackson 5ft 10in. 'Before the match, critics didn't give Scotland much chance,' captain Jimmy McMullan told *Charles Buchan's Football Monthly* in 1958. 'Height and weight, they said, were against us. But those two attributes can be nullified when the ball is kept on the ground, and that's the way it was.'

The night before the match Robert Campbell, the SFA president, encouraged McMullan to have a few words with his players. McMullan told his colleagues he didn't want any backchat from them, not to the referee and not to their opponents. 'I think you all know as well as I do what's expected from you tomorrow,' he said. 'So get off to bed, put your head on the pillow and pray for rain.'

The Scots felt that on a heavy pitch they had the advantage as with several skilful players they could confidently turn the English defenders, who were risking being left in the mud every time they attempted a challenge. 'It gave them the perfect footing for their skill,' England goalkeeper Ted Hufton said.

HRH Duke of York, later becoming King George VI, and his guest King Amānullāh of Afghanistan, then on a European tour, were presented to the teams. While King Amānullāh was in Europe, an uprising began in his country, and on his return he was forced to abdicate, fleeing in May 1929 and living out the rest of his life in exile.

The match kicked off in the sunshine, but within minutes dark clouds had descended, and the rain came on. 'Our plan was to attack,' McMullan said, 'backed up by our wing-halves – Jimmy Gibson and myself. Our full-backs Jimmy Nelson and Tommy Law came up with us, leaving that big fellow Tom "Tiny" Bradshaw to dominate the middle. Thus each section backed up the one in front.'

The result of the game could have been so different without a swift turnaround in play early on. 'For the opening 20 minutes, it was all England,' Jack Harkness told Geoffrey Green of *The Times.* Harkness recalled Billy Smith bearing down on his goal early on and hitting a shot that struck the post. 'From there, it rebounded to McMullan … a quick flick found James who released Alan Morton … over came a pinpoint centre and into the net it went like lightning from Jackson. In those seconds, the wizards were born, and there was no holding us.'

'Not an England player touched the ball from the time Smith fired it against the Scottish woodwork,' said Hughie Gallacher.

James evaded two defenders to beat Hufton from the edge of the penalty box just before half-time to take Scotland in two up.

Scotland's third came when Jackson once again got his head to another Morton cross on 65 minutes. A minute later, Gallacher beat Wilson and shot at goal. It was blocked but James got on to the rebound to make the score 4-0. With five minutes remaining Morton and Jackson combined again, with Jackson burying another accurate cross. Jackson became the fifth player, all Scots, to have scored a hat-trick against England.

England took the gloss off the result slightly with Bob Kelly's 25-yard free kick with a minute remaining to make the final score 5-1.

'The inferiority of the England side,' wrote J.H. Freeman in the *Daily Mail*, 'was so marked that the confusion and bewilderment of individual players against the science and skill and pace of Scotland's dazzling team became positively ludicrous.'

The Guardian wrote, 'It was thought that in going to English League clubs for eight of their players the Scots would depart from their usual style of play and tactics, but the eleven … showed rare craft, speed and strength, and when they had gained the upper hand they did much as they planned with their well-beaten rivals.'

In his book *Football Fever*, John Moynihan wrote that the match 'emphasised the real delights of Scottish football with its carpet manners and intricate passing between the forwards, backed up by a solid, uncompromising half-back line'.

Looking around for excuses for the heavy loss, some members of the English press felt that England's four Huddersfield players were tired, having played in an FA Cup replay against Sheffield United on the Monday leading up to the game. However, Alec Jackson had also been in that Huddersfield side.

The Wembley Wizards never played together again. There were five changes to the team for the next match, a 4-2 win over Wales at Ibrox in October. Tom Bradshaw wouldn't earn another cap, while Nelson, Law and Dunn would all only play once more. But the legend they created that day lives on.

12

Hughie Gallacher Scores Five – 1929

HUGHIE GALLACHER was born in Belshill, Lanarkshire, in February 1903. On the night of his first call-up to the Scotland team in 1924, a journalist knocked on the door of the family home he shared with his mother. 'Are you eligible to play for Scotland?' the pressman asked, telling a bemused Gallacher that he had a source in Belfast who had proof positive Gallacher was Irish-born.

Gallacher's father, an Ulsterman, had moved to Scotland to work in the mines. Hughie's indignant mother fetched his birth certificate, which confirmed his birth in Belshill. 'I shall not forget the awful moment I had,' Gallacher said in 1932, 'when someone tried to prove I was not Scots, of Scottish parentage, and qualified to play for the country that has so far produced the world's greatest footballers.'

Scotland's 7-3 win over Ireland on 23 February 1929 was the highest score in an international between the countries since 1901 when Ireland lost in Glasgow 11-0.

Alex Jackson on the right 'had a field day … doing pretty much as he pleased against Steele,' wrote *The Scotsman*, 'and his work helped to produce five of Scotland's seven goals.'

A crowd of 35,000 were there in Belfast to see Jackson put Gallacher in with only three minutes gone to make it 1-0. After ten minutes Morton centred; the ball struck the crossbar and came out to McMullan, who played it back into an empty goalmouth. Gallacher only had to tap into the net for his second. Liverpool's legendary Elisha Scott was in Ireland's goal.

Jackson centred again for Gallacher to complete his hat-trick and only 14 minutes had gone. Ireland pulled a goal back through Bamerick but 12 minutes before half-time Jackson made it 4-1. Rowley made it 4-2 just ahead of the interval.

His fourth came early in the second half. Bambrick got another back for Ireland, and Gallacher scored again on 76 minutes. Alex Jackson completed the scoring with six minutes left.

Gallacher had also scored five goals for the Scottish League against the Irish League in a 7-3 win in November 1925.

Working down the mines from the age of 15, Gallacher commonly worked ten-hour days. Alex James was a school friend, and they played in their first match together. 'Hugh and I hit it off right from the start,' James said. 'We scrapped together and dogged [school] together, and we romped the streets together … the two of us would do anything for a game.'

Starting his career in the Western League with Queen of the South, Gallacher signed for Airdrie in an undertaker's office. His new club parted with a fiver for his services. Newcastle United would pay £6,500 to Airdrie in December 1925, and it was at St James' Park where his legend was made.

Chelsea signed him for £10,000 in 1930, then moves to Derby County, Notts County and Grimsby followed.

Gallacher had lived in Gateshead since he signed for the club in 1938. He had missed the area since he left Newcastle for Chelsea. 'No place can compare with Tyneside and its people,' he said to the *Evening Chronicle* on signing.

He had been working as a machinist in a chemical factory, also writing as a football columnist for the *Evening Chronicle*. His second wife had passed away in 1950, marking the beginning of Gallacher's sad decline.

On 11 June 1957, Adam Cook and Gordon Glaholm were two 14-year-olds who saw a man pacing up and down on a bridge. As a train approached, he climbed a fence on to the embankment. Glaholm told the coroner, 'The man jumped and just disappeared.'

Leslie Spicer, a Newcastle journalist, met Gallacher the day before his death. 'My life is finished now,' Spicer said Gallacher told him. 'Drink has been my downfall. If I could have kept off the drink this would never have happened.'

The young boys had witnessed Hughie Gallacher walking on to the rail track at Down Bell Vue Bank in Gateshead, between Low Fell Station and Chowdene Bank, where he stepped in front of the London-Edinburgh train.

An incident at home in May where Gallacher lost his temper with his 14-year-old-son Matthew led to a report to the NSPCC. With a trial the following day at Gateshead Magistrates' Court, Gallacher couldn't live with the shame and the ruining of his reputation. A Scotland international scarcely had a more tragic end.

He's still the only player to have scored five goals in an international for Scotland.[2]

Newcastle legend Alan Shearer recalled in 2014 something his father had said to him as he started out on his career. 'No matter how many goals you score, son, you'll never be as good as Gallacher.'

---

2 Joe Harper is credited with scoring five times in an unofficial international in Canada in 1967. This match has subsequently been upgraded to a full international. Reports conflict on whether Harper scored three or five.

13

Norway 3 Scotland 7 – 1929

26 May 1929
Brann Stadion, Bergen
Friendly
Attendance: 4,000

Scotland: McLaren (St Johnstone), Crapnell (Airdrieonians), Nibloe (Kilmarnock), Imrie (St Johnstone), A. Craig (Motherwell), T. Craig [C] (Rangers), Nisbet (Ayr United), Cheyne (Aberdeen), McCrae (St Mirren), Rankin (St Mirren), Howe (Hamilton Academical)

Norway: Hofstad (Brann), Walde (Brann), Lund (Fredrikstad), Tollefsen (Stavanger), Olsen (Brann), Kjos (Brann), Kongsvik (Brann), Danielsen (Kvik Halden), Brodahl (Stavanger), Lie (Frigg), Berg-Johannesen (Stavanger)

Referee: Fredrik Schieldrop (Norway)

Goals:
Norway – Kongsvik (4), Berg-Johannesen (37), Kongsvik (76)
Scotland – Rankin (6), Craig (27), Cheyne (30, 64, 68), Nisbet (47, 52)

THIS WAS the first international Scotland played overseas. The beginning of a continental tour, it was also the first Scottish international played on a Sunday.

With eight changes from the 1-0 win over England in April, seven players were making their Scotland debuts – McLaren, Imrie, Allan Craig, Nisbet, McCrae, Rankin and Howe.

At 18 years, five months and one day, Sandy McLaren was, and remains, the youngest goalkeeper to appear for Scotland.

The Norwegian press expressed disappointment with the ticket sales and pondered if the lack of take-up was due to high prices or an expected walkover for Scotland. After the game, the party travelled to Oslo to play another Norwegian select side.

This game is considered a full international by the SFA, while the Oslo match is not. Their Norwegian counterparts don't consider either match to be a full international.

14

The Hampden Roar

HAMPDEN PARK was a formidable ground. It may have lost something in recent years, but the venue has proved intimidating for opposition players. So much so that once the notion of the 'Hampden Roar' was born, it was always prevalent in match previews and vaunted as something for visiting players to fear.

There's some debate about when precisely the Hampden Roar came into existence. Some have cited 1929 in a match with England. Alex Jackson sustained a dislocated elbow in a collision in the 40th minute and had to go off, leaving the Scotland side a man short. The crowd of 110,512 offered more support to make up for the loss of a man.

With the game goalless in the 89th minute, Scotland were awarded a corner. As Aberdeen's Alex Cheyne placed the ball to take the kick, cheering grew louder and louder. When he took the corner, the wind caught the ball and it sailed into the England net. The *Glasgow Herald* wrote, 'When Cheyne scored the only goal two minutes from the end, the crowd gave vent to its pent-up feelings and roared itself hoarse with delight. Hats, caps and handkerchiefs were thrown in the air.'

The other popular theory is that the Roar began in 1933. The goal that sparked it was scored by Celtic's Jimmy McGrory and made by Rangers' Bob McPhail. 'Bob was a great fellow to have alongside one in an international,' McGrory said in 1961, 'one of the best forwards I have ever known. We played together nine times and came to regard each other as team-mates, looking forward to playing together.'

The match was another international against England. The crowd numbered 136,259, a new world record. The gates had been closed long before kick-off, and many in attendance complained that their view offered little of the actual football.

Scotland had taken the lead through McGrory in four minutes, only for England to equalise through debutant Tottenham's George Hunt on the half-hour. With eight minutes remaining, England were on the attack when McPhail took the ball and strolled through the visiting defence. He hammered a shot which skimmed the crossbar as it went over. The unexpected chance released a swell of encouragement from the crowd. McPhail picked up the ball again. He ran down the middle as the noise from the crowd rose. McPhail sent in what McGrory called 'a beauty of a pass'. Tom Cooper tried unsuccessfully to tackle McGrory, but the Celt was past him and ran in on keeper Henry Hibbs. McGrory shifted his body to the left, and as Hibbs came out, McGrory, still running full pelt, lifted the ball over the Birmingham man's left shoulder and into the far corner of the net. The *Glasgow Herald* wrote, 'Then the hush of expectation was shattered by one of the mightiest roars ever heard at Hampden.'

The Roar became notable among opposition players. In his 1960 autobiography, Stanley Matthews recalled hearing that he had been selected to play against Scotland in April 1937, 'My father-in-law Jimmy Vallance said, "Congratulations, Stanley. But when you get there, watch out for that Hampden Roar; it's worth two goals' start any day."' Vallance, a Scot, played for Queen's Park and St Johnstone before later becoming a coach at Stoke City.

Matthews went on to write about the match itself, 'When I walked on to the Hampden turf for the first time in my life, I took one look at the ground and stopped dead in my tracks. The noise from the crowd was terrific, but the people! There were 149,407 people in the ground that day, the biggest crowd I had ever seen in my life. What a sight and what a sensation it gave you. Then the whistle went, and I heard the Hampden roar for the first time. It sounded like a tearing hurricane, and I felt as if I was going to be suddenly picked up off the playing pitch and flung into its roaring jaws.'

England were one up at half-time. 'We took to the field for the second half full of confidence,' Matthews wrote. 'We had, however, underestimated the fighting spirit of Scotland; but the biggest mistake we made was underestimating the Hampden roar. If ever a match was won and lost by the roar, it was this game. As soon as we started the second half, that roar started and never stopped until the end of the game. Believe me, a roar from 149,407 people is some noise indeed. You could say that it injected itself into the veins of those Scottish players, and within minutes they were playing like supermen.'

On his debut, Preston North End's Frank O'Donnell equalised two minutes into the half. 'The roar gained in volume after this goal, and I am afraid that it shook the confidence of some of our players,' wrote Matthews.

Bob McPhail scored twice to complete the win. 'Collectively, we thought the Hampden Roar had beaten us,' Matthews continued.

England's Tommy Lawton wrote about his experience of the 1939 international in his book *My Twenty Years of Soccer*, 'When England play Scotland at Hampden, England come out first and have to stand on the field while the famous roar greets the Scots. And that roar is really something. It seems to start behind one goal and then sweep right round the vast bowl that is Hampden. It makes your heart thump and your knees go weak. You can almost see and feel the roar.'

In a 1954 article in the *Evening Times*, Alan Breck wrote, 'It was England who discovered we had a roar. The thing had never occurred to us at all.' Breck suggested that England, whose win in 1939 was only their third at Hampden since 1906, were at a loss as to why their teams struggled at the ground. Looking around for a reason, they arrived at the sound. 'So that was it. We could not beat them at football, so we terrified them!' said Breck.

Whatever the noise, it certainly left an impression on English players through the years. Bobby Charlton said in 1976, 'I'll never forget the experience of coming out of the tunnel and hearing the Hampden Roar for the first time. I have played all over the world, but that Scottish sound is fantastic … and frightening for the opposition.'

15

Scotland 2 Austria 2 – 1933

29 November 1933
Hampden Park, Glasgow
Friendly
Attendance: 62,000

Scotland: Kennaway (Celtic), Anderson (Hearts), McGonagle (Celtic), Meiklejohn [C] (Rangers), Watson (Blackpool), Brown (Rangers), Ogilvie (Motherwell), Bruce (Middlesbrough), Macfadyen (Motherwell), McPhail (Rangers), Duncan (Derby County)

Austria: Platzer (Floridsdorfer AC), Janda (SK Admira), Szestak (Wiener AC), Wagner (SK Rapid), Smistik (SK Rapid), Nausch [C] (FK Austria), Zischek (SK Wacker), Bican (SK Rapid), Sindelar (FK Austria), Schall (SK Admira), Viert, (FK Austria)

Referee: J. Langenux (Belgium)

Goals:
Scotland – Meiklejohn (5), Macfadyen (49)
Austria – Zischek (41), Schall (53)

AUSTRIA WOULD be the first overseas nation to visit Scotland for an international. The match was proposed at the Scottish Football Association Council's meeting on 31 May 1933. Hampden was chosen as the venue when the other nominated ground, Ibrox, found no seconder.

Austria were managed by Hugo Meisl, a pioneer of the sport who had been first a banker and then a football referee. He had been in charge of the national side since 1913, initially alongside Heinrich Retschury, but from 1919 he took full control.

He had led his team to an unbeaten run of 14 games stretching from April 1931 to December 1932, including a 5-0 win over Scotland in Vienna in May 1931. Czechoslovakia ended the run with a 2-1 win in April 1933. Coming into the Scotland game, Austria played a further four times without defeat.

For Meisl, the result of the match wasn't the most important thing. More important, he said is 'that we should create a good impression in Scotland, for Scotland is the home of the sort of game we cultivate. Whatever the result of the match may be, we shall be delighted to play against opponents who will, we know, give us a rattling good game. We are happy to meet Scotland on their own ground. We, too, play football of the Scottish type, and I am certain that if our team can get into their stride and play their normal game, we will leave behind us a very profound impression, whatever the result.'

News agency Reuters reported that in the weeks leading up to the game, the interest in Scotland and Glasgow from the people of Vienna had grown. Tourist agencies were inundated with calls, and the chatter in cafes was all about 'Schottland', but the question most frequently asked was, 'Are they really so mean?' The Reuters correspondent replied, 'Das ist lauter Blödsinn.' It is all rot.

The Scotsman noted that the streets of Glasgow were thronged and resembled the city on the day of an international with England. Among those in attendance, which included 20 travelling Austrian fans, was Austrian minister Georg Baron Franckenstein.

The Scottish selectors chose their team on 22 November and had travelled all over England to consider Scots for all positions. There was much speculation and anticipation over this side. Several hundred people stood outside the offices of the SFA while the team was being chosen. Paisley-born Bobbie Bruce of Middlesbrough was a surprise inclusion. Four days earlier, his

Middlesbrough side had defeated Sheffield United 10-3, with Bruce hitting a hat-trick.

Goalkeeper Joe Kennaway was born in Montreal to Scottish parents. Capped for Canada in 1926, he had been selected to play against Wales, but the Welsh had objected due to his place of birth. As all the UK nations objected to him playing against them, this match would be Kennaway's only appearance for Scotland.

When the Austrians took the field, they were accompanied by a standard-bearer who carried the crimson and white flag of their country with the name Dr Dollfuss on it. Dollfuss was, at that time, chancellor of Austria and, according to Meisl, one of the team's keenest supporters.

It was Scotland who took the lead when Meiklejohn hit a free kick from about 40 yards out which took a deflection on its way in.

Austria equalised with four minutes of the first half remaining. Karl Zischek and Josef Bican exchanged passes, and when Zischek took a through ball, he controlled it and placed it wide of Kennaway.

The *Manchester Guardian* commented that Scotland built up attacks well, but their tendency to shoot from long range limited their lead.

But at the start of the second half Scotland were in front again. Ogilvie hit the crossbar, and Macfadyen latched on to the rebound to score from close range.

However, it was level again three minutes later when Anton Schall scored. Schall was described in *The Scotsman* as 'the Goalscoring King … one of the best-looking members of the team and wears a perpetual smile'.

The referee had to speak to several players for 'rough tactics'. *The Scotsman* noted, 'The Scots did not spare the shoulder.'

16

Tommy Walker

21 caps, 9 goals (1934–1946)

AT WEMBLEY in 1936, Tommy Walker had his finest moment in a Scotland jersey. Scotland had lost three times in a row at Wembley, and England were a goal up with around 15 minutes to go when Celtic's Johnny Crum was brought down in the box by home captain Eddie Hapgood. Walker, only 20, was elected to take the resultant penalty.

Calmly he placed the ball on the spot, but as he did so, a gust of wind blew it away. He replaced the ball, only for the small gust to take the ball away again. He placed the ball on the spot once more, only for the wind to move it a third time. Finally, Walker got the ball to sit still and converted the penalty to give Scotland a 1-1 draw.

Walker later said he could only vaguely remember the ball moving off the spot and couldn't even recall what end of the ground the kick took place. John Rafferty wrote in his book, *One Hundred Years of Scottish Football*, 'One of the great legends in Scottish football has persisted over the years because it was assumed that the young player must have been tortured by the distractions of the moving ball and all the time it had hardly recorded with him.'

The draw gave Scotland the British Home Championship.

Walker was a Scottish Schoolboy international and began his career with Livingstone Violet before a spell with Broxburn Rangers. In March 1932, he was taken on to Hearts' ground staff, playing in the junior ranks with Linlithgow Rose. He signed a professional contract for Hearts in May of 1932. At Tynecastle, he would enjoy a 14-year playing career.

He made his Scotland debut in 1934 in a 3-2 win over Wales at Pittodrie. In 1938 Walker scored the only goal at Wembley, on the day Bill Shankly made his international debut.

Walker also converted a penalty in a 3-1 win over Hungary at Ibrox in 1938. With that goal, he equalled Andrew Wilson's record of scoring in five consecutive internationals. In November, he scored against Wales in the 83rd and 84th minutes to help Scotland to a 3-2 win.

The outbreak of the Second World War curtailed the number of caps he would receive. Walker volunteered for the Royal Corps of Signals and went to India, where he played in Combined Services football.

Walker played in ten wartime or Victory internationals, although he only recorded one victory over England in that time, a 3-2 win in Newcastle in 1941.

In 1942 for an England-Scotland Aid to Russia match, there were insufficient clothing coupons to purchase new shirts for the Scotland team. Walker kitted the team out in shirts from his own international career. The gesture was greatly admired by his team-mate Shankly.

He played his last international, days away from his 31st birthday, in May 1946 in front of 111,899 fans as Scotland beat Switzerland 3-1.

In the *Evening Times* Gair Henderson called Walker 'one of the greatest players and the greatest gentlemen ever to wear a Scotland jersey'.

17

Scotland 2 Germany 0 – 1936

14 October 1936
Ibrox Park, Glasgow
Friendly
Attendance: 50,000

Scotland: Dawson (Rangers), Anderson (Hearts), Cummings (Aston Villa), Massie (Aston Villa), Simpson [C] (Rangers), Brown (Rangers), Delaney (Celtic), Walker (Hearts), Armstrong (Aberdeen), McPhail (Rangers), Duncan (Derby County)

Germany: Jakob (SSV Jahn), Münzenberg (TSV Alemannia), Munkert (1. FC Nürnberg), Janes (TSV Fortuna), Goldbrunner (FC Bayern), Kitzinger (1. FC Schweinfurt 05), Elbern (SV Beuel 06), Gellesch (Schalke 04), Siffling (SV Waldhof), Szepan [C] (Schalke 04), Urban (Schalke 04)

Referee: Harry Nattrass (England)

Goals:
Delaney (66, 83)

GERMAN PLAYERS arrived by air into Croydon Airport before travelling on to Renfrew Aerodrome. This was the first occasion a swastika-marked aeroplane had come to Scotland. SFA secretary George Graham and Rangers manager Bill Struth were at Renfrew to meet the Germans. Staying at the Central Hotel in the evening, the players saw a show at the Pavilion Theatre.

A large group of German spectators were also heading to Scotland. Their Hamburg-Amerika liner *Reliance* arrived at South Queensferry on the morning of the game. They then travelled by car to Glasgow. After the match, the passengers would cruise around the north of Scotland and then sail to Dublin for Germany's game with the Irish Free State.

Several newspapers commented that none of the travelling party wore Nazi emblems. They had with them snacks in small cardboard boxes, which the *Leicester Evening Mail* wrote 'were offered and accepted by unemployed men' in the crowd that had gathered to meet them.

Some people within Scotland were in opposition to a Nazi German team playing in Scotland. The Glasgow Independent Labour Party planned a protest. Glasgow's Lord Provost John Stewart said that sports were international and that to attempt to drag politics into it was absurd.

The Glasgow Trades and Labour Council wrote to George Graham. The letter said that the council 'deplores the action of the Scottish Football Association. The Nazi policy of intolerable pogrom against law-abiding Jewish citizens and its pitiless campaign of terror and murder against trade unionists and their families continue to be a destroyer of all freedom.'

It was well known through the British press that the Jewish people in Germany had been persecuted. David Lloyd George, the former prime minister, had visited Germany only in September 1936. *The Scotsman* reported his comments on his return, 'I have always thought and still think that the persecution of Jews in Germany has been a great misfortune. But Germany is not the only country that has persecuted Jews.' Lloyd George claimed that Hitler was 'a most remarkable personality, one of the greatest I have ever met in the whole of my life, and I have met some very great men'.

An application by the BBC for 'permission to broadcast a running commentary in whole or part' was refused by a majority at an SFA meeting in September.

Germany were not expected to provide much of a challenge for Scotland. 'Few people … the Germans included, expect that our continental visitors can do more than put up a fairly stout resistance to what is recognised as a very good Scottish team,' wrote *The Scotsman*.

German football didn't become professional until the 1960s, and there wasn't even a national league in place yet. German coach Otto Nerz had been travelling over to Scotland and England since the 1920s to study tactics and methods. He had visited Rangers in 1922 and stayed for a fortnight, becoming friends with Bill Struth. Nerz hosted Rangers when they toured Germany in 1933.

'They are all keenly interested in English and Scottish football,' Nerz said of his team to the *Derby Daily Telegraph* in 1935, 'and players with such teams as Arsenal, Glasgow Rangers, Derby County, Everton, Glasgow Celtic, and Sunderland are well known to them.'

The German team were held up in traffic and arrived on the pitch 18 minutes late. The Germans lined up and gave the Nazi salute to the main stand and then turned around and repeated the gesture to the opposite stand. *The Scotsman* reported that they received 'a warm welcome'. German journalists in the press box also gave the Nazi salute.

'The Nazi flag with its black swastika floated serenely above the Ibrox stand at the opposite end from the Union Jack,' reported the *Dundee Evening Telegraph*.

Footage from the game was released by the Associated Press and British Movietone in 2015, showing the Nazi salutes and the swastika flying. *The Independent* newspaper asked historians and academics to put some historical context on to something that seems abhorrent by modern standards.

Professor Neil Gregor from Southampton University said the footage of the flag was easy to explain simply because the Nazi banner was the national flag of Germany, and protocol dictated that it be flown at certain events, such as football matches. 'It doesn't signify sympathy or appeasement on the part of British participants,' he added. 'Naturally, it's striking to us now to see such a symbol becoming part of the fabric of everyday life in British society, but its presence doesn't always imply pro-fascist attitudes. Such attitudes were undoubtedly there, as many historians have shown, but this is not evidence for them.'

Dr Helen Roche, a research fellow at Lucy Cavendish College, Cambridge, said, 'All we can say is that people probably didn't know or care enough about what was going on in Nazi Germany to feel moved to protest at the fact that the swastika was being flown.'

It was a fine, clear afternoon with mild weather. In the first half Germany were the better team, and in the third minute they were unlucky to have a goal by Rudolf Gellesch disallowed for offside. Jerry Dawson, in the Scottish goal, made two good saves from Franz Elbern.

Two men were arrested on the north-west terracing after they unfurled a banner on the stroke of half-time. The large red banner contained an inscription in large white letters which read 'Who Murdered Jewish Footballers?'

In the second half, with a strong wind behind them, Scotland gained the advantage. The first goal came when a Matt Armstrong shot was parried by Hans Jakob. Attempting to clear, Reinhold Münzenberg kicked the ball off the in-rushing Jimmy Delaney, and it rebounded into the net for 1-0.

Ten minutes from the end, Delaney latched on to a through ball from Tommy Walker and thumped the ball home to give Scotland a 2-0 win.

Before they left the field, the German players gave the crowd another Nazi salute. 'When they repeated their little ceremony at the close of the game, they received an ovation which was thoroughly deserved,' wrote *The Scotsman,* who named Fritz Szepan as the player of the match.

'I knew we could prove ourselves as a team,' Otto Nerz said to Charles Buchan of the *Daily News*. 'What pleased me most was that we played real Scottish football in Scotland.'

The following year Germany beat Denmark 8-0 with a team that was famously known as *Breslau-Elf.* Nine of the 11 had played at Ibrox.

The German team's forward, Adolf Urban, was killed in combat in Demjansk in May 1943. Due to his Nazi Party membership, Otto Nerz was arrested as a prisoner of war after the Battle of Berlin and later interned in a camp in Sachsenhausen. After four years of imprisonment, he died in April 1949 and was buried in a mass grave on the site of the camp.

18

Scotland 3 England 1 – 1937

17 April 1937
Hampden Park
British Home Championship
Attendance: 149,547

Scotland: Dawson (Rangers), Anderson (Hearts), Beattie (Preston North End), Massie (Aston Villa), Simpson [C] (Rangers), Brown (Rangers), Delaney (Celtic), Walker (Hearts), O'Donnell (Preston North End), McPhail (Rangers), Duncan (Derby County)

England: Woodley (Chelsea), Male [C] (Arsenal), Barkas (Manchester City), Britton (Everton), Young (Huddersfield Town), Bray (Manchester City), Matthews (Stoke City), Carter (Sunderland), Steele (Stoke City), Starling (Aston Villa), Johnson (Stoke City)

Referee: William McLean (Ireland)

Goals:
Scotland – O'Donnell (47), McPhail (80, 89)
England – Steele (40)

IT HAD been proposed that the players would wear numbers on their shirts for the match, which would have been the first instance of their use in a full international. The English FA had been using numbers in amateur internationals. However, at the 3 February 1937 meeting of the SFA, the idea was turned down.

The SFA also turned down a request from the BBC to broadcast the match live on the radio. The sticking point was the BBC's request for free facilities. George Graham, the SFA secretary, told the press, 'We certainly have refused the BBC permission. But if they want to talk business we are prepared to do so.'

The attendance was a new world record for a football match; 149,407 tickets were issued. This figure didn't include complimentary tickets, press tickets and police. The gate receipts were £24,303. *The Scotsman* suggested that the attendance was over the 150,000 mark.

The Guardian wrote of the crowd, 'Hampden Park is said to be able to hold 180,000. It has shown that it can take 150,000 in comfort.' Hampden Park's enclosure was extended in 1936.

Preston North End's Andy Beattie and Frank O'Donnell were making their debuts. Selection Committee members Provost David Gray of Airdrieonians and Robert Williamson of Greenock Morton prepared a report after Preston's 4-1 FA Cup semi-final win over West Bromwich Albion, which led to their selection.

England opened the scoring when Steele accepted a pass from Starling and shot home from ten yards out.

Scotland were level two minutes into the second half when Walker, cheered by the crowd every time he was on the ball, crossed for O'Donnell to finish.

With ten minutes remaining, Bob McPhail pounced when Vic Woodley in the English goal failed to hold a Dally Duncan shot, putting Scotland into a 2-1 lead. With two minutes remaining, McPhail headed in an Andy Anderson free kick.

In the *Daily Record*, columnist 'Waverley' wrote that the proudest man in Hampden was George Graham, who was 'wearing his bowler at a jaunty angle'. He had, 'Waverley' wrote, 'staged the greatest event in the history of the game'.

The question of overcrowding was put to an unnamed SFA official who replied, 'Anyone at Hampden who did not see the match had only himself to blame. There would always be people who would not look for a place.'

Only 46 people required medical attention, and as none of that was due to crushing, the SFA believed overcrowding was not of any concern. The *Daily Record* commended the SFA on their 'magnificent organisation'.

In May of 1937, after the Scottish Cup Final, where there was an attendance of 144,000, the question of overcrowding at Hampden Park was raised at a meeting of Glasgow Corporation. It was revealed there that the master of works estimated the capacity of Hampden Park at 149,969 and that the reported figure of 180,000 was incorrect.

A subcommittee of Glasgow magistrates recommended that all matches of that nature be an admission by ticket only.

Brazil v Uruguay in the final match of the 1950 World Cup set the attendance record with 199,854 present, but Scotland v England in 1937 remains a high in Europe.

19

Scotland XI 5 England 4 – 1942

18 April 1942
Hampden Park
Wartime international
Attendance: 91,000

Scotland XI: Dawson (Rangers), Carabine (Third Lanark), Beattie (Preston North End), Shankly (Preston North End), Smith (Preston North End), Busby [C] (Liverpool/wartime guest Sept. 1941, Hibernian), Waddell (Rangers), Herd (Manchester City/wartime guest Feb. 1942, Hamilton Academical), Dodds (Blackpool), Bremner (Arsenal/wartime guest Apr. 1942, Blackburn Rovers), Liddell (Liverpool)

England: Marks (Arsenal), Bacuzzi (Fulham), Hapgood [C] (Arsenal), Willingham (Huddersfield Town), Mason (Coventry City), Mercer (Everton), Matthews (Stoke City), Edelston (Reading), Lawton (Everton), Hagan (Sheffield United), Kirchen (Arsenal)

Referee: Robert Calder (Rutherglen, Scotland)

Goals:
Scotland – Liddell (25), Dodds (29, 57, 70), Shankly (85)
England – Lawton (21, 75, 87), Hagan (51)

AN ARMY vs SFA Select game was held at Tynecastle ten days earlier to act as a trial for selection. Newspaper reports suggested that the match was played in too sporting a manner and that players acted like 'polite little gentlemen'. Matt Busby and Alec Herd had appeared for the Army side, while Jerry Dawson played for the SFA Select.

An editorial in the *Daily Record* on the day of the game made light of England's position as 'the auld enemy'. The only enemy, the paper said, was Hitler, and it should do much to dampen his spirit to learn that 75,000 would watch the pick of Scotland and England's footballers. The occasion would, the *Record* hoped, provide an audible expression of a spirit Hitler could never defeat in the famous Hampden Roar.

The attendance was recorded as 91,000 and was the biggest crowd at that point in wartime.

Scotland made six changes from their Wembley defeat three months earlier. Tommy Walker of Hearts, who had played against England for the last five years, missed out due to picking up an eye injury against Motherwell.

There were four debutants in the Scotland side, while George Mason was making his debut for England.

Everton's Joe Mercer was asked about the Scots' selection of 20-year-old Billy Liddell. 'I don't think Scotland have made a mistake in picking him,' Mercer said. 'He's a good 'un and one of the gamest boys in the country. He'll go into anything and keep in.'

The Scottish selectors had never heard of Liddell, who had joined Liverpool from Lochgelly Violet in July 1938. That was until the *Daily Record*'s 'Waverley', going off a tip-off from Matt Busby, gave the selectors a strong recommendation.

George Graham made the trip to Anfield to watch Liddell play for Liverpool against Burnley on Easter Monday, 6 April, when his side won 4-1.

The Scotland and England players stayed at the same hotel. On the night before the match, Liddell went to the cinema with Joe Mercer, Jimmy Hagen, Alf Kirchen and Maurice Edelston.

Scotland attacked England from the off, so it was something of a surprise when Jimmy Hagan broke away and crossed for Tommy Lawton, left free by Tom Smith, who headed past Dawson.

Scotland were level two minutes later when Liddell headed in Willie Waddell's corner. It was Liddell who was the provider five minutes later when after latching on to a Busby pass, he played the ball into Jock Dodds, who smashed the ball home.

Mercer was hit in the face by the ball and played much of the game with one eye closed.

Liddell tormented the English left-back, Fulham's Joe Bacuzzi, buzzing past him regularly and whipping crosses into the penalty box.

The game roared from one end to another at a terrific pace. Hagan made the score 2-2 seven minutes after the interval, then Dodds put Scotland back in front on 57 minutes, then completed his hat-trick on 65 minutes.

Dodds had spent part of his upbringing in Leadgate in County Durham and spoke with an accent that led many people to consider him a Geordie. With his given first name of Ephraim, Dodds acquired the nickname of 'Jock' during his time with Huddersfield. At the outbreak of war, Dodds joined the RAF and, based in Blackpool, became a physical training instructor, training aircrews.

Lawton made it 4-3 with 20 minutes remaining. Three minutes later, a long ball from Shankly bounced over George Marks's head and into the net for 5-3. A newspaper report of the time said Shankly had 'the blood of Bruce in his veins and the skill of the football ace in his feet'. A minute later, Lawton, too, had a hat-trick. Dodds and Edelston both went close late on, but the Scots hung on for a 5-4 win.

Jock Dodds wouldn't earn a cap for Scotland outside wartime, but no one has scored more goals against England for Scotland than his seven.[3] 'Happy, happy days,' he said in 1995 of his playing career. 'I enjoyed every minute of it. I'm pleased to say I have left my memory on quite a number of people in a good way.'

---

3 John Smith and George Kerr also both scored seven in total against England.

20

Billy Liddell

29 caps, 8 goals (1946–1955)

BORN IN Townhill, near Dunfermline, in 1922, Billy Liddell began his career at Kingseat Juniors; his coal miner father determined that he would not have a career down the pits.

He first represented Scotland at the age of 14 when he was selected to play for Scotland Schoolboys against Ireland at Somerset Park, Ayr, in May of 1936, where Scotland won 3-1.

One morning Liverpool's half-back Matt Busby intended to play golf with his ex-Manchester City team-mate Alec Herd. When Herd failed to show up, Busby joined Hamilton Academical manager Willie McAndrew to watch Lochgelly Violet. Here Busby encountered a 15-year-old Billy Liddell, who had joined the club after Kingseat folded.

McAndrew wanted Billy to sign for Hamilton; however, Billy's father insisted his son also get a part-time job. The club couldn't come up with one. Busby stepped in and recommended the player to Liverpool.

Liddell signed for Liverpool in July 1938, signing a professional contract in April of the following year. He began work as an accountant at Simon Jude and West in the city.

When the Second World War broke out, Liddell enlisted in the RAF. He served with the Pathfinders and with Coastal Command becoming a Bomber Command pilot officer and pathfinder.

His debut in wartime football came on New Year's Day 1940 in a 7-3 win over Crewe. Billy would play eight wartime internationals for Scotland, scoring three goals. Liddell made 152 appearances for Liverpool in wartime football before he made his official debut in January 1946, having missed the first half of the season completing his service in the air force.

His full Scotland debut came in May of that year in a 3-1 win over Switzerland; Liddell scored twice in the first half. He would play another two times in 1946, in a defeat to Wales and a draw with Ireland.

Liddell broke England goalkeeper Frank Swift's ribs in the 1948 international at Hampden. 'It was fair,' Swift said, 'Billy doesn't know how to be anything but fair.' Liddell was never once booked in his career.

At Wembley in 1951, Liddell was part of the Scotland team that triumphed 3-2. This was only the tenth time the sides had met at the Twin Towers. Liddell was the only Merseyside-based player on the pitch, and the *Evening Express* suggested that 'most of the Anfield rootin' will be for Liddell and not for England'.

Alf Ramsey was England's right-back, and he had experienced numerous roastings from Liddell over his career with Tottenham. 'I always knew I was in for a hectic afternoon when I was marking Billy,' Ramsey said. 'The only way to try to hold him was to beat him to possession of the ball. Once he had it, he was difficult to stop.'

As an Anglo, Liddell felt the pressure to perform at Hampden Park. 'I don't know why it should be,' he told the *Liverpool Echo*, 'but I think the majority of Anglo-Scots have always felt they are more liable to be criticised than players with Scottish clubs. It is something peculiar to Scotland. Most of the critics there seem to think that a team of home Scots is preferable to a mixed one, and quite a lot of the supporters appear to think that once a man goes to England, he loses his birthright.'

Liddell earned his 24th cap in the 3-3 draw with Wales in November 1953 in the British Home Championship group that doubled as World Cup qualifying. Scotland finished runners-up to England but qualified for and accepted their place in the finals. By spring 1954, though, Liddell had lost his place at outside-left to Hibernian's Willie Ormond, so was left out of the squad to travel to the finals.

In 1955 Liddell returned to the Scotland side. Billy scored the third in Scotland's win over Portugal in May of 1955. He then joined the party for a tour of Yugoslavia, Austria and Hungary. In the 2-2 draw in Belgrade, Liddell collected a black eye from the Yugoslav goalkeeper, who objected to Billy's continuous challenges for crosses.

In Austria, Scotland raced to a 2-0 lead, only for the hosts' frustrations to boil over. The crowd invaded the pitch, and patrolling troops had to work hard to calm the situation down. After order was restored, Liddell got his name on the scoresheet as Scotland ran out 4-1 winners.

Liddell claimed that the first half against Hungary in Budapest in 1955 was the best he had ever played. Scotland took the lead, but in the second half Hungary had gone 3-1 up. With 15 minutes remaining, Liddell was brought down in the box. 'You should have heard the uproar which followed,' he said to the *Echo*. 'It was almost terrifying. A home player collared the ball and sat on it while the rest surrounded the referee shouting and arguing. The crowd was on its feet, stamping, screaming and giving that shrill ear piercing whistle which only the continentals can. In short, bedlam was let loose, and it was several minutes before order was restored and I had to face the ordeal of taking the penalty. And what an ordeal it was.' Liddell missed the kick. There was no more scoring. 'I have taken 44 penalties for Liverpool and scored from 36 of them,' Liddell wrote in his autobiography. 'Yet for Scotland I took only two penalties and missed them both! The other was in the game against France in Paris in 1950.'

The next international Billy played in was his final cap, a 2-1 defeat to Northern Ireland at Windsor Park in October of 1955.

After his career ended, Billy became a justice of the peace in 1958. He operated as a bursar at Liverpool University, attending Liverpool games as a season-ticket holder. Liddell died of Alzheimer's disease in 2001, aged 79. 'Scotland have had few greater players,' England captain Billy Wright said. 'He could conjure goals out of nothing.'

21

George Young

54 caps (1946–1957)

GEORGE YOUNG signed professionally for Rangers from Kirkintilloch Rob Roy in August 1941, playing well over 100 games during wartime before he made his league debut. He also played wartime football for Scotland, appearing against England twice in 1943. Both were heavy defeats, 4-0 at Hampden in April and 8-0 at Maine Road, Manchester, in October.

Tommy Walker's last match for Scotland against Switzerland, on 15 May 1946, was Young's first. Young was introduced as a 46th-minute substitute for Morton's Billy Campbell. The game was considered unofficial for many years until its standing was revised to a full international. Young made his first start for Scotland in a 0-0 draw with Northern Ireland in November of that year.

He was nicknamed 'Corky' due to a champagne cork he carried with him as a lucky charm. It was given to him by a waiter at a banquet celebrating Rangers' 1948 Scottish Cup win over Morton. Young kept it with him for Scotland's match with Wales the following season, a 3-1 win convincing him of its lucky properties.

At 6ft 2in tall, Young had a 48in chest and weighed upwards of 15st. For a big man, he was celebrated for a surprisingly nimble touch on the ball as well as precision timing and deftness in the tackle.

Young made 34 consecutive appearances for Scotland, a record until March 1980 when Kenny Dalglish passed it.

Captaining Scotland for the first time in 1948, he had the armband on a record 48 occasions. Willie Ormond described Young as 'the greatest captain of Scotland, and the greatest leader of men I ever encountered'.

It was once suggested to Sir George Graham, the secretary of the SFA, that Scotland should move with the times and appoint a team manager as England had done. He replied, 'We don't need a manager, we've got George Young.'

Young's responsibilities as captain differed from the modern-day skipper. He was responsible for much of the preparation for international matches. He would arrange training sessions, book local transport and organise team-bonding trips to the cinema. Young also saw to it that if there was a new player in the squad, he would room with him to ensure that the player settled in quickly. 'In the eyes of many I was an unofficial team manager,' he said.

Tom Finney described Young as 'like a giant octopus. You would beat him seven times in one move, and thought you were past him, then that eighth leg would come out to reclaim the ball.' Finney said that the two exceptional Scottish footballers of his era were Young and his Rangers team-mate Sammy Cox, 'They were classy defenders who liked to try to outwit rather than outmuscle you, and I had some real tussles with them both.'

Young, having just recovered from injury, missed out on travelling to Switzerland for the 1954 World Cup finals. 'Excuses were made that I was not chosen because there was a doubt about my fitness,' he wrote in his autobiography. 'This was untrue. I was fit and could have played had the selectors wished to include me.' Instead, he travelled with Rangers on a tour of Canada.

Young was such a personality that he appeared in a newspaper advert for Quaker Oats, where he declared that the product was his food for action, 'It gives me match-winning fitness.'

Young played in Scotland's 2-1 World Cup qualifier win over Switzerland in May 1957. Newspapers reported that Young had decided to make the qualifying match against Spain in Madrid later that month his final game for his country. Young contended that he made no public announcement, and what the newspapers printed wasn't down to him. He travelled with the squad to a friendly with West Germany in Stuttgart and then on to Madrid. An injury ruled him out against the Germans, but he felt he would be fit to play in the qualifier.

Preston's Tommy Docherty had taken over the captaincy in Young's absence, but Young realised in the team hotel that Docherty was now being treated by the selectors as the captain even off the pitch, as he watched their chairman ask Docherty to organise a team photograph. 'In my heart, I knew I was out on my ear,' he said.

After training in the morning before the game, Young returned to his room at the hotel. He answered a knock on his door. There stood some of his team-mates. A newspaper reporter had been handed the Scotland team and had passed it on to some of the players. Young was missing. Bobby Evans would be at centre-half. 'I had been dropped, and the Scottish selectors hadn't made any excuses for leaving me out of the side,' he explained.

It was a sour end to a fine Scotland career, and perhaps typical of the unfeeling bureaucracy that existed within the Scotland set-up at that time.

In addition to his 54 Scotland appearances, Young also played 22 times for the Scottish League. Although he signed another one-year contract with Rangers, he didn't play again after the 1956/57 season and retired from the game at the age of 34.

22

Jimmy Cowan

25 caps, 8 clean sheets (1948–1952)

BORN IN Paisley, Jimmy Cowan began playing school football as a centre-forward. He was coached as a goalkeeper by Harry Rennie, who had won 13 caps in goal for Scotland between 1900 and 1908. Rennie had developed the practice of marking his goal area so that he always knew where his posts were. Cowan became a student of Rennie's theories, which also included a focus on angles.

Beginning his career with St Mirren, Cowan signed for Morton after an accidental meeting with Noel Davies, the son of Morton's manager James Davies. Army service delayed his debut, and it was only when he was on leave from Germany on 4 January 1947 that he went into the Morton team to play Hibs at short notice. Cowan had an outstanding game in the 1-1 draw, where he saved two penalties, the first from Gordon Smith and the second from Eddie Turnbull. His inclusion came so late that most newspapers credited the goalkeeper as regular Archie McFeat. 'The fact that McFeat's name appeared in the reports instead of Cowan's would not have mattered a great deal had Cowan not put up such a magnificent display which earned headlines,' wrote the *Port Glasgow Express*.

While in the Army, Cowan played with a BAOR (British Army of the Rhine) team who defeated a Scotland side, causing the *Sunday Post*'s reporter, former Scotland goalkeeper Jack Harkness, to cable back home saying there was a goalkeeper 'about whom we'll hear more'.

Morton, with Cowan in goal, lost 1-0 to Rangers in the 1948 Scottish Cup Final after a replay. One week later, on 28 April, Cowan's first cap came as a 21-year-old in a 2-0 friendly win over Belgium at Hampden.

The 3-1 win over England in April 1949 in his fifth international would forever be known as 'Cowan's Match'.

Team-mate Lawrie Reilly told the *Daily Record* in 1988, 'England should have been 5-0 up at half-time but for Jimmy Cowan who gave the greatest display of goalkeeping I have ever seen. He completely broke England's hearts.'

'Never shall I forget Cowan pushing out a [Jackie] Milburn drive while standing on one side of the goal,' wrote George Young in his autobiography, 'and, like a deer rising in the air to tip over the bar a Mortensen header which would have been made a goal a few seconds later.'

In the *Sunday Mail*, Rex Kingsley wrote, 'Cowan's saves were classics. One from [Stan] Mortensen that saw him leap sideways to grip the ball and crash to the ground with it jammed to his chest was fit for the National Gallery.'

'Jimmy Cowan was rightly hailed as the hero because of a string of wonderful saves in the first 20 minutes,' said England's captain Billy Wright.

Wright suggested that Scotland's win that day was also down to Sammy Cox at left-back, 'He usually played as a wing-half and everybody expected Stanley Matthews to give him a roasting. But Sammy cleverly cut Stanley out of the game by intercepting many of the passes meant for the Maestro. It was the first time I had seen poker-face Stanley looking so frustrated.'

Billy Steel had suggested pre-match that the key to shutting down England was to focus on goalkeeper Frank Swift and centre-half Neil Franklin. Steel felt that both players built quickly from the back.

'Frank likes time to look up, select the man he can see in the best position and throw the ball to him,' Steel said to his colleagues before the game. 'We've got to make him work quickly all the time.' Queen of the South's Billy Houliston was the man tasked with keeping on top of both Englishmen. This, of course, was the era when forwards sending goalkeepers through the air with a shoulder charge was perfectly acceptable.

Jimmy Mason, Billy Steel and Lawrie Reilly scored the Scottish goals in front of 98,188 fans, as Scotland won the British Home Championship for the 18th time. Jackie Milburn scored England's consolation with 15 minutes left.

Under his Scotland shirt that day, Cowan wore a blue-and-white hooped Morton jersey, as he did in every Scotland game.

Cowan won again at Wembley in 1951 when Scotland defeated England 3-2 to win the British Home Championship for the 19th time.

In remembering Cowan, Hugh McIlvanney wrote in 1999, 'For some of us Jimmy Cowan gained as much immortality as is available to footballers by defying England.'

With his final cap coming in May 1952, before he was even 26, he remains the most recent Greenock Morton player to have appeared for Scotland.

Cowan passed away aged only 42 in 1968.

23

Lawrie Reilly

38 caps, 22 goals (1948–1957)

LAWRIE REILLY'S debut came at Ninian Park, Cardiff as Scotland beat Wales 3-1 in a British Home Championship match. He was informed of his call-up to the national team by a fan he met at a bus stop.

His second cap came at Wembley on 9 April 1949. Both Scotland and England could win the British Home Championship that day. Scotland had finished the previous season with the wooden spoon, having lost all three matches. With an inexperienced team on the pitch – nine players had caps only in the low single figures – England were strong favourites. 'Unlike other postwar years, there is a solidarity about this team which may upset the calculations of some of England's older players,' wrote the *Yorkshire Post* before the match.

Thanks to Jimmy Cowan in goal, holding back England when they were at their strongest, Scotland got a grip of the game. Reilly made the first goal for Jimmy Mason. In the second half, Billy Steel had put the Scots 2-0 up.

In the 61st minute came Reilly's moment. Waddell ran down the right wing, evaded Howe and put over a cross into the centre. Reilly, coming in like an express train, threw himself at the ball and sent a downward header into the net.

'Even though that goal came very early in my career, I consider it one of my best,' Reilly wrote in his 2010 autobiography. 'It is still talked about today and looking back on it gives me almost as much pleasure now as scoring it did at the time.'

Jackie Milburn managed a consolation for England, but the 3-1 win would be a famous victory. 'It is no exaggeration to say that we were treated like national heroes,' Reilly wrote. The result was England's first postwar home defeat.

In Reilly's first 12 caps until May 1951, Scotland won every match, including another win over England at Wembley in 1951 and three friendly victories over France. He had also scored nine goals.

Reilly, at 5ft 7in, wasn't an obvious centre-forward, but making up for his lack of height were many other strengths, including his speed and power. Reilly was also fearless, with a dogged determination to get on the end of a cross. Always on the move to shake off markers and find space, he was most deadly in the six-yard box.

On Wednesday, 30 April, Scotland played a friendly against the United States in front of a crowd of 107,809. Reilly scored a hat-trick with goals in the ninth, 11th and 37th minutes.

In 1953 Reilly was back at Wembley for another match with England. Ivor Broadis had put England ahead in front of 97,000 spectators with 18 minutes gone. Reilly equalised in the 54th minute as he beat Alf Ramsey to a rebound, but Broadis put England ahead again in 69 minutes. In the 90th minute Bobby Johnstone delivered a pass on to Reilly, who sent a right-footed lob into Gil Merrick's far corner to make the final score 2-2.

Late goals were typical of Reilly's never-say-die spirit, and while this wasn't the only notable one in his career, it would be the goal that would earn Reilly the nickname 'Last Minute Reilly'. 'I knew that my last-minute goal had been something special, but I had no idea that it would earn me the nickname by which I am still known 57 years later,' Reilly wrote. The draw meant England and Scotland shared the British Home Championship.

Reilly missed out on going to the 1954 World Cup after having contracted pleurisy.

His unbeaten record for the national team at Wembley came to a juddering halt in April 1955. Scotland were already 2-0 down before Lawrie ran on to Bobby Johnstone's through ball in the 16th minute to score. England went on to win 7-2.

Reilly's final cap came on 6 April 1957 at Wembley. Reilly almost missed that match due to Tommy Docherty dropping a cup in the training ground's dressing room the day before. The cup shattered, and a piece embedded itself into Reilly's foot. With stitches in his foot on the day of the game, Reilly could barely walk, far less run. He was offered a painkilling-injection from the doctor and took it. 'The foot was agony before he inserted his needle into it,' Reilly wrote, 'but the pain very quickly receded. I never felt a thing during the match and I have never felt it since.' Scotland would lose 2-1.

By now, Reilly had a long-standing knee injury, and he counted himself out of Scotland's 1958 World Cup qualifiers in an attempt to do something to rectify it. The operation wasn't a complete success, and at the age of only 29, Reilly had to concede that he would never be as good as he was and called time on his career. It was a great loss to Hibs, the national team and Scottish football as a whole.

In 2023, Reilly stands fourth on Scotland's all-time scorers list, and no other Hibernian player has won more caps.

24

The SFA Refuse to Accept Scotland's Place at the 1950 World Cup

SCOTLAND ORIGINALLY joined FIFA in 1910, six years after the international governing body was established. Along with England, Wales and Ireland, Scotland left FIFA in April 1920, stating that they could have 'no relations with the football associations of Austria, Germany or Hungary'.

In April 1946, a meeting was held in London between FIFA and the British football associations. The aim was to mend the broken relations. The outcome was that the English FA recommended to its council that they rejoin FIFA. The other associations were similarly minded.

At a meeting in Geneva on 16 January 1949, the International Football Association announced that England, Scotland, Wales and Ireland would make up a qualifying group for the 1950 World Cup finals in Brazil. The annual British Home Championship would double as Jules Rimet Group One. The top two teams would join six others from the Europe and Near East Group to qualify for the 16-team tournament.

Scotland declared that they would only travel to Rio as British champions. Wales also made the same condition. England, however, made no such stipulations. They would head for the World Cup even as runners-up. The SFA estimated the cost of taking part in the finals would be £3,000. 'Brazil is not too popular, and many countries have not entered, because it is so far away,' George Graham, the secretary of the SFA, said.

Scotland opened their group on 1 October 1949 in Belfast, where Ireland[4] were routed 8-2. That victory was followed up in November with a 2-0 win over Wales at Hampden. 'I said we would only go as champions,' Graham said to journalist Clifford Webb, 'and we're going.' The win meant Scotland had confirmed at least the runners-up place in the group. England defeated Wales 4-1 and Ireland 9-2. So the game in April would decide who won the championship.

George Graham and Bob Kirkwood, the SFA's honorary treasurer who sat as the Scottish delegate on the FIFA Committee, returned from a meeting in Paris in December, insisting Scotland had not moved from its position. The SFA also said they wanted nothing to do with floodlit football, although the perception was the players had no such concerns.

In January, the *Sunday Sun* reported, 'There is already a feeling of regret in certain quarters across the border that the Scottish FA should cling so rigidly to their uncompromising attitude.'

In February, the World Cup organising committee in Zürich announced the known finalists so far. Both England and Scotland were included in the 13 teams named.

Some of the SFA committee, including John Lamb of Arbroath, the SFA president since 1948, favoured sending a Scottish team to Brazil. Among those who appealed to the SFA to change their minds was Sir Stanley Rous, the secretary of the English FA. The Brazilian Sports Federation asked the SFA to reconsider its stance before the deciding match.

In April 1950, Scotland went into the game with England at Hampden knowing that a draw would allow them to win the British Home Championship. Scotland hadn't beaten England at Hampden since 1937 but had won at Wembley the previous year. Roy Bentley scored the only goal of the game for England on 64 minutes.

---

4 In June 1954 FIFA ordered that the IFA name their international team Northern Ireland and the FAI name their side Republic of Ireland.

At a dinner after the match for the two teams, an appeal was made for Scotland to reconsider. There was, however, concern that a reversal of the decision would mean a loss of prestige for the SFA.

Brazilian coach Flávio Costa was at the England game at Hampden. He suggested to the Brazilian Sports Federation that they invite Scotland to play a friendly in Rio before the World Cup. In May, the federation extended the invitation to the SFA. Pedro Polzin, the Brazilian Consol in Southampton, travelled to Glasgow to talk to George Graham about Scotland playing a friendly in Brazil. Graham said the talks did not get beyond 'the friendly session' stage, adding, 'It was found impossible to accept such a generous offer.'

A final decision was made on 26 April 1950 at a meeting of the executive committee in Glasgow. The SFA felt that having entered the British Home Championship under certain conditions in the agreement with the other international associations, they could not now depart from their previous decision.

In his autobiography, Scotland captain George Young said the SFA's decision was one of the few bitter memories of his career. 'I shall always believe they erred,' he wrote. 'Had we gone to Brazil, the Scottish team would have put up a good show, and just as important, everyone who made the trip would have returned home a better and more experienced player.'

Graham attended the 1950 World Cup finals. He returned confident that the SFA had made the correct decision, highlighting what the travelling teams had to do to get to Brazil, changing their diets and training to adapt to the heat, while the season left them out of practice for a July World Cup, 'Obviously, in any World Cup competition, the conditions cannot be equal to all the competitors.' He also suggested that he was not inclined to change his mind in future, 'The British Associations are likely to ponder deeply before taking any decisions with regard to 1954.'

25

Bobby Collins

31 caps, 10 goals (1950–1965)

'I WENT out and tried to be the best,' Bobby Collins said of his career in an interview with the *Liverpool Echo*.

Growing up in Polmadie in Glasgow's southside, Collins idolised Scotland internationals Jimmy Delaney of Celtic and Third Lanark's Jimmy Mason. At 16 he began his career with Pollok, moving on to Celtic for £8 per week in 1948.

Collins was a cobbler before he became a footballer, and on his last day at his trade he re-soled two pairs of boots to take with him. 'I always cobble my own boots,' he told the *Daily Mirror* in 1955, 'and I know they will be exactly as I want them.' At 5ft 3.5in tall, he wore a size-four boot.

Making his debut against Rangers on the opening day of the 1949/50 season, Collins quickly became a regular in the number seven shorts. He performed his national service in Fife, catching a bus to play for Celtic at the weekend.

His Scotland debut came in front of 60,000 at Ninian Park in Cardiff against Wales in October 1950, when he was still only 19. Collins played against Northern Ireland in November of that year and against Austria in December. After that, he didn't win another cap until May 1955, when he played against Yugoslavia in a 2-2 draw in Belgrade.

The Scottish selectors picked the team while standing on Mount Avala waiting for officials from the Yugoslav FA to arrive to lay a wreath on the Monument to the Unknown Hero. Collins replaced Archie Robertson, the only change in the team from the previous match against Portugal. When Collins was told he was in the team, he crossed the dining-room floor at the Avala Hotel and apologised to Robertson for taking his place at inside-right. He told the *Evening Times*'s Gair Henderson that his selection was his biggest break in football. Collins kept his place in the team for the remaining games of the May tour away to Austria and Hungary.

In May 1957, Scotland took on West Germany in a friendly at the Neckarstadion in Stuttgart. The Germans were the World Cup holders at the time, although Helmut Rahn was the only player facing Scotland that day who had also played in the 1954 World Cup Final. 'Two of the best goals I ever scored came in this match,' Collins said in David Saffer's biography of him. 'Jackie Mudie set me up for the first; as for the second, that was a result of a throw-in routine I had with Tommy Docherty. It worked to perfection, and I hit an absolute screamer.'

The *Glasgow Herald* described Collins's second as 'a crashing right foot shot from 25 yards that left the goalkeeper aghast at both the temerity and the power of the effort'. The newspaper noted that the Germans, who made up the bulk of the 80,000 crowd, appreciated Collins's play, 'His readiness to run for an open space after he had made the pass frequently tore gaps in the home defence.'

'My attitude always centred around winning,' Collins told the *Evening Times*. 'That, after all, is the point in playing.'

At the 1958 World Cup finals in Sweden, Collins played in all three matches.

With 320 appearances and 116 goals for Celtic, Collins moved to Everton in 1958, becoming their record signing. He made six more appearances for Scotland as an Everton player, including a 3-2 friendly win over West Germany at Hampden in May of 1959.

At 31, he joined Leeds United. Liverpool boss Bill Shankly, taken by surprise at the news, called Collins, hoping that there was still a chance he could go to Liverpool, but the deal had already been done.

In 1970 Don Revie, then Leeds manager, told *The Times*, 'The real turning point for Leeds came when Bobby Collins, that great pint-sized Scot, joined us from Everton as inside-forward to become the midfield organiser. He cost us £25,000, but he gave us £300,000 value as teacher on the field and captain to a group of youngsters.'

Among those youngsters was Billy Bremner. The 19-year-old had been playing on the right wing, but Revie moved him into midfield alongside Collins. 'We clicked from the start,' Collins said in 1997. 'People used to say I was a bit of a father figure for him. I never saw it that way but I like to think he learnt a bit from me. It would be nice if he had.'

In 1965, with his Leeds team finishing second in the First Division and losing in the FA Cup Final, Collins was voted as the Football Writers' Association Footballer of the Year. He was the first Scot to win the award. His form that season led to a recall for Scotland, almost six years since his last cap. He played at Wembley in a 2-2 draw with England in April, then two matches in May, a friendly draw with Spain and a World Cup qualifier away to Poland that ended 1-1.

Billy Bingham played against Collins for Northern Ireland and with him for Everton. 'He could turn so quickly and use the ball so well,' he told the *Liverpool Echo* in 1995. 'He was a very aggressive midfielder who worked from box to box. He was terribly competitive, but an inspiration to his team-mates.'

26

The Scotland Badge – 1953

IN 1927, the British golf team, before leaving for America to play in the inaugural Ryder Cup competition, discussed what emblem would be on their shirts. It was decided it should be a rose but, at the fitting, George Duncan, the 1920 Open champion who was from Methlick, Aberdeenshire declared he wouldn't wear a rose. He would wear a lion or nothing. As the only Scot in the party, it was at first suggested that he alone would wear a lion, but eventually it was decided that all the team would wear the lion in recognition of the fact that golf came from Scotland.

From the beginning, Scotland's football shirts have been adorned with a red lion, most often on a blue or yellow background. The first lion rampant was sewn on each player's shirt before the 1872 match with England, by forward David Wotherspoon's elder sister Marion.

In 1890 a decision was made to change the badge to a thistle. Twelve years later, the lion rampant returned and has remained on the Scottish jersey ever since.

For the game at Wembley with England in April 1953, the Scottish team had a new badge on their shirts. The *Daily Mirror* described it as 'a yellow lion-rampant surrounded on a purple ground, the whole thing surrounded by eleven thistles – quite enough to terrify any opposing football team'. The crest featured the name of the Scottish Football Association. The badge was a modification of the Royal Banner of Scotland; an exact copy would have been illegal.

The badge was granted by Lord Lyon, King of Arms, responsible for all matters appertaining to Scottish heraldry. Under the authority of an act of 1672, he granted arms on application to persons who could show no hereditary right but were judged to socially occupy a position entitling them to coat armour.

The design has been modified over the years but is familiar now as the crest regularly used on Scottish sides' shirts.

27

Uruguay 7 Scotland 0 – 1954

19 June 1954
St. Jakob Stadium, Basel
World Cup finals Group 3
Attendance: 43,000

Scotland: Martin (Aberdeen), Cunningham [C] (Preston North End), Aird (Burnley), Docherty (Preston Noth End), Davidson (Partick Thistle), Cowie (Dundee), McKenzie (Partick Thistle), Fernie (Celtic), Mochan (Celtic), Brown (Blackpool), Ormond (Hibernian)

Uruguay: Máspoli (Peñarol), Santamaria (Club Nacional de Football), Martínez (Rampla Juniors), Andrade (Peñarol), Varela [C] (Peñarol), Cruz (Club Nacional de Football), Abbadie (Peñarol), Ambrois (Club Nacional de Football), Míguez (Peñarol), Schiaffino (Peñarol), Borges (Peñarol)

Referee: Vincenzo Orlandini (Italy)

Goals:
Borges (17, 47, 60), Miguez (30, 83), Abbadie (55, 85)

'UNBELIEVABLY, WE had travelled to the World Cup with a squad of 13,' Tommy Docherty recalled, 'two of whom manager Andy Beattie confided in me were only there on standby should injuries occur to the selectors' preferred 11 – which, by the way, Andy Beattie was not yet privy to.'

In April, Uruguay sent over a representative, Marcelino Pérez, to watch the Scottish League play the English League at

Stamford Bridge. Pérez had played for Nacional and the national team in the 1930s. He spoke with journalist Colin Glen. 'How can they take such a risk?' Pérez asked Glen when he heard Scotland would only take a party of 13, even though FIFA allowed a squad of 22. 'How can they expect to win with such a small reserve? Surely they have made up their minds that they cannot win.'

Despite Rangers providing captain George Young, Sammy Cox and Willie Waddell to the Scotland side, the Ibrox club informed the SFA that none of their players would be available for Switzerland as they were going on a tour to Canada.

The Scotland players' equipment was ill-suited to the conditions. Tommy Docherty told *The Scotsman* in 2010, 'Imagine playing in a Crombie overcoat. Our shorts went past our knees, the socks were double-knit, and of course, we had big, clumpy Mansfield Hotspurs on our feet.' Johnny McKenzie would say that he lost half a stone during the match.

Andy Beattie, the first Scottish team manager, announced his resignation the day after the opening game, a 1-0 defeat to Austria. SFA officials refused to confirm or deny it to the press. In his autobiography, *The Doc*, Tommy Docherty recalled, 'He told me he was totally fed up with the way the Scottish FA ran the show, "There are more SFA officials here than players. It's a nonsense."'

Author John Moynihan wrote of Beattie's predicament, 'His value to his team was undermined by the verbal and dictatorial strength of the Scottish football establishment which overlorded his authority.'

Blackpool's Allan Brown was the most experienced international in the side with 14 caps, having made his debut in 1950 while with East Fife. The rest of the team all had appearances in single figures.

Uruguay were the World Cup holders, and playing in hot conditions on a dry pitch favoured the South Americans.

'That game still sticks in my gullet,' Willie Ormond said in 1974. 'We played well against Austria in the previous match, but Uruguay were brilliant, and we took a thrashing. The temperature was up in the nineties. I remember we played football for the first

20 minutes but then blew up. Five of the goals came in from the near post. We were overrun … beaten in all departments. That's how it goes sometimes.'

'We simply didn't think anything like that could happen to us,' Neil Mochan said in 1986. 'It's not that we were big-headed. We just didn't know anything about the Uruguayans. Fair enough, they had won the World Cup, but we didn't know anything about that either. We knew nothing. We went into it blind. It was a complete revelation what these boys could do.' Mochan also cited the heat as being a factor in the heavy loss, 'In that dressing room, we felt sick, even humiliated.'

Reflecting on the debacle, Docherty noted, 'I was sure the SFA and the English FA didn't fully grasp the magnitude of what had happened. They appeared to consider the World Cup something of a gimmick, a tournament that still played second fiddle to our domestic competitions.'

28

Scotland 2 Hungary 4 – 1954

8 December 1954
Hampden Park
Friendly
Attendance: 113,146

Scotland: Martin (Aberdeen), Cunningham [C] (Preston North End), Haddock (Clyde), Docherty (Preston North End), Davidson (Partick Thistle), Cumming (Hearts), McKenzie (Partick Thistle), Johnstone (Hibernian), Reilly (Hibernian), Wardhaugh (Hearts), Ring (Clyde)

Hungary: Farago (Honved), Buzanszky (Dorogi Banyasz), Lorant (Honved), Lantos (Voros Lobogo), Bozsik (Honved), Szojka (Salgotarjani Banyasz), Sándor (Voros Lobogo), Kocsis (Honved), Hidegkuti (Voros Lobogo), Puskás [C] (Honved), Fenyvesi (Kinizsi)

Referee: Leo Horn (Netherlands)

Goals:
Scotland – Ring (36), Johnstone (46)
Hungary – Bozsik (20), Hidegkuti (26), Sandor (44), Kocsis (89)

THE NEWS that Hungary, victors over England by scores of 6-3 in 1953 and 7-1 in 1954, and that summer's World Cup runners-up were coming to Glasgow caused great excitement.

Former Rangers director George Brown was a Scottish selector in 1954 and described himself as technical adviser to the

Scotland team. 'It became apparent this was a match everyone wanted to see,' he said in 1979. 'For days before, nothing else was talked about. The excitement even spread to the dressing room, for when the players gathered for the match, the talk was different to that before any other international.'

The Hungarians were also the 1952 Olympic champions, with six of the starting line-up here playing in the gold medal game.

'We went with foreboding to our match against Scotland,' wrote Ferenc Puskás in his autobiography. 'The whole team was tired after the hard fights of the year.' Puskás's transfer to Real Madrid was four years away, and at this point he was an officer in the Hungarian army.

Scotland at the time would be confident of beating anyone at Hampden Park in front of a strong, noisy crowd. But not this day. 'We all knew we were meeting supermen,' said Lawrie Reilly.

Twenty-two tons of straw were scattered over the pitch to ensure overnight frost and the snow that had fallen didn't impact the surface. More snow fell as the players, dressed in tracksuits, stood for the national anthems.

For this match, Scotland wore a one-off shirt which had white sleeves. This was down to the match being filmed, as in black and white Hungary's red would have looked similar to Scotland's dark blue. The BBC was granted permission to film the game once 80 per cent of ticket sales had been achieved.

The Hungarians opened the scoring in 20 minutes when József Bozsik's shot was deflected past Martin by Haddock. Six minutes later, Puskás evaded Docherty's sliding tackle to send a lovely through pass for Nándor Hidegkuti to double the lead.

Scotland came back into the game in 36 minutes when Johnstone beat Lorant and passed to Ring, who beat Farago with a nice shot from 12 yards out. With a minute to go before half-time, Puskás and Sándor Kocsis worked together to provide Károly Sándor with a chance, which he converted on the second attempt after Martin had saved his first shot.

In his autobiography, *Hallowed Be Thy Game*, Tommy Docherty wrote, 'Willie Cunningham and I spent most of the interval geeing-up our team-mates. "Leave Puskás to me, I'll sort him out," I heard myself saying, though I had no idea how. In the second period, I knew my job was to stick as close as I could to Puskás and "get a foot in". Easier said than done.'

Johnny McKenzie was brought down near the right corner flag at the start of the second half. He took the free kick himself and flighted over a perfect cross for Johnstone to head home. It was now 3-2.

The SFA had held firm with regard to substitutions that only the goalkeeper could be replaced at any point in the game, and that only for injury. One other position could be replaced, Scotland insisted, but only in the first half. Therefore it was quite unfortunate when Cunningham suffered an injury preventing Hidegkuti from getting a shot on goal and had to leave the field. Wardhaugh went to right-back, and Ring moved to the left wing. Around five minutes later, Cunningham, to everyone's surprise, returned, putting in a challenge on Kocsis within seconds.

Scotland's standout player was McKenzie, earning his third cap, who showed his pace down the wing and frequently sent over crosses into the middle. 'Johnny nearly ran riot,' his Partick Thistle team-mate and centre-half that day, Jimmy Davidson, recalled in 1979, 'though once they realised how dangerous he was going to be, the Hungarians cleverly forced him to stay on the wing and wouldn't let him cut inside.'

Wardhaugh just failed to connect with a McKenzie cross to make the score 3-3 with two minutes left. A minute later, Kocsis, who later won two Spanish titles with Barcelona, made it 4-2.

'At least her players had the satisfaction of proving that hard tackling and quick covering can reduce the speed and skill of their illustrious visitors to the level of the human mortal,' Harold Mather wrote of Scotland's performance in *The Guardian*.

'We won 4-2, but our play was not up to the standard expected of us,' Puskás wrote.

After the game, Puskás said that 'after Stanley Matthews' McKenzie was the best right-winger he had seen. 'That was a fantastic thing to say,' McKenzie said in 1987. 'To receive such a compliment from him was really the icing on the cake for me to a display which I rate as my best in a Scotland jersey in the nine games I played.'

Puskás was also impressed by Hampden Park, saying, 'It is the most magnificent stadium I have ever seen, the life and essence of football.'

Willie Cunningham said after the match, 'Some of the boys were afraid to try their favourite tricks of beating the man with the ball in case they lost it. But as the game wore on, they discovered the Hungarians were only human after all and could be beaten like any other players. Perhaps we realised this too late.'

29

Sir George Graham

Secretary of the Scottish Football Association (1928–1957)

GEORGE GRAHAM succeeded John K. McDowell, the first SFA secretary, a position he had held since 1882. In that time McDowell had missed only one council meeting, and that was two weeks before his death. McDowell died at home in Crompton Avenue, Cathcart, in September of 1928, at the age of 67.

Graham was educated at Allan Glen's School and had been with the SFA since 1912. Graham had a lot of ideas on how football should be run and how it could be developed. He had backed plans for an Anglo-Scottish floodlit league containing Partick Thistle, Hibs, Hearts, Newcastle United, Manchester City and Tottenham Hotspur. The SFA Council rejected the plan by 23 votes to 12. The Scottish League banned any competitive floodlit football under their jurisdiction, and the proposed league didn't take off.

Appointed an OBE in 1947, he was knighted for his services to Scottish football in 1952.

Graham retired from his post in June 1957, the same day that Hughie Gallacher was found dead on the railway line. 'Hughie Gallacher was one of the finest centre-forwards we ever had,' Graham said.

Graham had advocated in his final year for a British Championship Cup, where the Scottish Cup and FA Cup winners would play each other in a final in Glasgow.

The SFA collected £1,200 for a retirement gift, and he was handed the keys to a new car. He was succeeded as SFA secretary by Willie Allan. Graham continued in his role as chairman of the organising committee for the European Cup.

Having left the SFA, Graham signed a deal to provide the *Scottish Sunday Express* with a series of exclusive articles. When published, they did not go down well with his former employers. 'The Executive Committee feel it is their duty to report to the council that they deplore the articles appearing in a Sunday newspaper under the name of the past secretary Sir George Graham,' an SFA Council statement read. In September 1957, the SFA unanimously decided to rescind a previous minute which read that Graham would always be an honoured guest at all future home internationals and Scottish Cup finals.

In retirement, Graham travelled across Europe to look at the inner workings of football in each country and wrote a series of newspaper articles on how clubs in Spain and West Germany trained, paid their players and developed their youth prospects.

In 1966, at the age of 74, Graham went over to the US and became executive secretary of the new National Professional Soccer League. The league's president Robert Hermann called Graham 'one of the world's foremost soccer administrators'. Graham worked to have the league recognised by FIFA. Brigadier E.G. Eakins, who headed the Vancouver branch of the rival North American Soccer League, said Graham was involved with 'an illegal soccer organisation. He should hand back his knighthood.' Despite having secured TV coverage, the NPSL could not become sanctioned and merged with the NASL in December 1967.

In January 1971, the SFA overturned their decision of 1957 and welcomed Sir George as the association's guest at home international and cup final matches.

Graham died at his home in Largs in January 1974 at the age of 81.

30

Scotland 4 Spain 2 – 1957

8 May 1957
Hampden Park
World Cup qualifying Group 9
Attendance: 88,873

Scotland: Younger (Liverpool), Caldow (Rangers), Hewie (Charlton Athletic), McColl (Rangers), Young [C] (Rangers), Docherty (Preston North End), Smith (Hibernian), Collins (Celtic), Mudie (Blackpool), Baird (Rangers), Ring (Clyde)

Spain: Ramallets (Barcelona), Olivella (Barcelona), Campanal (Sevilla), Garay [C] (Athletic Bilbao), Vergés (Barcelona), Zárraga (Real Madrid), González (Atlético Madrid), Kubala (Barcelona), Di Stéfano (Real Madrid), Suárez (Barcelona), Gento (Real Madrid)

Referee: Albert Busch (West Germany)

Goals:
Scotland – Mudie (23, 70, 79), Hewie (41, pen)
Spain – Kubala (30), Miramontes (50)

THIS WAS Scotland's first game in the three-team group, after Spain and Switzerland had drawn 2-2 in March.

The match, kicking off at 6.45pm, should have been live on BBC; however, due to poor ticket sales the SFA pulled out of the TV deal. Live coverage, though, did go ahead in many European countries.

Spain were seen by many as the strongest side in Europe, and the Scots were given little to no chance. But that didn't sit well with captain George Young, who spoke to the press on the eve of the tie, 'The Spaniards are described to us as the greatest team in the world, and we are expected to go to Hampden feeling very much inferior. They are just 11 men in jerseys. We are as good as, if not better than them.'

Lawrie Reilly and Willie Fernie had both lost their places in the team after the 2-1 loss to England a few weeks earlier. There was, therefore, a place for Blackpool's Jackie Mudie. The *Daily Telegraph* felt he 'could be the surprise of the match'. Mudie had received an FA Cup winners' medal in 1953 as Blackpool beat Bolton Wanderers in the match known as the 'Stanley Matthews Final'.

Hampden had been baked in the sun for the week previous to the match, but on the day there was steady heavy rain. Queen's Park officials reported that the ground was 'softening up nicely' in conditions that would suit the Scots more than the visitors.

Alfredo Di Stéfano, with six caps for his native Argentina, had taken Spanish nationality in 1956, making his debut for his adopted country in January 1957. This would be his fourth Spanish cap. Barcelona's Martín Vergés was making his debut.

From a corner on 22 minutes, Mudie hit the crossbar and then headed the rebound past Ramallets for 1-0. It only took four minutes, however, for Spain to level. Zarraga passed to Kubala, who swept the ball past Tommy Younger.

With five minutes to go until half-time, Olivella pulled Ring down and Scotland had a penalty. John Hewie made it 2-1 from the spot. Scotland then won a succession of free kicks as the Spanish resorted to petty fouls.

In the second half, although Scotland played with much confidence, the equaliser arrived from Spain. Di Stéfano back-heeled to let Suarez in. Younger pushed his shot out, only for Kubala to knock in the rebound. Younger then had to save from Gento, while the offside flag came to Scotland's rescue after González had the ball in the net.

Collins played in Mudie on 70 minutes; he shot from the edge of the box, and Scotland were 3-2 up. Nine minutes later, McColl and Collins combined with a one-two and Collins squared for Mudie to side-foot the ball in to make it 4-2. 'The brilliance of the movement that led up to it must have proved to [the Spaniards] that Scotland had assets of ball control and judgement that even Scottish football followers had not thought possible,' wrote the *Glasgow Herald*.

The following day Spain's *Marca* wrote that Spain's defeat was deserved due to 'the constant superiority of the play of the Scots over our team'.

'I could not tempt Young out of position,' Di Stéfano said. 'I used all my ingenuity, but there he was, always looming up as a barrier, impossible to pass.'

Tommy Docherty recalled the game in 2007, 'Spain were a great team with fantastic players, but we never let them play. We didn't have a manager at the time because the Scottish FA were too mean to hire one. But the trainer, Clyde's spongeman, Dawson Walker, gave the team talk. It was along the lines of, "Never mind the ball, get on with the game. Roll your sleeves up and get into them." And that's exactly what we did. We got among them and played a physical game. They hated it and spent the whole game complaining to the referee.'

Eric Caldow spoke to the *Sunday Mirror* in 2007, 'I was directly against Gento, who they claimed was the fastest winger in Europe at that time and he was tough to face. But if I had anything, I had pace, and I felt that I matched him. I didn't need to tackle a lot as I was blessed with natural pace. But we were a strong side that night, and Spain didn't like it.'

Scotland would beat Switzerland 2-1 in Basel 11 days later, and although they would lose 4-1 to Spain in Madrid at the end of May, a 3-2 win over Switzerland at Hampden would be enough to top the group on six points and qualify for the 1958 World Cup finals.

31

Matt Busby as Scotland Manager – 1958

AT A two-hour meeting of the SFA at Park Gardens in Glasgow on Thursday, 9 January 1958, a decision was made to appoint a national team manager. 'We have agreed in principle to the appointment, but no one has been asked yet to take the post,' an SFA official said to the press.

Among those suggested for the role were Tommy Walker, manager of Hearts, and Manchester United boss Matt Busby. In 1956 Rex Kingsley of the *Sunday Mail* asked Busby if he would manage Scotland alongside the United job. 'I'd take it as one of the greatest honours to come my way,' he replied. The SFA didn't make any moves at that point. United chairman Harold Hardman said, 'If the SFA ask Mr Busby we will not only consider it a great compliment to our manager, but to the Manchester United club itself.'

'It's the best step Scotland have taken for years,' remarked Ireland boss Peter Doherty. He suggested, however, that the new manager would have a three-year rebuilding job ahead of him.

On Tuesday, 14 January, members of the SFA's Selection Committee attended the Manchester United-Red Star Belgrade European Cup quarter-final first leg at Old Trafford. United won 2-1.

The following night, Busby attended the Scotland under-23s game with England at Goodison Park. The young Scots lost 3-1. After the match Busby announced that, subject to the agreement of United's directors, he would become Scotland's new manager, 'I am delighted to accept the invitation. It is a great honour.' Busby was the second national team manager after Andy Beattie.

Busby had won a full cap for Scotland against Wales in 1933 and had captained the team in several wartime internationals.

The appointment was met with enthusiasm from the press. The work Busby had done with Manchester United, the reigning English champions, indicated he could only improve the national side's fortunes. How he would do it, he told the *Sunday Mail*, was by building a team. 'This doesn't necessarily mean five years,' he said, 'but it means making every young player of quality believe and understand that there's a place for him in that Scottish side if he can prove he's worthy of it.'

The goal was to build the Scottish squad for the World Cup finals in Sweden that summer. Busby was happy that Scotland was still breeding good young players 'who only need guidance – maybe firm guidance – to bring us back to top class. We'll find them. We'll use them. And one day, we'll be proud of them.'

Jimmy Delaney, who was taken to United from Celtic by Busby in 1946, said, 'I think Matt could take Scotland's international team to the very top. Scotland will feel the master's touch. The touch that made Manchester United one of the world's greatest ever teams.'

In the first trial game, Scotland beat the Scottish League 3-2, with Nottingham Forest's Stuart Imlach the standout performer. Busby wasn't in attendance as United were in Belgrade for their European Cup quarter-final second leg, where a 3-3 draw took United into the semi-finals. The draw for the World Cup finals groups was set to take place in Stockholm on Saturday, 8 February.

On returning from Belgrade on 6 February, the plane taking the Manchester United squad home stopped in Munich to refuel. It was snowing when the Airspeed AS-57 Ambassador taxied to take off at 2.45pm. The pilot turned back, and an engineer looked at the engine. Around 15 minutes later there was a second attempt at take-off, but this was also abandoned. On its third attempt, the plane took off in a snowstorm. Slush on the runway slowed the plane too much to enable take-off. The aircraft ploughed through a fence beyond the end of the runway, and the left wing was torn off when it struck a house. The tail section broke off and hit a barn with a parked fuel truck in it, which caught fire and exploded.

Twenty-one people died, while the plane's captain and Manchester United's Duncan Edwards later passed away from their injuries.

Busby was severely injured. As he recovered in hospital, he admitted to wishing he had died and initially blamed himself for not stopping the pilot from attempting the third take-off.

By 21 February, he was reported to be out of danger. Gradually he would stop feeling he was to blame, but he decided he never wanted anything to do with football again. His wife, Jean, convinced him to carry on, telling him that the loved ones of those who perished and those who died themselves would surely wish him to carry on. 'From that moment, I wanted to live,' he wrote in his book.

Scotland kept the post open for him until the start of the 1958/59 season.

Busby left the Rechts der Isar Hospital in Munich on 17 April and returned home. He was asked at a press conference if he would be in charge of Scotland at the World Cup in Sweden in June. 'It will depend how well I am,' he replied.

Scotland lost 4-0 to England days later, with Clyde's trainer Dawson Walker put in charge of the team. 'I am very disappointed,' Tommy Docherty said. 'We did miss Matt Busby.'

Busby was still convalescing at home while Scotland played in Sweden. He travelled to Old Trafford when he was well enough for exercises with the physiotherapist Ted Dalton.

Willie Allan of the SFA and Willie Watters, chairman of the Selection Committee, visited Busby in Manchester at the end of August. On their return, they issued a statement saying that he was fit and had accepted the position of Scottish team manager.

Busby took charge of Scotland for the first time at Ninian Park, Cardiff, on 12 October. He gave first caps to Hibernian's John Grant, Willie Toner of Kilmarnock, David Herd of Arsenal, and Huddersfield's 18-year-old striker Denis Law. Busby, who had a 'magnanimous offer of £10,000' for Law turned down by Huddersfield, described him at that time as 'an elf with a wallop'.

Despite the presence of the experienced Tommy Docherty, Hearts' Dave Mackay was made skipper. It had been noted that on Docherty's four appearances as Scotland captain, he had changed from a demonstrative player to someone more timid. 'Tommy is one of those people worried by a title,' Busby told Sam Leitch of the *Daily Herald*. 'If we gave him the captaincy, the same thing might happen again.'

When Busby took over the Scotland job, he insisted that the players got a jersey and a cap after each match and kept them. The press reported that the gesture lifted the mood of the players.

Despite Mackay missing a penalty, Scotland won the match comfortably, with Graham Leggat, Law and Bobby Collins getting the goals in a 3-0 win.

'There is not a chance at all of me leaving Manchester United to do this or any other job,' Busby said when he was asked if he would become Scotland's full-time manager. 'I love both jobs. And the present arrangement is a perfect one, a happy one and one which I hope will last for a long time.'

Busby's next match in charge was at Hampden Park in November, where Northern Ireland were the opposition. Busby fielded an unchanged team. Arsenal's Jackie Henderson would win the last of his seven caps, while John Grant and Willie Toner both made their second and final appearances for their country.

All the goals came in the second half, Scotland taking a 2-0 lead with Herd and Collins scoring in the 53rd and 57th minutes. An Eric Caldow own goal let Northern Ireland back in, and with only seven minutes remaining Burnley's Jimmy McIlroy equalised.

Before Busby had really got started, rumours began circulating that United's directors believed his focus should be solely on his club job. Manchester United hadn't won since a 4-1 victory over West Ham on 17 September, and the 2-1 defeat to West Bromwich Albion on 25 October was their seventh game without a win. Busby told Rex Kingsley he was aware of the rumours but added, 'No one at Old Trafford has even hinted of such a thing.'

Busby, though, resigned from the Scotland job in early December 1958. 'Mr Busby has resigned for health reasons only,' the SFA announced. 'He has expressed his willingness to help us in any other way possible, but he was forced to give up the job on doctors' orders. If circumstances change in the future, he will reconsider the position.'

'Mr Busby's doctors feel he is trying to do too much,' Willie Allan said. 'Travelling is particularly bad for him. It is too early to say whether [the SFA committee] will consider appointing a successor.'

In his 1973 autobiography, Busby said he gave up the job for health reasons and 'because of my many commitments with Manchester United'.

32

France 2 Scotland 1 – 1958

15 June 1958
Eyravallen, Orebo
World Cup finals Group 2
Attendance: 13,554

France: Abbes (AS Saint-Étienne), Kaelbel (AS Monaco), Lerond (Olympique Lyonnais), Penverne (Stade de Reims), Jonquet [C] (Stade de Reims), Marcel (Olympique de Marseille), Wisniewski (RC Lens), Fontaine (Stade de Reims), Kopa (Real Madrid), Piantoni (Stade de Reims), Vincent (Stade de Reims)

Scotland: Brown (Dundee), Caldow (Rangers), Hewie (Charlton Athletic), Turnbull (Hibernian), Evans [C] (Celtic), Mackay (Hearts), Collins (Celtic), Murray (Hearts), Mudie (Blackpool), Baird (Rangers), Imlach (Nottingham Forest)

Referee: Juan Brozzi (Argentina)

Goals:
France – Kopa (22), Fontaine (45)
Scotland – Baird (66)

THIS WOULD be the final match of Group 2. Both sides had lost 3-2 in their previous match; France to Yugoslavia and Scotland to Paraguay.

Scotland had held Yugoslavia to a 1-1 draw in the opening game, where Jimmy Murray became the first Scot to score in the World Cup finals, while France had hammered Paraguay 7-3.

The results left Scotland sitting bottom of the group with one point. A win would guarantee joint second place in the group and a play-off to determine who went to the quarter-finals.

Scotland had a good record against France. They had won the last three internationals against them, in 1949, 1950 and 1951. France only had one win in six encounters. Robert Jonquet was the only player from the two sides to have played in that 1951 game.

Captain Tommy Younger was replaced in goal by debutant Bill Brown. Dave Mackay came into the side, while Bobby Evans was handed the captaincy.

Scotland went a goal down after 22 minutes when Just Fontaine crossed for Raymond Kopa to net. However, Scotland had a lifeline after half an hour. Mackay hit a shot which Claude Abbes dived to his left to save, but as Jimmy Murray ran in he was pushed to the ground. The referee pointed to the spot.

There followed a delay as the French players protested. John Hewie stepped up and cracked his shot against the post. As the French and Scots went for the rebound, a fight broke out with fists and feet flying. Referee Juan Brozzi called the two captains together and told them to cut it out.

'John Hewie almost broke the post with a penalty,' Murray told the *Sunday Mirror* in 1998. 'We were ready to chase the ball in, just in case it broke loose but it was going so fast, it flew back over our heads.'

'It was a stressful moment, obviously too stressful for me,' Hewie said to *The Independent* in 2006. 'I didn't just boot it anywhere, I was very deliberate. I belted it towards a chosen spot, the left-hand side. I can still picture it hitting the post. It had some force to it, and it bounced straight back out, over my head. I'll never forget it.'

France hit the crossbar twice, and Scotland were saved by Bill Brown, who made several great stops. 'He will never play a better game,' Cyril Horne wrote in the *Glasgow Herald*.

Just before the end of the first half, however, it was 2-0. Bobby Collins was tripped and Scotland were awarded a free kick. As the French regrouped when the kick came in, the defence cleared the danger, and suddenly Fontaine was flying through on the right and fired the ball past Brown. In the 66th minute, Scotland got back into the game. Murray played the ball long for Sammy Baird, who collected it on the run. He shrugged off a French challenge and shot home from 20 yards out.

Jackie Mudie had a chance a few minutes later when Baird played him in, but from only six yards his left-footed shot was too weak and Abbes gathered.

An equaliser wouldn't come, and the 2-1 defeat saw Scotland eliminated.

'Scotland more than matched the Frenchmen for football skill,' wrote the *Daily Telegraph*, 'but they made the mistake of passing sideways – which slowed them down.'

'The preparations were shambolic,' Mackay said. 'Why the authorities did not replace [Busby] is beyond me. Can you imagine an international side being allowed to travel to the World Cup finals without a manager nowadays? Had we taken a squad, had we employed a manager and invested in some weeks of preparation, it is hard to believe that we would not have done better than we did.'

33

Scotland Under-23s 4 England Under-23s 4 – 1960

2 March 1960
Ibrox Stadium
Friendly
Attendance: 25,000

Scotland: Blacklaw (Burnley), Mackay (Chelsea), Riddell (St Mirren), Gabriel (Everton), Martis (Motherwell), Higgins (Hearts), Hunter (Motherwell), Cousin (Dundee), St John (Motherwell), Law [C] (Huddersfield), Weir (Motherwell)

England: Marshall (Hearts), Cohen (Fulham), Allen (Stoke City), Setters [C] (Manchester United), Swan (Sheffield Wednesday), Kay (Sheffield Wednesday), Crowe (Leeds United), Eastham (Newcastle), Charlton (Manchester United), Greaves (Chelsea), Sydenham (Southampton)

Referee: Clifford Kingston (Newport, Monmouthshire)

Goals:
Scotland – St John (25, 54), Cousin (38), Mackay (40, pen)
England – Greaves (42, 55, 71), Eastham (76)

SCOTLAND'S FIRST under-23 match was in February 1955, against England at Shawfield, where an ill-prepared team were thrashed 6-0 with Duncan Edwards netting a hat-trick. There had been another seven under-23 internationals since then; three with England, two with the Netherlands and two against Wales.

This would be the first under-23 match between the countries since January 1958, when England won 3-1 at Goodison Park.

The 19-year-old Jimmy Gabriel was transferred just before the game, from Dundee to Everton for a reported fee of anything between £22,500 and £30,000. Goalkeeper Adam Blacklaw played for Burnley in a 2-0 win over Tottenham Hotspur only the night before, although his club-mate John Angus had dropped out of the England squad to play in the same game. This was the first time Denis Law had captained a senior side.

In the England side were goalkeeper Gordon Marshall and outside-right Chris Crowe, English by birth but brought up in Edinburgh. Crowe won three Scotland Schoolboy caps, including an appearance against England at Wembley in 1954. His cap from that match fetched £360 when it was auctioned in 2021.

Scotland, lining up in a 2-3-5 formation, started the 7.30pm kick-off smartly in the torrential rain. Law was crunched early on by Maurice Setters. It only spurred him on to a first half where he pinged passes all around the English defence.

The two had a personal feud throughout the game; Setters was no real match for Law as the Aberdonian continually lost him with ease. Law and Setters later played two and a half seasons together at Manchester United.

With 25 minutes gone, Gabriel lobbed a ball into the England box. Law jumped with Marshall, who fumbled. Ian St John picked up the scraps and hammered the loose ball home. It was 2-0 when Cousin darted on to a St John pass and put the ball away 13 minutes later.

A minute later, Setters grabbed Law around the waist for a penalty, which Mackay converted. Scotland were coasting, but then Jimmy Greaves got on the ball. Weaving and darting, he passed three Scots defenders in a run that resulted in England pulling a goal back just before half-time.

With nine minutes of the second half gone, Gabriel crossed a 40-yard free kick into the box for St John to head in to make it 4-1. That should have been that for a strong Scotland side, but Greaves responded with two solo goals before George Eastham headed in John Sydenham's cross on 77 minutes to tie the match at 4-4.

The FA's yearbook noted that 'for long periods play was dominated by Scotland'. England had been poor, with the notable exception of Greaves. 'A scoreline has never told a more ludicrous lie,' wrote the *News Chronicle*. Greaves's goals were noted by the *Motherwell Times* as 'three of the sweetest goals it has been our fortune to see'. The Chelsea striker was only in the team due to the unavailability of Joe Baker, who was required by his club Hibs. It was Greaves's third hat-trick for the under-23s.

Law played in every outfield position on the pitch that night, from right-back to outside-left. His performance was 'one of the really great inside-forward displays of recent years' according to *The Journal*. The *Evening Times* reported that Rangers fans in attendance were asking why their club couldn't sign Law.

Of the 11, only Riddell, Higgins and Cousin didn't go on to win full caps. The England goalkeeper Gordon Marshall's son, also called Gordon, earned one cap for Scotland against the United States in 1992.

34

England 9 Scotland 3 – 1961

15 April 1961
Wembley Stadium
British Home Championship
Attendance: 97,350

Scotland: Haffey (Celtic), Shearer (Rangers), Caldow [C] (Rangers), Mackay (Tottenham Hotspur), McNeill (Celtic), McCann (Motherwell), MacLeod (Hibernian), Law (Manchester City), St John (Motherwell), Quinn (Motherwell), Wilson (Rangers)

England: Springett (Sheffield Wednesday), Armfield (Blackpool), McNeil (Middlesbrough), Robson (West Bromwich Albion), Swan (Sheffield Wednesday), Flowers (Wolverhampton Wanderers), Douglas (Blackburn Rovers), Greaves (Chelsea), Smith (Tottenham Hotspur), Haynes (Fulham), Charlton (Manchester United)

Referee: Marcel Lequesne (France)

Goals:
England – Robson (9), Greaves (21, 30, 83), Douglas (55), Smith (73, 85), Haynes (78, 82)
Scotland – Dave Mackay (48), Davie Wilson (53, 75)

'I TIP Scotland,' England legend Stanley Matthews said before the match. 'They are poised to break that long and dismal Wembley record. I have a hunch they can beat England.'

It's perhaps the most infamous Scotland game of all time, although it went on to have competition in later years. When you look at the side that lined up that day, it's by no means understrength. England were undoubtedly strong, but the Scottish side should have been a match for them.

Scotland hadn't beaten England since a 3-2 win in 1951, with six defeats and three draws over the decade.

The Scotland side had four players making their international debuts: Pat Quinn, Bobby Shearer, Billy McNeill and Johnny MacLeod. The Scotland squad had no training together before leaving on the sleeper on Thursday night to arrive at their headquarters in Sonning, where they would go on to have a training session at Reading's Elm Park ground. 'Scotland's preparations go back to the Ark,' wrote Bernard Joy in the *Evening Standard*, noting that surely the new caps needed to develop an understanding.

The Queen was in the crowd, watching her first international between the countries. The *Birmingham Mail* reported touts selling a pair of 25s tickets for £11.

In goal should have been the twice-capped Lawrie Leslie. However, an eye injury sustained while playing for Airdrie against Ayr United ruled him out. Celtic's Frank Haffey was selected in his place.

'Always the English will believe the genius of captain Johnny Haynes earned glorious victory,' Donald Saunders wrote in the *Daily Telegraph*. 'Scotsmen will forever blame goalkeeper Frank Haffey's shortcomings for ignominious defeat.'

'He might have made a couple of mistakes but not half as many as the defenders around him,' England's Jimmy Armfield said to *The Guardian* in 2001. 'It is always too easy to blame your keeper.'

'The goalie might have stopped a couple but we'd have run amok whoever was in goal,' Johnny Haynes said. Five of England's goals came in the last 17 minutes of the match. 'It was very competitive until we hit that purple patch,' Haynes continued. 'Then even the best keeper in the world wouldn't have denied us.' Haynes said he regretted not saying anything to Haffey at the end of the match.

'I think that the big difference between the two sides was that England had a settled team which played like a club side,' wrote Denis Law in his autobiography *The Lawman*, 'whereas we were a disjointed set of individuals who met only a few minutes before the match.'

'I remember getting kicked in the air in front of the Royal Box by Denis Law,' Bobby Robson said in the TV programme *Faith, Hope and Calamity* in 1994. 'Oh, did I? Did I? Did I?' Law said with mock surprise on the same programme. 'In front of the Queen as well. What a liberty.'

Davie Wilson had a great chance to put Scotland in front in the first minute but slipped. Robson put England ahead after nine minutes with a shot from 20 yards, a goal he would say was the happiest memory of his 20 England appearances. Wilson and Dave Mackay had chances to equalise before Haynes sent Greaves clear for 2-0. Haffey saved from Bobby Smith but was helpless to prevent Greaves from knocking in the rebound to make it 3-0. Law then had the ball in the net but was ruled offside.

Scotland had chances but squandered them. Haffey made a great save from Greaves to prevent England from extending their lead before half-time.

'I don't know why England did not score a lot more before half-time,' Law recalled. 'We were there for the taking but the scoreline remained the same.'

'Walter Winterburn didn't say a great deal,' Jimmy Greaves said of England's half-time talk. 'Like the supporters, I think he was stunned. He just told us to keep playing football and make certain we kept it tight during the opening ten minutes of the second half because he was certain the Scots would come out all guns blazing and give it a go.'

'Our dressing room was more than a little animated during half-time,' Law wrote. 'We were not just in disarray on the pitch, for those few minutes we were in a state off it as well. Blame was being handed around as if it was a grenade with the pin removed.'

'Defensively, we were awful,' Ian St John said to *The Times* in 2011. 'I partially blame our manager, Ian McColl. It was only his second game in charge, and, for me, he hadn't a clue. At half-time, with us 3-0 down, Ian could not sort us out. He was out of his depth.'

In the second half the Scots were more determined and pulled a goal back three minutes into the second period through Mackay. Mick McNeil fouled Law, and Mackay hit the free kick through English legs and into the net. In the 52nd minute, the deficit was cut to one when Mackay sent MacLeod down the wing. He sent over a cross for Wilson to head home.

A few minutes later, and England had a free kick on the edge of the Scots' box after Billy McNeill and Smith had challenged for a high ball. It looked soft, and Scots fans felt the decision should have gone against Smith. As the Scots defence were preparing to line up, Greaves took the kick from where the ball lay, yards away from the offence. Douglas collected the ball and shot. Haffey slowed the ball down, but it squirmed out of his hands and over the line for 4-2.

The Scots team surrounded the referee in protest. But he would not be moved. Minutes later, Scotland had a free kick. On this occasion, as on others previously, the referee held on to the ball and paced out the distance for the wall. Scots in the ground couldn't help but feel aggrieved.

'The goal was an injustice as we were getting back into the game,' Scotland coach Ian McColl said, 'and it took the heart out of the lads. That was the turning point.'

'This should be the end of continental referees for games like this,' Eric Caldow said afterwards. 'The referee let Greaves take the free kick from the wrong place. I thought it was an injustice.'

'To this day, it seems to us that Jimmy Greaves gained an unfair advantage by taking the free kick several yards nearer to the goal than he should have done,' recalled Law.

The referee called both captains together due to the number of fierce tackles flying in. Law, in particular, was noted for the ferocious challenges he was making, being booed by the English crowd. 'There's no doubting that Law was a very good player,' Peter Swan wrote in his 2006 autobiography, 'but if he went into a tackle, he always went over the top. He'd have his foot up, and that sort of thing could break your leg.'

It's possible that the disputed free kick may have contributed to the Scotland team losing focus, but from that point on, they folded.

Haynes and Greaves then worked a move allowing Bobby Smith to take up the ball. Smith beat Billy McNeill and fired past Haffey. It was now 5-2.

Scotland had some hope again two minutes later. Mackay back-headed a MacLeod corner to Wilson, who shot first time. There has been some debate over the years whether Quinn got the final touch, but the consensus now appears to be that, although it may have looked like Quinn got something on it, the ball went straight in from Wilson, who scored his second.

The roof, though, was about to fall in. Greaves beat McNeill with a pass, Haynes latched on to the ball, feinted to pass, but then whipped it past Haffey for 6-3. Douglas went on a run and played Haynes in to shoot home from 16 yards in 82 minutes. Greaves toyed with the Scots' defence before knocking in his hat-trick.

With only a few minutes remaining, Greaves played through Smith for the ninth. The only piece of luck for the Scots was that the referee spotted a hand used by Greaves just before he lashed the ball in for what would have been England's tenth.

Law wrote that Frank Haffey was in tears, 'I think we were all close to tears in our morgue of a dressing room, but Frank gave way to his.'

In *Ireland's Saturday Night,* Malcolm Brodie wrote that England's late four goals 'make Scotland losers by a much greater margin than they deserved'.

In *The Scotsman*, Hugh McIlvanney wrote that Haffey 'erred with the clumsiness and regularity of a substitute in a second-class works team'.

Lawrie Leslie travelled with the team and watched the game from the stands. 'It was a terrible game for me to watch,' he said. 'Then, as now, the goalkeepers tended to stick together, so that night, I found myself wandering around central London with Frank, trying to cheer him up. But, in truth, we were both suffering and couldn't get back up the road quickly enough.'

Haffey said to the *Evening Times* in 2003 that his club manager Jock Stein sat him down with a film of the game at Celtic Park, and Stein's opinion was his keeper was only at fault for two of the goals. Bobby Robson also said the same in a TV interview in 1999. 'I feel I was maybe at fault for three,' Haffey said.

'Your defenders haven't done very well if you face nine shots on goal,' Dave Mackay said to *FourFourTwo* in 2009.

'I have to admit the scoreline was a bit of a freak,' Bobby Charlton wrote in 2009. 'There wasn't *that* big a gulf between the two sides.'

'In footballing terms, it was the worst day of my life,' Mackay said years later. 'We played crap ... I felt such shame for letting my country down so dramatically, and I did not know how I could face anyone. It was a freak result and is the only game people seem to remember me playing at Wembley.'

35

Czechoslovakia 4 Scotland 2 (AET) – 1961

29 November 1961
Heysel Stadium, Brussels
World Cup qualifying Group 8 – play-off
Attendance: 7,976

Scotland: Connachan (Dunfermline Athletic), Hamilton (Dundee), Caldow [C] (Rangers), Crerand (Celtic), Ure (Dundee), Baxter (Rangers), Brand (Rangers), White (Tottenham Hotspur), St John (Liverpool), Law (Torino), Robertson (Dundee)

Czechoslovakia: Schrojf (Slovan Bratislava), Hledík (Spartak Hradec Králové), Pluskal (Dukla Prague), Popluhár (Slovan Bratislava), Tichý [C] (CH Bratislava), Masopust (CH Bratislava), Pospichal (CH Bratislava), Scherer (CH Bratislava), Kučera (Dukla Prague), Jelinek (Dukla Prague), Kvašňák (Sparta Prague)

Referee: Gérard Versyp (Belgium)

Goals:
Scotland – St John (37, 72)
Czechoslovakia – Hledik (70), Scherer (82), Pospichal (94), Kvašňák (105)

THE PLAY-OFF in neutral Belgium came about as Scotland and Czechoslovakia were tied on points at the top of their qualifying group. An oddity of the rules said that with a better goal average, if the play-off was drawn, Czechoslovakia would go through.

The Czechs wouldn't allow Scotland to call up West Ham's Lawrie Leslie to deputise for Bill Brown, as he wasn't in the original squad, which was within FIFA's rules. Instead Eddie Connachan made his debut in goal. In a countermove, Scotland insisted that the referee should not allow the game to be played with a Czech ball.

Torino demanded that Scotland insure Denis Law for £200,000 before they would allow him to play.

The game kicked off at 2.30pm local time (1.30pm UK time) in a 65,000-capacity stadium.

'It was a dump even back then,' Ian St John said of the ground in 2011. 'Very dilapidated and there was nothing of a crowd there. Fans didn't travel to midweek games the way they do now.'

Ian Ure recalled the match in his 1968 autobiography *Ure's Truly*, 'The crowd were not much help to either side – there weren't many present in the Heysel Stadium because of live television coverage. Though there was no atmosphere on the terraces, it must have been one of the most exciting games of the year.'

The first goal came when Popluhár fouled St John just outside the penalty area. Baxter took the free kick and lifted the ball into the box for St John to head into the net.

In the 54th minute, White went down holding his leg in an off-the-ball incident with Jelinek, who got a talking-to from the referee. White, normally calm on the pitch, had to be restrained by his team-mates as he sought to exact retribution.

The equaliser came as Czechoslovakia forced three corners in a row, and Hledík came up from the back to head in from the third on 70 minutes.

But Scotland were soon back in front as, two minutes later, Schrojf misjudged a Brand free kick leaving St John to knock the ball into the empty net.

'Then the Czechs equalised with a goal that was dodgy to say the least,' wrote Denis Law in his autobiography. Scherer hit a shot-cum-cross which struck the underside of the bar and came flying back out. There was some dispute about whether the ball had actually gone over the line, but the referee had no doubt. 'There was absolutely no way he could have had clear vision,' wrote Law.

The game now went to extra time.

'My morale nosedived,' Ure recalled, 'because of the behaviour of two of our players. They started a scuffle, and all they were fighting over was a sponge.'

St John also recalled the incident in his autobiography, 'Suddenly, Paddy Crerand and Jim Baxter were exchanging blows. I pulled them apart and said, "For God's sake, let's fight them, not ourselves." The issue was which one of them got first use of a wet sponge. It was not the most encouraging signal.'

Crerand explained what happened in his autobiography *Never Turn the Other Cheek*, 'The trainer passed me a sponge and Jim Baxter tried to grab it out of my hand. We finished up on the ground trying to punch each other. We were about to play the most important half-hour in Scotland's football history and yet we were fighting with each other over a sponge. We were both pals, but we were so angry because they had equalised so late on that we took it out on each other in the heat of the moment.'

'I stood watching all this with my mouth open,' recalled Ure. 'I was new to the international level of football and did not expect anything like this. I thought to myself, if they are as desperate as that, what chance had we got in extra time?'

'Paddy got the sponge,' Baxter recalled in 1994. 'I said, "Come on, let us have some water." He turned away and I grabbed him and we're tussling to get this bloody stupid sponge in the middle of the Heysel Stadium.'

Scotland had a great chance in the sixth minute of extra time, as White hit a 20-yard shot which hit the junction of post and crossbar.

Scotland's luck, however, was not in. Jiří Tichý punched St John after he had challenged the keeper for a cross from Brand. The referee awarded a foul against St John.

Law recalled, 'On the heavy, muddy pitch, the Czechs who were a much bigger and physically stronger side than Scotland wore us down.'

Pospichal scored in the fourth minute of extra time while Kvašňák added a fourth in the second period.

In the *Evening Times*, Cyril Horne wrote, 'Of all the continental or foreign teams I have ever seen, this Czech side was the worst for unfair, and even brutal tactics. This was not merely a case of the Scots having to suffer pushing and body checking, there was hardly a player in the Scottish team who did not have his ankles rapped from behind.'

'There was much shared anger as we flew home,' St John wrote. St John and Crerand were of the opinion that this was the biggest opportunity for Scotland to make a name for themselves on the world stage. The Czechs went on to reach the World Cup Final, losing to Brazil, which for some Scots provided a crumb of comfort; for others, it seemed like a missed opportunity.

36

Denis Law Scores Three Hat-Tricks in a Year and a Day – 1962/63

'My heart pounds when I pull over my shoulders the dark blue jersey of Scotland. This is the proudest moment of all, the prelude to 90 minutes which represents more than a game of football. It is an expression of one's deepest loyalties and convictions, a giving of oneself wholly to the task of proving Scotland's everlasting greatness.'

Denis Law, in his 1963 autobiography *Living For Kicks*

Scotland 5 Northern Ireland 1
7 November 1962

Against the run of play at Hampden, Northern Ireland scored first in this British Home Championship match, Jimmy McIlroy picking Paddy Crerand's pocket and playing in Billy Bingham to score after eight minutes.

The equaliser came with four minutes remaining of the first half. Willie Henderson cut the ball back for Law to score with a back flick.

Although Tottenham's Danny Blanchflower was immaculate, particularly at keeping his club-mate John White in check, he had little answer to Law. Denis put Scotland ahead with a shot from close range after Henderson had crossed on 64 minutes.

The Irish defence were now looking for the final whistle as Law completed the hat-trick with 13 minutes remaining. Willie Henderson made it 4-1 two minutes later. Law's fourth, with five minutes left, went in off a defender.

In the *Evening Times*, Gair Henderson wrote, 'Denis Law is the nearest thing to the perfect footballer – and Scotland must be the luckiest country in the world to have him on call.' Henderson wrote that Hampden had never witnessed a greater one-man show than that put on by Law.

Cyril Horne in the *Glasgow Herald* wrote of Law's 'remarkable display of skill, speed and stamina. Without the superb combination of craft and exuberance that the inside left produced, Scotland would have had great difficulty in winning.'

In his autobiographies, Law wrote about his scoring exploits that week, where he had also scored four for Manchester United. 'After my experience of tight marking in Italy, I was finding it far easier to score goals in British football because there was so much more time and space available. I was very happy to be back in Britain, and I think it gave my football a new lease of life. I no longer felt so restricted.'

In December 1962, Alfredo Di Stéfano, asked to name his ideal successor when he was to leave Real Madrid, said, 'Denis Law. He is the best inside-forward in the game.'

Norway 3 Scotland 4
4 June 1963

Brian Glanville wrote that Scotland's friendly defeat to a team of amateurs in Bergen was 'the biggest soccer upset of the year'.

Olav Nilsen opened the scoring on five minutes. Law equalised eight minutes later before putting Scotland in front after 22 minutes. Erik Johansen made it 2-2 after 59 minutes, but Law completed his hat-trick with 76 minutes gone. Five minutes later, Arne Pedersen equalised, while John Krogh made it 4-3 with seven minutes left.

'If Law had been in the same form in the second half as he was in the first, the result might have been different,' Norwegian coach Ragnar Larsen said. 'At the interval, I told the team to close up on the Scottish forwards and throw everything into attack. This we did successfully, and I am only surprised that the Scots had no counter to our all-out offensive.'

Press reports suggested that Scotland had at least three good chances to add to their goal tally, and Law was the man who missed them all. SFA secretary Willie Allan remarked, 'A very poor Scottish team. They deserved to lose.'

Scotland 6 Norway 1
7 November 1963

In the first minute of this friendly, postponed for 24 hours due to fog, Law hit a drive that was tipped over for a corner by Sverre Andersen in goal. However, Norway took the lead through Per Kristoffersen in the eighth minute, reacting to a pass from Arne Pedersen.

The equaliser came in the 20th minute. Dave Mackay passed to White, who played the ball to Alan Gilzean, on his debut, who knocked it on to Law, who prodded home. Law then scored a solo effort past Andersen in goal one minute from half-time to put Scotland 2-1 up.

Being well aware of his capabilities, at times Norway had three men marking Law. 'Nobody requires the same amount of close attention on the field as Denis,' Gianni Rivera, the Milan and Italy midfielder, once said.

On the hour, Law made it 3-1. He controlled a corner from Willie Henderson before thrashing the ball into the net. Mackay scored from 25 yards and followed that up with another piledriver from a similar distance for 5-1. With three minutes to go, Law rounded substitute keeper Kjell Kaspersen to complete the scoring.

'Seven goals in two matches against the Norwegians gave me something of a reputation in Scandinavia,' Law wrote in *The Lawman*, 'and I still get mail from there reminding me of those two games.'

Two days later, on 9 November 1963, Law scored three for Manchester United against Tottenham Hotspur in a 4-1 league win. 'You just can't keep that little so-and-so down,' the Tottenham goalkeeper, Law's international colleague Bill Brown, said.

'Big crowds lift me out of myself,' Law said in 1964, 'I could hug them. Atmosphere is everything in football. I wear my confidence like wings.'

37

Mr Baxter Goes to Wembley – 1963

'Just the mere thought of Jim Baxter brings a smile to my face. I always grin at the memory of him, whether it was taking the piss out the English at Wembley or joking about a life that he never took very seriously.'

Jimmy Greaves, 2008

WHILE JIM Baxter's 1967 performance against England is the one that has become the most famous, it's his display in the 1963 game at Wembley that was perhaps his best in a Scotland jersey.

Bobby Moore believed the team that day was the best side Scotland ever had.

After five minutes, Scottish captain Eric Caldow sustained a multiple leg fracture following a collision with England's Bobby Smith. Team boss Ian McColl was sat in the Royal Box, hoping to get a better overall view of the game. 'The visiting royals, though, must have got the fright of their lives … when I dashed downstairs to check out my team captain Eric Caldow,' McColl said in 1999. 'He'd been struck down by the worst tackle I'd ever seen.'

With no substitutes available, the team now had to be reorganised. 'Ian McColl shouted at Dave Mackay to go to left-back,' Davie Wilson said to *The Scotsman* in 2016. 'I didn't think that was the best idea, so I did it.'

The injury to his friend and colleague lit a fire in Baxter. In the *Press and Journal*, Norman MacDonald wrote, 'Baxter made every move look simple – the mark of the supreme artist. And, in the 29th minute, he showed his forwards that England's defence was by no means impregnable.'

Willie Henderson sent a cross into the England box. It missed the head of Ian St John and fell nicely for England captain Jimmy Armfield who decided to dribble it out of the area. Baxter easily dispossessed him and ran in on goal.

Gordon Banks, the 25-year-old Leicester City goalkeeper, was making his England debut. In his book *Banksy* he recalls the moment, 'Heaven knows what Jimmy thought he was doing. Scotland's left-half, Rangers' Jim Baxter, thought it was Christmas. Latching on to the gift we had presented him with, he bore down on my goal. I raced off my line to cut down Baxter's vision of my goal, but he swayed like a bird on a twig. I put all my weight on my left foot, and Jim rolled the ball to my right and into the net.'

'Normally, I played for myself,' Baxter said in 2000. 'But when it came to England-Scotland games at Wembley, I played for the fans as well. They helped make these occasions special.'

'Jim Baxter was strolling arrogantly around Wembley as if he owned the place,' recalled Banks, 'and we were giving him far too much room in which to operate.'

England had been staring wide-eyed at Scottish passes for 30 seconds when Henderson jinked and swerved his way into the box. Ron Flowers of Wolves could only body check the Rangers winger as he went past him. Dutch referee Leo Horn pointed to the penalty spot.

Eric Caldow had been the designated penalty taker. Dave Mackay retrieved the ball and had only one thought. 'I just threw it to Jim,' Mackay told Ken Gallacher for his biography of Baxter, 'and said to him, "Just you tuck that away in the net."'

Willie Henderson recalled, 'He might have been getting ready to take the kick on a public park in a bounce game for all the emotion he showed.'

'Facing penalties could be like participating in the Leicester City card school,' wrote Banks. 'Sometimes you try and bluff your way through even when you know you haven't a strong hand. The cool Jim Baxter, however, called my bluff: he approached the ball as if he was on a leisurely stroll in the park and casually placed it into the left-hand corner of my goal as I dived the wrong way.'

It was the first penalty Baxter had ever taken.

England pulled a goal back through Bryan Douglas, but Baxter and Scotland were triumphant.

'For all true lovers of football, Baxter's artistry that day was a joy to behold,' wrote Banks. 'It was just my luck that he had chosen my England debut as the occasion on which to produce the greatest performance of his career!'

'Alf [Ramsey] was sick about losing to the Scots from that day on,' Bobby Moore told Jeff Powell, 'but most of the players appreciated the way Scotland played.'

'[Baxter] cleverly and completely ran the game from his midfield command post,' wrote Greaves, who was England's number eight that day, 'swaggering off at the end with the ball famously stuck up his jersey. He had owned the match so it was only right that the ball should also belong to him.'

'The feeling I got that afternoon could never be repeated,' Baxter said to journalist Jim Black in 2000. 'I just wish it had been a hat-trick.' Baxter cheekily suggested he thought of putting through his own net to claim three goals that day. 'Believe me, I would have done had they not pulled it back to 2-1. I had made up my mind to score again – for England. When I told [goalkeeper] Bill Brown what I had in mind, he clearly thought I had flipped. But I was deadly serious. I was capable of doing that sort of thing, believe me.'

38

Spain 2 Scotland 6 – 1963

13 June 1963
Estadio Santiago Bernabéu, Madrid
Friendly
Attendance: 40,000

Spain: Vicente (Real Madrid), Rivilla [C] (Atlético Madrid), Mingorance (Córdoba), Reija (Real Zaragoza), Aguirre (Athletic Bilbao), Glaría (Atlético Madrid), Amancio (Real Madrid), Adelardo (Atlético Madrid), Veloso (Deportivo de La Coruña), Guillot (Valencia), Lapetra (Real Zaragoza)

Scotland: Blacklaw (Burnley), McNeill (Celtic), Holt (Hearts), McLintock (Leicester City), Ure (Dundee), Baxter (Rangers), Henderson (Rangers), Gibson (Leicester City), St John (Liverpool), Law [C] (Manchester United), Wilson (Rangers)

Referee: Giulio Campanati (Italy)

Goals:
Spain – Adelardo (8), Veloso (43)
Scotland – Law (15), Gibson (16), McLintock (18), Wilson (32), Henderson (51), St John (83)

SCOTLAND TRAVELLED to Spain as British Home Championship winners, but defeats to Norway and Ireland had demoralised the squad. 'By the time we got to Madrid, Ian McColl didn't have a clue what he was doing,' Ian Ure said to journalist Graham Spiers in a 2020 piece for *The Herald*. 'He was done in by these two defeats. We played a makeshift team in Spain, and yet, look at the players we fielded: Billy McNeill, Jim Baxter, Willie Henderson, Denis Law, Ian St John, Davie Wilson and more. Terrific players.'

McNeill was selected at right-back while Ure was centre-half. McNeill hadn't played right-back for Celtic since a 3-0 league victory over Raith Rovers in September 1959.

The Spanish were a relatively inexperienced side with two debutants in Mingorance and Lapetra. Their most experienced international was first-time captain Rivilla, who was earning his 15th cap at the age of 26.

Spain had taken the lead through inside-right Adelardo with only eight minutes played. '"Here we go again," I thought,' wrote Frank McLintock in his 1969 autobiography. The equaliser, though, was only seven minutes in arriving as Baxter combined with St John, who passed for Law to score.

From the restart, Scotland retrieved the ball, and Baxter played in Gibson, who hit a shot from 20 yards for 2-1. 'Even the Spaniards stood up and cheered a gem of a goal,' the *Daily Record* reported.

Denis Law stood out as a truly world-class performer. He excelled in both attack and defence, and his distribution was sure-footed and insightful. Henderson and Wilson down the wings gave the Spanish defence a torrid time.

'We were dead flash that night doing what we term in Scotland keepy-uppy,' Ian Ure wrote in his autobiography.

From a Henderson corner, Frank McLintock made it 3-1. Spain attempted to quell the onslaught by taking off Mingorance for Zoco after only 32 minutes. Those 32 minutes would count as the Córdoba defender's only experience of international football. Zoco was on the field just in time to see the imperious Baxter play in Wilson, who scored Scotland's fourth.

'I played behind Baxter,' Davie Holt, who had also played for Great Britain in the 1960 Olympics, said to the *Daily Record* in 2019. 'I could have strolled through the 90 minutes in full Highland regalia and playing the bagpipes.'

With two minutes remaining in the first half Veloso pulled a goal back. Vicente, who, despite recently winning his third La

Liga title in a row with Real Madrid, had looked uncertain in goal, and was replaced by Atlético Bilbao's Carmelo at half-time.

In the Scottish goal, Blacklaw made two excellent saves to maintain Scotland's lead before St John cut the ball back for Henderson to make it 5-2 in the 51st minute. The sixth goal came from St John with seven minutes remaining.

The *Glasgow Herald* noted that its only criticism was that after the sixth goal, the Scots slowed the game to a walking pace and tried to humiliate the Spaniards. 'The Spanish crowd didn't like it one bit,' said Ure. 'Stuff was being thrown on to the pitch.'

'I don't think I can remember a match in which the Scottish defence played so well,' wrote McLintock, 'and though we scored six times, we were great at the back. This was easily my best performance for Scotland and to be fair to the Scottish press, they said so in print. This was practically the only time they managed to say anything nice about me, and it made sweet reading.'

'This is one of the greatest teams ever to wear the Scottish jersey,' manager Ian McColl said afterwards. Denis Law, too, said it was the greatest national team in which he had played. 'I do not think a Scottish side has ever been tighter in defence,' Ure wrote.

39

John White

22 caps, 3 goals (1959–1964)

'THE WORST thing for all of us in those 1960s was losing dear John White,' Jimmy Greaves said in a 1970s conversation with Dave Mackay included in Norman Giller's book *Jimmy Greaves The One and Only*. 'Yes, I still well up when I think of it,' Mackay replied. 'He had asked Cliffie Jones and me to play golf with him but we turned him down because there was a lot of rain around. He went out on his own and got hit by lightning. It was a tragedy that affected everybody at the club, particularly his best mate Jonesie and me. He was a magnificent footballer, a real players' player who always put the team first.'

Those who saw White play often reminisce about him and about what could have been. White was a Falkirk player when he made his international debut on 6 May 1959 in a friendly against West Germany at Hampden in front of 103,500.

White had a start to dream of when with only 50 seconds gone, he raced into the box to meet a knockdown from Ian St John and fired home past Günter Sawitzki. 'Taken with the icy calm of a veteran of 50 internationals,' wrote Gair Henderson in the *Evening Times*.

Five minutes later, Andy Weir had made it 2-0. White's quick and accurate passing that night ripped right through the opposition, and although West Germany came back, Scotland won 3-2.

Later that month White played in Amsterdam as Scotland beat the Netherlands 2-1.

Born in Musselburgh, White was a slight 5ft 7.5in, leading to him being rejected by both Rangers and Middlesbrough. He got his chance with Second Division Alloa Athletic, and after a couple of seasons at the Recreation Ground, he signed for First Division Falkirk in August 1958.

Tottenham captain Danny Blanchflower played against White for Northern Ireland on 3 October 1959. Scotland won 4-0, with White scoring the third. Blanchflower told Spurs manager Bill Nicholson he had to sign him. Less than a week later, White joined Tottenham for £20,000. He was still a serving soldier with the King's Own Scottish Borderers at Berwick-on-Tweed at the time.

One of White's notable skills was using open space, leading to his nickname, the 'Ghost of White Hart Lane'. In 1960/61, John played every game as Tottenham won the First Division and FA Cup double.

For Scotland, White played against England three times and won on each occasion: 2-0 in 1962, 2-1 at Wembley in 1963 and 1-0 in April 1964.

In 1962 White scored twice as Spurs defeated Rangers in the European Cup Winners' Cup 5-2 at White Hart Lane, following it up in the second leg with a 3-2 win at Ibrox. Spurs would go on to win the trophy, White scoring in the final as they beat Atlético Madrid 5-1.

Rangers fans didn't forget what White had done to them, and in subsequent internationals at Hampden, particularly the game against Norway in November 1963, White was barracked from the terracing. It was not uncommon in this era for Celtic players to receive this treatment when playing for Scotland.

The May 1964 friendly with West Germany in Hanover was White's final appearance for Scotland.

On 21 July 1964, he was playing golf at the Crews Hill course in Enfield, Middlesex. When a lightning storm came on, he took shelter under an oak tree. He was playing alone. Two groundsmen found him dead on the ninth fairway.

'He will be missed as much as a man as a player,' Tom Reid, the president of the SFA, said.

40

Alan Gilzean

22 caps, 12 goals (1963–1971)

ALAN GILZEAN joined Dundee as an amateur in 1956 before signing professional terms the following year. He had won the Scottish First Division title in 1962 and played in a European Cup semi-final against AC Milan the following year before making his Scotland debut. It came in a 6-1 win over Norway. The *Glasgow Herald* reported, 'He seldom wasted a ball and there were more shots from a Scottish centre-forward than have been seen for some time.'

His first goal for Scotland came in his third international, and it was a moment that forever sealed his place in Scottish football folklore. England were the visitors to Hampden and came into the game having won their last six internationals. Archie Macpherson was early in his broadcasting career. 'As far as I can recollect, the game was scrappy, untidy, and Scotland seemed to have more possession although with a developing sense of frustration rising around the stadium,' he said to *The Times* in 2018. 'But what still stands in sharp relief is the 72nd minute of the game.'

'There was a gale-force wind blowing throughout the match, and ball control was really difficult,' Gilzean said. 'We were deadlocked without a goal when we forced a corner on the left.'

John Greig was making his debut that day. He said, 'What a goal that was. Davie Wilson swung over a corner from the Mount Florida end. Gillie running in from the penalty box timed his jump to perfection and the ball went in like a bullet.'

'I timed my jump just right and managed to head the ball wide of that fantastic goalkeeper Gordon Banks,' said Gilzean.

'I was at fault for the goal that beat us,' Gordon Banks said in 1976. 'I'm not making excuses, but the cover on the enclosure behind that goal had still to be erected and the Hampden swirl was at its worst. I came out to meet the ball, well off my line, and never got to it, allowing Gilzean to knock it over the line with his head. I hadn't had a bad game … but I know I should never have lost that goal.'

The goal gave Scotland a run of three victories in a row over England for the first time since the 1880s when England were beaten five times in a row from 1880 to 1884.

'I hate talking about my goals,' Gilzean said. 'I always saw it as my job to put the ball in the net, so I could never understand all the fuss.'

In the following international, a month later, Scotland faced West Germany in Hanover. With Scotland behind by two Uwe Seeler goals, Gilzean hauled his team back into the match with a goal in the 66th minute. He notched an equaliser with eight minutes left to seal a 2-2 draw.

In December 1964 Gilzean's form earned a transfer to Tottenham Hotspur, where he formed an instant understanding with strike partner Jimmy Greaves. 'He was a master of the flick pass and glancing header,' Greaves said. '[He] was always graceful on the ball, no matter how great the pressure. A genius of a touch player.' Greaves acclaimed Gilzean as the greatest player he played with.

Gilzean's last game for his country was a 2-0 defeat against Portugal in Lisbon in April 1971. He continued to play at the top level, with Tottenham winning the 1972 UEFA Cup.

In the *Evening Standard*, journalist Patrick Barclay, a Dundee supporter, said of Gilzean, 'He was a better passer with his head than many a striker can manage with his feet – and his feet were balletic.'

41

Austria Abandoned – 1963

ONE OF the oddest endings to a Scotland match took place at Hampden Park on 8 May 1963 as Austria visited for a friendly before a crowd of 94,596.

Jimmy Millar, David Gibson and David Holt made their debuts. Scotland's line-up was: Brown, Hamilton, Holt, Mackay (captain), Ure, Baxter, Henderson, Gibson, Millar, Law, Wilson.

Austria picked this 11: Fraydl, Kolarik, Hasenkopf, Gager, Glechner, Koller, Linhart, Hof, Nemec, Fiala, Rafreider.

The referee was Jim Finney from Hereford, who had taken charge of the Scotland vs Ireland game earlier in the season.

The first goal came on a quarter of an hour when Jimmy Millar and Davie Wilson worked a routine that ended in Wilson netting.

In the 25th minute, Millar passed inside the right-back, and Wilson cut in and scored for 2-0. The Austrians appealed unsuccessfully for offside. Finney consulted his linesman before confirming the goal.

In the 28th minute, after Wilson made it 3-0, Finney ordered Horst Nemec off for spitting in his face. Nemec refused point-blank to go. Finney walked over to speak with the Austrian officials on the bench. They offered little encouragement to their player to obey the referee's instructions. After two or three minutes, finally the Austrian relented and made for the dressing room.

With 19 minutes remaining, Denis Law had scored to make it 4-0. However, Toni Linhart pulled a goal back a moment later.

'The game was ludicrous,' Ian Ure recalled in his autobiography *Ure's Truly*. 'The Austrians wouldn't accept any decisions. And I can best sum them up by saying they were a crude bunch of cloggers, and their mood was not helped by the fact that we were playing well. The Austrians had come to Scotland with a big reputation after an impressive string of results on the continent.

'I do not know if they had a premonition that they were going to come a cropper at Hampden, but it was clear after the first five minutes that they were going to have to rely on crunching rather than skill to beat us.'

'The Austrians' attitude worsened in the second half,' wrote Denis Law. 'They kicked anything that moved and were ridiculously petulant, engaging in time-wasting even though they were three goals down.'

In the 78th minute, Erich Hof charged Henderson. Finney said that he had performed a 'diabolical waist high tackle'. Finney ordered Hof from the field. The Austrian refused to leave. Austrian officials encroached on the pitch, pushing Hof back on to the field, and Hof's team-mates surrounded the referee in support of their colleague. It took the police to come on and escort Hof to the dressing rooms; even then, a policeman was manhandled by one of the substitutes.

In the *Evening Times*, Gair Henderson wrote, 'When order was finally restored and play restarted, the remaining nine Austrians went berserk. They tried to kick everything and everyone in sight.'

Dave Mackay recalled the game, 'I could have sworn they were on a mission to injure Denis Law. We really had to look out for him. Denis could well look after himself, of course, but with five or six maniacs chasing him around the field, the odds were not good.'

A moment later, Linhart kicked Law. The Manchester United forward responded by punching Linhart, who in the 1970s would change sports to play in the NFL with the Baltimore Colts and New York Jets. The referee was then besieged by Austrians demanding that Law be punished.

'I'm still young enough to be unable to prevent showing how I feel,' Law said in 1964. 'Retaliation in some form has been the cause of any trouble I've been in.'

Finney's response was to abandon play. He ran from the field, ensuring that no one could mistake that he had finally had enough of the misconduct. 'He went off the pitch first,' Ure recalled, 'and after a minute to take in what had happened, we followed.'

Jack Mowat, chairman of the Referees' Supervisory Committee, said after the game that the referee was '100 per cent correct' in his decision to abandon the game. Although Scottish and Austrian officials didn't think the game would have descended into serious injury and potential crowd trouble. FIFA also backed Finney.

Jock Stein, then Dunfermline manager, who was there watching, was pleased with how Finney had controlled the game, 'For too long British teams have gone abroad to be pushed around, booted all over the park by foreigners who disobey the rules. I know that Mr Finney has been criticised, but to my mind, he showed great courage.'

'What could I do?' Finney was reported as saying after the match. 'I felt I had to abandon the match, or somebody would have been seriously hurt. I ordered Nemec off for spitting and Hof for a diabolical tackle at waist height. I absolve the Scottish players from all blame.'

Anton Mayerhofer, the Austrian FA's vice president, said, 'The referee in last night's game was not good. We do so much want to come back to Scotland to show your supporters that we can play good football in a sporting manner. It was a great pity last night's game had to end as it did. The Scotland team played world-class football, especially in the first half. Your Scottish supporters are very fair. We return to Vienna full of sorrow that they were not able to enjoy 90 minutes of the wonderful football which the Scotland team played in the opening stages.'

Nemec said after the match, 'Your Queen is so correct, so proper. Why also was not the referee? I did not spit at him. I did spit on the ground, but it was only to clear my mouth, as most footballers do at some time during a game.'

In Austria, the press were on the defensive. *Kurier* quoted team coach Karl Decker as saying that Nemec 'never spat at the referee – the referee needs a psychiatrist'. Herr E. Mayerhofer, a representative of the Austrian FA who watched the game, blamed only the referee for the 'ugly scenes'. 'The brilliant Scottish team deserved a correct and fair victory. The Scottish players are not to be blamed for the scandal,' *Kurier* quoted him as saying.

Jim Finney recalled the occasion when speaking to the *South Wales Echo* in 1995. 'It all started from Scotland's second goal. When we got back to the middle, the Austrian player, Nemec, spat at me and told me it was offside. When he did the same again, I sent him off, but it took four minutes to get him off the field. Their manager Karl Decker was telling him to stay on, but he eventually went. At half-time, their manager came into my room with an interpreter and told me Nemec had a medical condition which meant he had to spit. I told him there was ten acres of room outside and he should spit somewhere else.'

After the second sending-off, Finney said things just started getting worse, 'From then on, they just wanted to bring the game into disrepute. If I gave a corner, they would put it on the 18-yard line, and they tried to take goal kicks from the penalty spot. Then when Denis Law broke away, one of the Austrians raced 30 yards to chop him down. I knew the Scottish Cup Final had to be replayed the following week, and there were a lot of Rangers and Celtic players in the Scottish team. I was worried somebody could have had a broken leg, anything could have happened. So I just walked off and abandoned the game because they were bringing the game into disrepute. Everybody acclaimed me and said it was time somebody showed these players they could not get away with what they wanted. The Scots were great. As I got into the taxi, the crowd clapped and said they admired my guts. I was banned from Austria and couldn't even go there on holiday!'

The appearances and goals stand in the records, and indeed Law's brace that night contributes to him jointly being Scotland's record scorer with 30 goals.

42

Scotland 1 Italy 0 – 1965

9 November 1965
Hampden Park
World Cup qualifying Group 8
Attendance: 101,293

Scotland: Brown (Tottenham Hotspur), Greig (Rangers), Provan (Rangers), Murdoch (Celtic), McKinnon (Rangers), Baxter [C] (Sunderland), Henderson (Rangers), Bremner (Leeds United), Gilzean (Tottenham Hotspur), Martin (Sunderland), Hughes (Celtic)

Italy: Negri (Bologna), Burgnich (Inter), Facchetti (Inter), Guarneri (Inter), Salvadore [C] (Juventus), Rosato (AC Torino), Lodetti (Milan), Bulgarelli (Bologna), Mazzola (Inter), Rivera (Milan), Barison (Roma)

Referee: Rudolf Kreitlein (West Germany)

Goal:
Greig (88)

IN A four-team group also including Poland and Finland, only the winners would qualify for the following summer's World Cup finals in England. Italy had trounced Poland 6-1 in Rome on 1 November. Scotland now sat in third, two points behind Italy and one behind Poland.

Celtic boss Jock Stein, who had been placed in temporary charge of Scotland, made six changes to the team from the last game, a 2-1 defeat against Poland at Hampden in October. That result was Scotland's first defeat in a World Cup tie at Hampden in 11 years.

Stein had selection problems to contend with. Eddie McCreadie had been suspended for 14 days, having been sent off while playing for Chelsea in an Inter-Cities Fairs Cup tie against Roma. Bans in those days were for days not matches and covered both club and international fixtures. Billy McNeill was out through injury.

It was a relatively inexperienced team in regard to international appearances. Ronnie McKinnon of Rangers and Celtic's Bobby Murdoch both made their debuts. Five of the other players still only had caps in the single figures.

John Hughes was selected ahead of Willie Johnstone shortly before kick-off.

Jim Baxter claimed to be amazed when Stein told him he was skipper. In the *Evening Times*, Gair Henderson called the appointment a masterstroke, '[Stein] may get from Baxter a brilliant and, at the same time, responsible performance. In the Army, many a difficult-to-handle private was turned into a good soldier by the simple process of making him a lance-jack, and this looks like the Stein psychology with Jim.'

'I had the pleasure of playing with Baxter,' Billy Bremner said in 1994. 'He had this arrogance. I remember we played in '65 against Italy, and he was walking about the dressing room before the game saying, "Rivera? Who the fuck is Rivera? Wee man, I tell you what. If I don't get four or five nutmegs on him tonight, I'm a bad player." And during the game, this is true, during the game, as he's nutmegged Rivera, he's going, "Wee man. One! Wee man, that's two!" And he thought that to take the mickey out of Rivera was better than scoring a goal.'

'Gianni Rivera was the golden boy, a really fabulous player,' Baxter said in 1992.

'Jock Stein had two good full-backs in his Celtic team, Jim Craig and Tommy Gemmell,' David Provan recalled for the *Sunday Times* in 2007. 'I thought they would be picked, but his actual selection was a Rangers pair of John Greig and myself. I was more than happy to play under him, and it showed the mark of the man that he did what he thought was right for Scotland and not for his own club.'

This would be John Greig's first game at right-back for his country. He said in 2007, 'Jock wanted the wingers, Willie Henderson and John Hughes, to go inside when they got the ball because the Italians were renowned for man-marking, and that would leave room for myself and Davie Provan to overlap.'

The Italians were managed by 43-year-old Dr Edmondo Fabbri. 'I have always feared the Scots,' he said before the match, 'I do so again in tonight's game.'

In the first half, Italy came closest to scoring when Greig had to head off the line from Paolo Barison. Although the Italians, who could settle for a draw, played a defensive game, their counterattacks were swift and skilful, and Bill Brown had more to deal with than William Negri.

'I played alongside Alan Gilzean and the Italians were so quick and skilful we didn't get many chances,' Neil Martin said to *The Scotsman* in 2007. 'I remember thinking, because of the ability they had, Italy didn't need to play that way. They could easily have been more attack-minded.'

Stein had spotted that goalkeeper Enrico Albertosi always rolled the ball to sweeper Tarcisio Burgnich to play out from defence. Martin told the *Sunday Mirror* in 2007, 'Every time the Italians built from the back, it started with the sweeper. Jock pushed me up right on him, and that had the effect of playing one up front with a five-man midfield. I was marking him rather than him marking me. I had a lot of running about to do, and it was a fairly thankless task. I had the job of making sure that he did not have time on the ball, that the keeper did not have the option of finding him every time, and he would have to kick from hand which they hated to do.'

Both teams had chances to take the lead. Gilzean overstretched when just a prod would have knocked in Baxter's flashing cross. Giacinto Facchetti shot from 30 yards only to see Brown gather the ball, while Rivera missed what looked like a golden opportunity.

Greig realised that time was running out when he saw that the lights in the Hampden stands had been turned on to allow spectators to leave safely. 'I knew then we were short of time. Suddenly, I got a last chance to go into midfield and play the ball to Jimmy Baxter. Wee Willie sprinted inside and took Facchetti with him, which left me vital space.'

Baxter recalled in 1992, 'These were Jock's pre-match instructions and they worked a treat.'

Greig continued, 'Baxter gave me it back with a perfect pass, as only he could. It landed perfectly for me to have a shot. If I hadn't taken advantage of it, I think Big Jock would have shot me.'

'It was a very intense game, and it carried on for the whole 90 minutes,' Willie Henderson said in 2007, 'but the fans were fantastic. There were 100,000 supporters, and they backed us for the whole game and that contributed to us scoring in the last two minutes. We were playing against world-class players, but we weren't overawed. They had guys like Facchetti, Mazzola and Rivera, but we had a few good players ourselves, and we were up for it.'

The players were awarded a £100 win bonus, the first time the SFA had allowed such a payment. Rangers defender Provan recalled, 'It was a great gesture, £100 could buy a lot in those days. But it honestly didn't make any difference to us. As far as I was concerned, and I'm sure for the rest of the lads too, just playing against the Italians was fantastic.'

STV screened 45 minutes of highlights in the evening.

The win put Scotland's hopes of qualifying for the World Cup in England in 1966 back on track, as they were now level with Italy on seven points with one match left to play. However, the dream was shattered in Naples for the return match when Scotland lost 3-0, and Jock Stein stood down from his temporary role in charge.

43

Pelé Comes to Glasgow – 1966

WHEN BRAZIL won the World Cup in 1958, the 17-year-old Pelé was their star. However, in the 1962 finals in Chile, an injury sustained in Brazil's second game put him out of the tournament.

By 1966 he was undoubtedly football's biggest name. Pelé had played one game in the UK previously, as his club side Santos beat Sheffield Wednesday in a 1962 friendly, but this would be the first time Scottish fans could see him on their soil.

So famous was Pelé that on away trips Brazil packed a hamper that contained 48 number ten jerseys so that the demand for a souvenir from their talisman never left them running short of his shirt number.

Preparing for that year's World Cup in England, Brazil began with a series of friendlies at home, then travelled to Europe to play first Scotland and then, five days later, Sweden in Gothenburg.

Brazil trained at Troon Juniors' Portland Park, while Scotland based themselves at Largs. Through an interpreter, Pelé told the press that all he knew of Scottish football was what he had seen on television.

The game took place on Saturday, 25 June 1966, and Hampden entertained a crowd of 73,933, around 50,000 more than the previous Saturday when Eusébio was the star attraction in a 1-0 defeat to Portugal.

'It was a friendly match, but I remember there being a huge, passionate crowd, and the game was competitive,' Pelé told the *Daily Record* in 2016. 'We had the World Cup to think about, but we had to deal with a few tackles.'

'What a player he was,' Stevie Chalmers recalled in 1998. 'I remember singing his praises before the match in the dressing room to Jim Baxter, who replied, "Pelé? Wait until you see me out there." Jim didn't let me down – he was brilliant.'

Hereford's Jim Finney was the referee, the same man who had abandoned that match against Austria in 1963.

Brazil opened up with some short passes, but John Greig intercepted and found Baxter. 'It was early in the match, and Jim Baxter sent through one of his perfect passes,' Chalmers said in 1987. 'I recall moving in on goal and thought sure I was going to score.' Chalmers let fly and Scotland were a goal up after only 43 seconds.

Palmeiras striker Servílio equalised on 15 minutes and the match ended 1-1. Highlights were shown on BBC1 the following afternoon.

'That was a fabulous night,' Greig remembered in 1987. 'The weather was perfect, and there was a great crowd. What better opposition could you get than the world champions with Pelé in their side? He played well, and apart from the obvious skill, it was very noticeable that he was big and strong and could look after himself. Mind you, he had to have those attributes. Myself and Billy Bremner were keeping an eye on him.'

The *Daily Telegraph* noted, 'Pelé was watched as closely by Bremner as anyone is likely to watch him next month.'

Bremner harassed and harried Pelé over every inch of the Hampden pitch. Alex Smith, who later managed St Mirren, grew up with Bremner. He said to the *Record* in 1997, 'Billy was told to mark Pelé, and he did it so well that the great man had a quiet day. Mind you, he gave Billy a black eye with his elbow which tells you something. But that was Billy, he never went on the pitch thinking anyone was better than him.'

Bremner detailed the experience in his book, *You Get Nowt for Being Second*, 'I was told to stick to him like glue. I decided that the best way to play him was to let him know I was there as soon as possible in the game. I figured that once he realised I was going to be almost standing on his toes for the whole 90 minutes, he might decide that this was no occasion for showing just how great he was. So the first time he went for a 50/50 ball, I put everything I knew into my tackle. I was fair – but hard. Very hard. I have never tackled harder in my life, in fact.'

Bremner felt that when he put the marker down in the English game, invariably opponents would get the message and back off. But he found that Pelé was made of stronger stuff, 'We're much of a muchness when it comes to size and weight, and so I can only assume that he figured the odds were even in a test of physical strength. And the next time we clashed, I was made very much aware of this. The ball came over through the air, and we went in together for it. From the corner of my eye, as I leaped to get my head to the ball, I could see Pelé taking off too. The next thing I knew was that I was lying on the ground, and one of my eyes was already beginning to swell. From that moment, I had got his measure, and I knew that I was facing an opponent who had courage and pure guts, two commodities which, in my book, are as much a part of greatness as fantastic ability.'

Bremner acknowledged that as tight as he stuck to Pelé, the Santos player could still find space, 'I do not think that there is a professional footballer in the game today, throughout the world … who could mark Pelé so tightly that he could eliminate him from a game completely.'

It was said that Pelé handed over his jersey not to his direct opponent but to the player he felt had performed best for his country.

'At the final whistle, it so happened I was quite close to Pelé,' Chalmers recalled. 'Without even asking, the great man whipped off his jersey and handed it over.'

The newspapers were disappointed in Pelé's performance. 'Pelé, he's here at last but what a flop,' read *The People*'s headline. In his report, John Blair highlighted Bremner's marking job, saying, 'He showed that Pelé and the Brazilian team can be shaken up by close marking, keen tackling half-backs.'

Back in Brazil, they looked on the tactics differently, 'Pelé was persecuted like an escaped convict,' wrote *Jornal dos Sports*. *Jornal do Brazil* said, 'Scotland's Bremner used his only accomplishments

– kicks and elbow jabs – to stop Pelé and referee Finney never even reprimanded him.'

Of Bremner, Pelé said in 1989, 'Yes, I remember my marker from that game. But we are friends now and have met since and talked about the game.'

44

England 2 Scotland 3 – 1967

15 April 1967
Wembley Stadium
British Home Championship/European Championship
Qualifying Group 8
Attendance: 99,063

England: Banks (Leicester City), Cohen (Fulham), Wilson (Everton), Stiles (Manchester United), J. Charlton (Leeds United), Moore [C] (West Ham United), Ball (Everton), Greaves (Tottenham Hotspur), B. Charlton (Manchester United), Hurst (West Ham United), Peters (West Ham United)

Scotland: Simpson (Celtic), Gemmell (Celtic), McCreadie (Chelsea), Greig [C] (Rangers), McKinnon (Rangers), Baxter (Rangers), Wallace (Celtic), Bremner (Leeds United), McCalliog (Sheffield Wednesday), Law (Manchester United), Lennox (Celtic)

Referee: Gerhard Schulenburg (West Germany)

Goals:
England – J. Charlton (86), Hurst (89)
Scotland – Law (27), Lennox (78), McCalliog (88)

Tommy Gemmell: From the moment we all met in our London headquarters, it was Baxter who put us in the right frame of mind. He had such a glorious contempt for the English team that we all began to think the same way. If anyone tried to indicate a strong point in the England team, Jim brushed it aside with his strong Fife accent.

Bobby Brown (Scotland manager): Going into that game as your first in charge of the team looked on paper to be fairly daunting. After all, we were playing against the reigning world champions. I suppose I did surprise some people, probably most people, by picking Jim McCalliog, who was almost unknown in Scotland. He had gone south when he left school at 15 and had played all his football there. However, I had seen him in an under-21 game, and we had watched him in his club games, and I thought he was the right type of player to go in against the English.

Jim McCalliog: I was more nervous about meeting Denis [Law] than playing against England. Honestly, I swear.

Billy Bremner: I always remember one London newspaper writing, 'I do not see it as being a repeat of the 1961 scoreline of 9-3. I cannot see the Scots scoring three goals.' That sort of reporting just made us all the more determined to do well.

Bobby Lennox: I remember the atmosphere in the dressing room before the match. My club-mate Ronnie Simpson, who was making his international debut at the age of 36, was feeling a bit edgy and said that he could do with a dram. Scotland's substitute that day, Stevie Chalmers … magically produced a bottle of malt whisky, and I promise you at least half the team had a nip before we walked out on to that magnificent pitch.

Ronnie McKinnon: I felt terrible, and I think I was in and out to the bathroom five times before going out for the game. It was the most nervous I had ever been, and yet Jim and Denis Law were behaving as if they were going out for a Sunday kickabout in the local park.

Billy Bremner: There had been some nerves in the dressing room, but I will always remember Jim Baxter quietly telling us what he was going to do to humiliate this player or that player. We knew that he meant every word, and he almost scared us.

Ronnie Simpson: To be honest, I was a little bit surprised at how sure he was that we were going to go there and win this game. Somehow though, it was contagious, and it began to rub off on the rest of us.

Denis Law: The spirit in the dressing room was just amazing. Jimmy Baxter kept talking about how he was going to make fools of the England defenders and was actually taking bets on how many players he would nutmeg – especially Ray Wilson.

Bobby Lennox: Our team manager was Bobby Brown, who until a few weeks earlier had been manager of St Johnstone. He simply spoke to the players individually and offered no tactical advice of any kind. I don't mean that as a criticism. He simply told us to play for each other, keep possession as much as possible and just 'Go out and enjoy it.' Which, of course, we did.

Tommy Gemmell: Bobby Brown sketched out how he wanted the game to be played, and then we were left talking among ourselves about which players we should be picking up when England had the ball and that kind of thing. Wee Billy did a lot of the talking there, and then Jimmy butted in, and I can still hear him saying, 'Don't ask me to do any of that. I'm not coming back to pick anyone up; they can come and look for me.' Funnily enough, that struck the right tone in the dressing room.

Bobby Brown: I did think we could outplay England, and it worked out that way. I also wanted a change in the way Denis Law had been playing for his club. At Manchester United, he had not been playing as an out-and-out striker, but I wanted him right up there on top of Jack Charlton and Bobby Moore. If he was snapping at them throughout the 90 minutes, then they were not going to have a comfortable afternoon, and he would cause them problems. Again, that worked.

Jim McCalliog: As soon as Tommy Gemmell clattered Jimmy Greaves with the first tackle, we were at them. Never gave them a minute to settle.

Tommy Gemmell: I got the ball away from Jimmy Greaves in the early minutes, and after that, my nerves disappeared.

Gordon Banks: We knew they were ready to run through brick walls from the moment we saw Denis Law come on the pitch. For the first time anyone could remember, Denis was wearing shin pads.

Denis Law: It was Baxter's match more than anyone else's. The England players just didn't know what to make of him, and he teased and tormented them without mercy.

Tommy Gemmell: It was amazing just how often he was on the ball. He was always available, always in space, and this against the World Cup holders, a team which was built to deny opposition players any room at all. Everything we did seemed to go through him, and he loved every minute of it. It became a day out for Jimmy, and he revelled in the whole affair.

Bobby Lennox: People talk about Jack Charlton being injured early on and that affecting England, but that's because he tried to do me. He broke his toe off my knee. I was still bleeding through my suit when we went out later that night.

Tommy Gemmell: I know he broke his toe … but I still can't shed a tear for him. In my opinion, the tackle which caused his injury was a desperate and dangerous one. Jackie Charlton had been injured, and since then, all of them, including Sir Alf Ramsey, have used this to explain away the defeat.

Jack Charlton: After that, I couldn't put any weight on my foot. Ray Wilson was injured as well, and Jimmy Greaves was suffering from a swollen ankle, so we were up against it.

Tommy Gemmell had to go off for treatment after being fouled by Ray Wilson and was lying behind the English goal when in 27 minutes Scotland took the lead. From a free kick on the left, the ball fell to Willie Wallace, whose shot was blocked. Denis Law was following in, Banks saved his first shot, but Law made no mistake with the rebound.

Billy Bremner: There was a tremendous roar when the ball hit the back of the net, and anyone outside the stadium would have thought that England scored.

With 12 minutes remaining, it was 2–0. The English defence struggled to deal with a loose ball. A cross came over for Lennox, who turned inside and drove the ball hard past Banks.

Bobby Lennox: I remember my goal like it was yesterday. The ball just broke to me at the edge of the box, and I got a good hit at it. I remember shouting, 'Don't bother diving Banksy, it's behind you!' That's a career highlight.

Billy Bremner: England became really desperate then, and I remember Alan Ball shouting so much that his voice went even higher than usual, and nobody could understand a word that he was saying.

Tommy Gemmell: There was one stage in the game when I joined in with wee Billy and Jim to pass the ball around between us with little Alan Ball in the middle of the three of us, and he was running from man to man, trying to get the ball. I've watched that on film, and we put together 14 passes as Bally became more and more angry.

John Greig: Wee Bally was going crazy, and Jimmy was just laughing at him.

Alan Ball: I tried very hard that day, but I have to admit that I could not get near him. The best side won on the day. Played terrific football. I got the biggest chasing of my life by Jim Baxter, who had a fantastic game.

Despite the gulf developing between the two sides, England came back. A low cross by Ball was driven in by Jackie Charlton. Scotland, though, were soon on the attack again.

Tommy Gemmell: I can remember one save Gordon Banks had from Denis Law. Denis chipped him from about 17, 18 yards, and it was going over Banksy's head, and … he was so acrobatic, he got back, and he knocked it out for a corner kick. How he got back to it, I'll never know. It was a magnificent save. It would maybe be even better than the save he had against Brazil, the Pelé save from the header. I put it in the same category.

It was 3-1 a few moments later when McCalliog worked his way into the box and hit a right-footed shot from close range.

Jim McCalliog: Scoring the third for Scotland was amazing for me because it was getting late in the game. I played a one-two with Willie Wallace, and I was determined to get my shot in before Bobby Moore could block me and to put it past Banks. I smashed it as hard as I could in the near post, and all I could see was the net rippling. I ran to where my dad was in the crowd and waved up there, and the first guy to come and embrace me was Denis Law. What an occasion.

Gordon Banks: I committed the cardinal sin of not guarding my near post properly as I came out to meet him after he evaded two half-hearted tackles.

Bobby Brown: Things only began to go a little bit adrift when Jim started the keepy-uppy routine. He had me tearing my hair out on the touchline when he started all that nonsense. But he was always a law unto himself, Jim, and anything I was shouting was being ignored.

Tommy Gemmell: Denis Law was a bit unhappy that Jim and wee Billy had decided to show off a bit rather than get goals, and he was screaming at Baxter to get the ball forward to him and stop messing around. But Jim wasn't listening to anyone that day; he was just out there to obey his own instincts.

Jim McCalliog: I think their attitudes were always a little different, but they were more marked that day because I think Denis had played in the 9-3 defeat, and the memory of that match still hurt.

Denis Law: I wasn't happy at the time, but I soon forgave him.

Jim Baxter: Naturally, I've had lots of arguments since with people who didn't like the way we took the mickey. I don't think they understood; I really don't. A team and a country can forget big scores against them. Our aim was to show England how easily we could beat them. We wanted to give them no excuses. We wanted the Scottish punters to laugh at the English as well as to enthuse over victory, which is exactly what happened. Now and again, one of us would put a foot on the ball and then walk away from it as if we were bored, but we always knew that a team-mate would get to it first.

Tommy Gemmell: This was Baxter in a class of his own. I can think of no other player, of any other nationality, who would have dared to treat England as he did before so many of their own followers, in Wembley Stadium of all places.

Ronnie Simpson: No one who was there will ever forget his performance, and I was very glad to be a part of it, I can tell you that.

England pulled another goal back right at the end when Geoff Hurst headed in a Bobby Charlton cross.

Tommy Gemmell: The record books will tell you it was 3-2 at the end, but we won out of the park, and if it had finished up six or seven, then that would have been a scoreline that would have reflected the amount of possession we had.

Bobby Charlton: I remember thinking as I walked off the field, and the goalposts were disappearing beneath a Scottish swarm, 'Oh, my God, we are the world champions but now we face a year of hell.'

Billy Bremner: The Wembley pitch was completely covered by dancing Scottish fans. I was dancing with them.

Bobby Moore: They went absolutely mad over it. The eyes of some of the players were wild. Their supporters came pouring off the terraces to cut up the pitch, waving lumps of earth at us and saying this was the turf on which they destroyed the world champions. Some of them were seriously suggesting we ought to hand over the World Cup.

Geoff Hurst: I can't dispute that the Scots deserved their win, but I've always felt it as something of a hollow victory. These were the days before substitutes were allowed in the Home Internationals, and for much of the game England were forced to carry three injured players.

Bobby Lennox: Jimmy Greaves had promised me his jersey, but only after the game. When I went into the England dressing room, it was like a morgue. But we swapped shirts, and he was gracious in defeat, like a true professional.

Jim McCalliog: After the game, we went and met the England team and had some drinks. Bobby [Brown] nipped out for some fresh air, and this Scottish guy came along, and he'd had a few drinks and started poking Bobby in the chest and said, 'We absolutely gubbed you today.' Bobby didn't have the heart to tell him he was the manager of the Scotland team. He said he didn't want to spoil the moment for him.

Tommy Gemmell: At the informal get-together before the meal, Bobby Moore sat in a corner and gave the distinct impression he wanted nothing to do with the smiling Scots in the room. Sir Alf Ramsey also did not look too pleased when SFA president Tom Reid made a couple of characteristic wisecracks; the England boss did not appear amused. Some of the other England boys, however, made a point of congratulating us over a beer. Nobby Stiles, Alan Ball and Bobby Charlton were very friendly, and that goes for Jackie Charlton too.

Jim Baxter: We're sitting in the Cafe Royal, Denis and I sitting at the banquet. Bored. So I says to Denis, 'Come on, let's go down to the bar.' We went down there, it was like Wembley all over again. There was the table, about 12 of them sitting round it. They had the Wembley turf on it. The kitty in the middle and all the drinks round about it. They'd all pinched a bit of turf.

45

Tommy Gemmell Boots Helmut Haller – 1969

SCOTLAND FACED a strong German side in the World Cup qualifying match at the Volksparkstadion in Hamburg. Sepp Maier was winning his 18th cap in goal with 22-year-old Berti Vogts and 24-year-old Franz Beckenbauer at the back. Wolfgang Overath was in midfield, while up front there was Gerd Müller, who had 16 goals from 15 caps, and Uwe Seeler, who had scored 38 times in 62 internationals.

Jimmy Johnstone put the Scots in front after three minutes. Eddie Gray ran through the German defence and cracked a shot from distance, Maier couldn't hold on to it, and the ball dropped nicely for Johnstone to run in and sweep it into the net.

It was Scotland's final qualifying game in Group 7 of the European section. A win would see the Scots reach for the 1970 finals in Mexico. A draw wouldn't be the worst result as it would lead to a play-off against Austria in Vienna.

Tommy Gemmell first came to the referee's attention when kicking the ball away at a throw-in during the first half. Gilbert Droz of Switzerland took Gemmell's name.

Klaus Fichtel of Schalke 04 equalised for West Germany ten minutes before half-time. But Scotland were playing well. John Greig was overlapping and outflanking a hesitant German defence, unsure who should be picking him up. In *The Guardian*, David Lacey noted, 'For every opening created by the Germans, the Scots would make three and waste two of them.'

Scotland hit the bar twice, only to see Müller put the hosts in front on the hour mark. However, two minutes later, Alan Gilzean equalised when Bremner crossed for him to head in.

With ten minutes remaining, Scotland were caught out. Pouring forward in an attack, there was a gap on the left of defence, so when Helmut Haller collected a clearance he pinged the ball into space. Reinhard Libuda collected it and ran from the halfway line. Gemmell tried in vain to pull him down just as Libuda reached the edge of the box, where he fired past Jim Herriot to make it 3-2.

With only a minute to go, Scotland were passing through the German defence in search of an equaliser. In the minutes leading up, there had been a couple of German players falling to the floor. Greig body checked one, and Johnstone left his boot in on another, doing an apologetic driving wave as the referee let play go on.

Gemmell intercepted the ball just inside his own half on the left, sending the ball down the wing to Gray. Gemmell had run on into the middle, and Gray slid the ball into him, around 35 yards out. Gemmell was famous for his 'Big Bertha' shot and was deadly from this sort of range. As two defenders crowded him, he twisted into the right in an attempt to create space for the shot. As he got away from his opponents around 25 yards out, a third defender, Haller, threw out his right foot with the sole intention of kicking Gemmell, connecting with his right leg.

Speaking to Kenneth Wolstenholme in 1968, Gemmell opined on playing against European opponents. 'They are a lot of nigglers,' he said. 'They body check and obstruct and pull your shirt and generally set out to irritate you.'

Gemmell, still running, turned and looked at Haller, and he ran towards him. Haller thought better of a confrontation and swiftly shifted to his left to avoid Gemmell. The big Celtic man gave chase and booted Haller on his legs sending him flying up into the air to gasps of astonishment from the 72,000 crowd. 'Oh dear! Oh dear. That was uncalled for,' said Archie Macpherson on commentary, his first overseas international.

In his autobiography *The Big Shot*, published the previous year, Gemmell had written, with reference to his kicking of

Racing Club's Norberto Raffo, 'If another player annoys you it is no solution to kick him deliberately.'

Haller, now on his knees, threw his hands on his head and then collapsed on the ground. Eddie Gray went over to check on him, only for Willi Schulz to push him away. Haller was then up on his feet, hobbling around as an ambulanceman ran on, wrapping Haller in a blanket for a few moments until the Juventus player assured him he was OK. Several photographers and backroom staff made their way on to the pitch. A furious Gemmell was led off the pitch by Scotland's coaching staff. The game resumed with a free kick to West Germany.

'He never went near the ball,' Gemmell wrote in his 2012 autobiography, 'he just took my legs away from me. I was raging because I had been in my favourite position just outside the D and ready to hit one from a part of the park from which I scored a lot of goals.' Gemmell's rage was increased as the referee failed to award Scotland a free kick. 'That didn't help my mood as I felt a rush of blood to the head in my anger at the incident. He went down as if he was dead. The person who retaliates of course is always sent off. Haller the instigator was not even spoke to by the referee. It was the first time in my career I had been sent off but you can only take so much punishment before retaliating.'

The game had been ugly throughout. At one point, Hottges of Werder Bremen kicked Colin Stein when the ball was dead, and the referee did nothing. Watching the game was the Brazilian manager João Saldanha, compiling a report on European football. He asked Droz why he had opted not to take action on some of the Germans' antics. The referee stated that the Germans began kicking when the game was going against them. He felt that letting play go on would benefit the better team. 'I think he was sincere, but he was wrong,' Saldanha told Hugh McIlvanney in *The Observer*.

The 3-2 victory was West Germany's first win over Scotland in what was the fifth match between the sides. Gemmell later received a three-match international ban. The Scottish FA Referees Committee fined him £60.

46

Peter Lorimer

21 caps, 4 goals (1969–1976)

PETER LORIMER was playing for Broughty YMCA and working as a printer's apprentice when Leeds United spotted him. Don Revie picked up a speeding ticket driving to Dundee to get him to sign. Lorimer became England's youngest peacetime league footballer when he made his debut at 15 years and 289 days old against Southampton on 28 September 1962.

A Scottish Schoolboy international with seven amateur caps, Lorimer's senior international debut came on 5 November 1969 as a substitute in Austria's 2-0 defeat.

It would be May 1971 before Peter's second cap in a 0-0 draw with Wales. A 1-0 defeat to Northern Ireland followed three days later.

Team manager Bobby Brown was preparing for the European Championship qualifying match with Denmark and a friendly in Moscow with the USSR in June 1971. He had to wait until six days before the match before he could name his travelling squad. The last two players he was waiting on were Lorimer and Billy Bremner, playing in the second leg of Leeds United's Inter-Cities Fairs Cup Final against Juventus on 3 June. Leeds won the trophy on away goals.

Brown called Leeds the morning after to ask why he had read in the newspapers that Lorimer and Bremner wouldn't be travelling to Denmark with the Scotland party. Brown was further incensed when he discovered that, instead, Lorimer was on a plane bound for South Africa to play and coach for six weeks with Cape Town City. Lorimer scored in a 1-1 draw against Johannesburg Rangers the day before Denmark got their first win in two years by beating Scotland 1-0. Lorimer was subsequently banned by the SFA.

Speaking to *Goal* magazine in March 1972, Lorimer said that he badly wanted to play for Scotland again, 'I got into bother with the SFA last summer, and I don't know whether they are prepared to forgive me.' He said he went to South Africa as he was recovering from a hamstring injury, 'I never realised that my decision would get me into so much trouble.'

'Probably I was naive,' he said years later. 'But I was made to feel like a traitor; my parents were very upset.' The ban only lasted for around 11 months.

Lorimer's first win in a Scotland shirt, along with his first goal, came as Northern Ireland were defeated 2-0 at Hampden in May 1972. He crossed for Denis Law to score the first with four minutes remaining. In the last minute, Lorimer cracked in his goal. 'It's the chance I had been waiting for,' Lorimer said to the press of his half an hour on the pitch. 'Today's brief appearance gave me the chance to show that I could do it.'

In a double-header with Denmark in October and November, Lorimer scored in both matches, a 4-1 win in Copenhagen and a 2-0 victory at Hampden. In the second game, however, Lorimer was sent off along with Per Røntved after 84 minutes, after retaliating when the Dane fouled him.

Lorimer played in all three matches in the 1974 World Cup finals. His final cap came in December of 1975 in a 1-1 draw with Romania at Hampden.

Peter's Leeds United testimonial came in November 1977 and was a match with a Scotland XI. The Scottish side was made up of Anglos as the Scottish League Cup quarter-finals took place the same night, but Lorimer lined up with full internationals such as Kenny Dalglish, Joe Jordan, Martin Buchan and Gordon McQueen. Leeds won 5-2.

47

Edna Neillis

Scottish women's national team (1972–1975)

EDNA NEILLIS didn't set out to be a pioneer. All she wanted to do was play the game she loved and was very good at. The attitudes of the era she played in necessitated her to become a rebel.

Edna blazed her trail through women's football with her best friend, Rose Reilly, by her side. Reilly has, in recent years, and not before time, been awarded her place in the Scottish Football Hall of Fame as well as in public consciousness. There's even now a pub named after her. However, Edna hasn't quite had the full acknowledgement she deserves.

'Edna was a wing-half, very technical,' Rose told *Nutmeg* in 2017, 'with the same skills and the same size as [Celtic's Jimmy] Johnstone – we called her "Jinky" but she didn't like it because she was a Rangers fan.'

Edna's love of football grew, as many children's did, from kicking the ball around in games in the streets. The difference was that Edna was the only girl playing with boys.

Having played organised football with boys' teams, Edna joined her local women's side Westhorn United.

Westhorn took part in the UK Women's Championship, a tournament organised by TV personality Hughie Green. The regional finals were at Butlin's in Ayr, where they beat Stewarton Thistle. This allowed Westhorn to represent Scotland in the national final played at Belle Vue Park in Manchester, where they lost to Foden Ladies.

At the age of 19, Edna played in the first Scottish women's international against England at Ravenscraig Park in Greenock in November 1972. Scotland led 2-1 at half-time with goals from Rose Reilly and Mary Carr. In front of a crowd of 400, England rallied in the second half to win 3-2.

The result wasn't as close in June the following year at Manor Park in Nuneaton, the home of Nuneaton Borough, who played in the Southern League. England hammered Scotland, with Edna and Rose both in the team, 8-0 in front of a crowd of 1,308.

'We had Rose Reilly and Edna Neillis who were our real star performers,' former Scotland team-mate Sheila Begbie said to Steven Lawther for his book *Arrival*. 'I suppose our team style was to get the ball to Edna or to get the ball to Rose. It was quite easy for opponents to shut that off.'

In September 1974, Scotland played two friendlies away to Italy, first in Pescara (the result of which is unknown) and then losing 3-0 in Milan before a 10,000 crowd.

On 23 November 1974, Scotland Ladies entertained Northern Ireland at New Kilbowie Park, Clydebank. This was the first time a senior ground had been used for a ladies' international in Scotland. It was also the first time a ladies' international had been played under floodlights. Scotland won 11-1, with Edna scoring a hat-trick.

'Edna was a better ball player than Rose,' Elsie Cook said to the *Daily Record* in 2015. Elsie was the first secretary of the Scottish Women's Football Association and sewed the badges to the Scottish shirts for that first game.

Elsie wanted Edna and Rose to achieve their dreams of playing professionally. They knew that would mean moving abroad, and Elsie had an idea, 'I put a portfolio together, and the girls took it to the *Daily Record*. They met a famous journalist called Stan Shivas, and he saw straight away it would make a great story.'

The paper paid for the girls to go to France to play a trial for Stade de Reims, a team managed by sportswriter Pierre Geoffroy. 'Stan and a photographer went with them.'

Shivas wrote, 'They spoke no foreign languages, had never even been abroad and were somewhat inhibited because, understandably, their horizons until then had been fairly narrow.' They signed for Reims and were soon spotted by Italian scouts and were both off to AC Milan.

'The Milan scouts wanted to sign us right away,' Rose said. 'Geoffroy must have seen a deal, he asked if we wanted to go to Italy, and we said, "Aye." When the plane landed at Linate Airport, the doors opened, the sun was out, and it was like a mother's embrace. We played at the San Siro, in front of more than 20,000 people, and we won the league.'

In 1975 AC Milan won the Serie A title and the Coppa Italia. The championship was secured with a last-day win against Lazio. In a 3-0 victory, Edna scored two, with Rose netting the other.

In January 1975, problems arose. Edna, Rose and Elsie were banned from the Scottish game by the Scottish Women's Football Association for speaking with the *Sunday People*. They had all criticised the methods by which the new national team manager Bill Cranston was appointed.

Charles Leggeit, the vice-chairman of the association, said, 'It is true the girls were banned because they talked to the *Sunday People*. They seem to want to do all the talking because now they have gone to a lawyer.'

Edna instructed Glasgow lawyer Thomas Brannigan to act for herself and Rose. 'Football means everything to Rose and me,' she said to the *Sunday People*. 'We are going to fight. Surely there is still such a thing as free speech in Britain.'

'I think it was about keeping people in their place,' Begbie said. 'That working-class thing of "Who the hell do they think they are?" That was maybe where Scotland was at, at that point, in terms of women in our society.'

Edna carried on despite her country's football association turning its back on her. She won two more Coppa Italias and went on to play for Gorgonzola, while Rose signed for Catania. 'They were best pals,' Elsie said, 'in one another's pockets. They were way above everybody else on the park, and off it they were joined at the hip.'

Edna learned the Italian language and was happy playing and living in Italy, but she always wanted to return home to Scotland. She retired from football in 1990 and moved to Cumbernauld. She met her partner Robert McKie while she worked as a stewardess for the Citylink long-distance coach service while Robert was a driver. In later years ill health led to the amputation of her legs. She passed away in August 2015.

48

Scotland 2 Czechoslovakia 1 – 1973

26 September 1973
Hampden Park
World Cup qualifying Group 8
Attendance: 89,028

Scotland: Hunter (Celtic), Jardine (Rangers), McGrain (Celtic), Bremner [C] (Leeds United), Holton (Manchester United), Connelly (Celtic), Hay (Celtic), Law (Manchester City), Morgan (Manchester United), Dalglish (Celtic) [Jordan (Leeds United), 60], Hutchison (Coventry City)

Czechoslovakia: Viktor (Dukla Prague), Pivarník (Slovan Bratislava), Samek (Dukla Prague), Zlocha (Slovan Bratislava), Bendl (Dukla Prague), Bičovský (Sklo Union Teplice), Panenka (Bohemians Praha), Kuna [C] (Spartak Trnava), Adamec (Spartak Trnava), Nehoda (Dukla Prague), Stratil (Sklo Union Teplice) Subs used: Čapkovič (Spartak Trnava), Dobiaš (Slovan Bratislava)

Referee: Henry Oberg (Norway)

Goals:
Scotland – Holton (41), Jordan (75)
Czechoslovakia – Nehoda (33)

FOR THE qualifiers for the 1974 World Cup, Scotland had been drawn in a three-team group with Denmark and Czechoslovakia. Scotland defeated Denmark 4-1 in Copenhagen in October 1972 and 2-0 at Hampden in November. In Copenhagen, in May 1973,

Denmark and Czechoslovakia drew 1-1, and although the Czechs won the return in June, 6-0, Scotland were in a great position. They were only required to win one of the two games with the Czechs to qualify for West Germany 1974.

In January 1973, Willie Ormond took over as manager after Tommy Docherty left for Manchester United.

In his book, *The Quiet Assassin*, Davie Hay recalled Ormond's pre-match team talk. 'Succinct and to the point. "Go out there and become legends. You have Scotland's destiny in your hands. Don't let down your country. Don't let down yourselves. Go on, get the job done."'

'With the calibre of player I had alongside me that night, I knew that we were going to win. I had no doubts at all,' Tommy Hutchison wrote in his autobiography.

Denis Law, who had now left Manchester United for Manchester City, hadn't played in either of the qualifiers and had not appeared for Scotland since the game against Brazil in July 1972, an absence of eight internationals. Ormond brought him back into the squad. 'I was both surprised and delighted by the news,' Law wrote in his 1979 book. With his selection in the starting 11 up front alongside Kenny Dalglish, Law would become the second player after George Young to earn 50 caps for Scotland.

In addition to recalling Law, manager Ormond gave two players their international debuts – Celtic's George Connelly and Tommy Hutchison of Coventry City. 'Big Hutch was the star of the whole game,' Dalglish wrote in his autobiography *King Kenny*.

Hay recalled the atmosphere he found when he was on the pitch, 'Every single one of that tartan-clad gathering seemed determined to make their voice heard. It was amazingly uplifting; pure, gorgeous, orchestrated mayhem.'

'As we came out on to the pitch, the noise of the crowd really did hit me,' Hutchison wrote. 'The Hampden Roar was something that I had heard about, but to experience it first-hand that night was really special.'

'It was a wonderful Hampden occasion,' David Lacey wrote in *The Guardian*. 'The chanting, singing Scottish standard-bearers gave the night colour and excitement.'

The Czechs took the lead when Zdeněk Nehoda cracked a shot across the face of goal that Hunter misjudged and turned into his own net. 'Suddenly there was a strange eeriness about Hampden Park,' wrote Law.

Hutchison recalled, 'There were a few moments of stunned silence in the stadium before a huge wave of encouragement came rolling down off the terraces. "We'll support you ever more" was the chant, and it was clear that the 100k watching on hadn't given up on us.'

'With so much at stake, no one would be surprised to learn it was an intensely physical match,' Sandy Jardine wrote in his 1987 autobiography. 'Denis Law and Billy Bremner artfully sorted out a number of gentlemen.'

Hutchison recalled, 'At Hampden, Billy Bremner had been getting "the treatment" from the Czech midfielder [Ladislav] Kuna. Billy was a fiery character who believed in giving back what he received. A clash between the two saw Kuna having to leave the field with blood pouring from a broken nose.'

With half an hour remaining, Joe Jordan was sent on for his fourth cap in place of Dalglish. In his autobiography *Behind the Dream*, Jordan recalled what happened next, 'Billy was playing at the limits of his skin, and his shot bounced off a post and wide for the winger Willie Morgan to pick up. Willie shaped to cross, and I anticipated the flight of the ball just right, slipping away from my marker and diving to head the ball, as sweetly as I would ever see or feel, into the bottom corner.'

'I can still picture it in my mind,' Jordan said in 2011, 'because it is something that has been spoken about so many times since. It was also my first international goal, and with everything that went around it, I don't think you could forget a moment like that.'

Late on, Denis Law pounced on a Czech defender's hesitancy and went in one-on-one with the goalkeeper. On *Scotsport*'s coverage, Arthur Montford threw all pretence of neutrality out the window as he commentated, 'Law's in the clear. Come on now Denis! Come on Denis!' Viktor tipped the ball away from Law's toe as he attempted to take it around the keeper. An executive later asked Montford of his commentary, 'Don't you think you were biased?' Montford replied, 'Of course I was.'

'The emotional impact Denis had at Hampden that night helped carry the team to the finals,' Dalglish wrote. 'What a night,' wrote Hay. 'It was what football was invented for.'

'Scotland deserved their victory for their persistence in attack against opponents who demeaned their own skills with frequent and cynical fouls of the sort that the English game is gradually stamping out,' David Lacey wrote in *The Guardian*.

Bremner went down the tunnel to get Willie Ormond out to take the acclaim from the fans who refused to leave. Scotland had qualified for their first major tournament since 1958.

49

Jimmy Johnstone Goes to Sea – 1974

IN APRIL of 1974, Jimmy Johnstone gave an interview to Alex Cameron in the *Daily Record* under the headline 'Jimmy Has Grown Up'. 'Football is a funny game,' he said. 'You can be either up there at the top or right down at the bottom. There are no half-measures it seems, for people like me.' Jimmy would go on to prove that a month later in spectacular fashion.

On 14 May, Jimmy was man of the match as Scotland bounced back from a 1-0 loss to Northern Ireland by beating Wales 2-0 at Hampden Park.

'Wee Jimmy puts new sparkle into Scotland's World Cup hopes,' the *Daily Record* raved.

It's worth noting that this was something of a comeback to the international scene for Johnstone. He hadn't played in any of the qualifying matches for the 1974 World Cup; this was his first appearance since May 1972. He had also fallen out of favour with Celtic, playing in the reserves from December 1973 until his return to the first team in April 1974.

After the match, the Scotland team returned to their base at Largs on the Ayrshire coast. Despite arriving back close to midnight, the players were given permission from manager Willie Ormond to go out for a drink, and they headed for the Royal Hotel on the seafront, where owner Ross Bowie arranged for them to have a few after-hours drinks.

The players departed several hours later in daylight. Walking along the seafront to the Queen's Hotel, where they were staying, they came across some row boats.

In *Celtic View* in 2004, Sandy Jardine recalled, 'Jimmy was a bit merry, and he decided, upon seeing a couple of rowing boats, that he'd have a shot in one of them.'

'In my drunken stupor, I looked at Sandy and mumbled, "Fancy a wee trip on the water?" "Nae bother," came the reply.' Johnstone climbed in, only to find that the boat was equipped with only one oar and no rowlocks.

He waited for Jardine to join him, but the Rangers man had other ideas. 'I actually kicked the boat further out into the water,' Jardine continues. 'But the tide began to take Jimmy out to sea very quickly.'

David Hay and Erich Schaedler went out in another boat to pull Jinky back in, but it began to take in water, and they quickly abandoned their rescue mission.

Hugh McIlvanney described the scene in *The Observer*, 'Johnstone, who was cheery enough to spend the first few minutes of his ordeal standing up in the boat, waving the single oar in his possession and chanting "Scot-land! Scot-land!", was soon reduced to a less-celebratory waving as he bobbed towards the horizon, pursued by the noisy advice of his team-mates on the shore.'

'Eventually, the coastguard had to be called to rescue him,' Jardine said. John and Tom Halliday were two brothers who ran boat hires. They were tasked with getting Jinky back to dry land. 'I asked him what he was doing,' John told the *Record*. 'He said, "I was just going out to fish." He said he was all right, but he had lost an oar. There was no fishing tackle in the boat.'

Johnstone recalled the incident in the documentary *Lord of the Wing*, 'The following morning I came down the stair thinking nothing had happened, nobody had seen it, and it would be swept under the carpet. I came into the breakfast room, and Denis [Law] is sitting in the corner at the table, and he goes, "What shall we do with the drunken sailor?"'

'After our morning training session was over, when we got back to the hotel, I think every journalist in Britain had laid siege to our headquarters,' Jardine wrote in his autobiography. 'Willie didn't fancy the press relations side of the job at the best of times, and we really landed him in it that time.'

Ormond, a Royal Navy man who had taken part in Second World War convoys to Murmansk, recognised that his leniency in allowing the players to go out made a bollocking seem churlish. 'I've told them that they've misused the trust I put in them,' he told the press, 'and that from now on, there would just have to be some kind of curfew system. And the next one to step out of line knows it's bingo, pack the bags and home.'

Despite some calls in the press for the end of Johnstone's Scotland career, he was selected in the number eight shirt for the match against England the following Saturday.

An attendance of 93,271 was at Hampden to see Jinky have one of his best games in a dark-blue shirt. In his book, Hay recalls, 'Willie Ormond would have realised that the wee man, with his dander up, was a frightening proposition for any unsuspecting defence. That was bad news for England left-back Mike Pejic who was never selected again for his country after being given a very public runaround by a little demon with something to prove.' He was at the centre of every move as Scotland won 2-0.

Jardine recalled, 'At the end of the game, the team did a lap of honour and as we're coming round to the press box wee Jimmy's getting the team, and he says, "Right lads, they gave us pelters during the week," and he's wanting to give them the V-sign, and we're having to calm him down.'

50

The Copenhagen Five – 1975

SCOTLAND'S HOPES of qualifying for the later stages of the 1976 European Championship had all but evaporated by September 1975. A 2-1 defeat to Spain at Hampden and a 1-1 draw in Valencia was followed up with a 1-1 draw with Romania in Bucharest.

The fourth game in Group 4 came on 3 September at Idrætsparken, Denmark's national stadium in Copenhagen. Scotland's win came courtesy of a goal from Joe Harper, who was earning his first cap since November 1972.

Scotland players were never shy to go for a night on the town, and that was what the win called for. The full squad were joined in a nearby nightspot, the Mariner Club, by members of the under-23 team, who had won the previous night in Frederikshavn.

Peter Lorimer recalled, for author Richard Sutcliffe, giving his Leeds team-mate Billy Bremner a word of advice before the match, 'I remember saying to him, "Billy, the young lads from Aberdeen have a bit of a reputation, so it's best to steer clear of them." So what does he do once we are back in the bar? He only heads straight over and joins them. Within 20 minutes, they were going to fight everyone. But that was Billy, he had to be in the middle of things.'

The Aberdeen boys Bremner joined were Arthur Graham and Willie Young, who were accompanied by Celtic's Pat McCluskey and former Aberdeen striker Harper, then with Hibernian.

A row with the bar staff over the price of drinks ensued. Bremner and his party left to find a nightclub. There the police were later called following complaints of rowdy behaviour and bad language. No arrests were made. Vigo Viggoson, the owner of Bonaparte's nightclub, was reported to say, 'I know Billy Bremner personally and was delighted to have him and his colleagues in my club.'

Back at the Marina Hotel where the players were staying, a room belonging to Jock McDonald, a member of the SFA Council and Inverness Thistle chairman, was trashed. He refused to comment to the press.

At breakfast, the mood was gloomy. Word had got around that an incident had taken place and that Bremner was in some degree of trouble.

When the squad returned to Scotland, SFA secretary Willie Allan announced an SFA emergency meeting 'to investigate the alleged incident'. Rankin Grimshaw, president of the SFA, said, 'If any players are found guilty, we would ban them from international football. We are trying to get the hooligan element out of spectating. We cannot tolerate this sort of behaviour.' Grimshaw said that they had received complaints from several sources, including one from the manager of the hotel.

Comments made by SFA Council members prompted the meeting, Grimshaw saying, 'It distresses me greatly that certain council members abused the privilege of travelling with the official party by making statements regarding the alleged misconduct of players.'

Hibs chairman Tom Hart had called publicly for certain players to be banned for life from the national team, while George Rattray, the Aberdeenshire representative, said, 'You should have seen some of them at meal tables. Some were just like animals. It was the same at the duty free shop. What we need is a good clean out.'

Bremner denied that there was a row in the nightclub or a fight or trouble over a bill, calling the allegations 'nonsense'. He also suggested that what players did in their spare time was no one else's business.

On Monday, 8 September, the Scotland International selection committee sat to decide what disciplinary measures would be taken. Bremner had been Scotland's captain for the past four seasons, coincidentally taking on the duties for the first time in Copenhagen in 1972. At the time Bremner was one cap short of Denis Law's record of 55.

The players were not told of the specific charges against them. Reports in the press and within the SFA varied. There was no clear indication, for example, that Arthur Graham was involved, with one report suggesting that he had left before the police were called and watched the commotion from a distance.

The SFA passed sentence that all five players would be banned from playing for Scotland for life.

Bremner, who played for Leeds in a 3-2 win over Ipswich the same night, told the *Yorkshire Evening Post*, 'I honestly never expected to be banned like this for something I still consider to be a small happening.' Bremner expressed sympathy for the three under-23s only at the beginning of their international careers. He stressed there was no fight at the nightclub and that the SFA hadn't listened to the players' side of the story.

The secretary general of the Danish Football Federation, Erik Hyldstrup, had compiled a report on the situation for his Scottish counterpart. He spoke to the Danish newspaper *Politiken*. 'My report indicated there was very little basis for the charges against the five,' he said. 'There was no police complaint after the incident in the nightclub, when the Scottish players were ejected, and no names were given in the police patrol's report.' Denmark's captain Ulrik Le Fevre said he found the verdict 'unreasonably hard'.

Bremner sat down with Ken Jones of the *Daily Mirror* a few months later. 'I didn't have many games left,' he said. 'But it would have been terrific to have the [caps] record. Look, I loved playing for Scotland. I did it wrong in Copenhagen, and not for the first time. But there you are; that's life.'

In July 1977 at a meeting of the SFA's Executive and General Purposes Committee, the minutes noted, 'The cases of the five players who were disciplined following the match Denmark v Scotland played on 3rd September 1975 were considered and having agreed that the sentences imposed had now served their purpose, it was agreed that the ban on their being again selected to represent Scotland be raised forthwith.'

Harper played against Iran in the 1978 World Cup finals, and Graham, uncapped in 1975, won 11 caps between 1977 and 1981, scoring two goals.

In 1988 it was announced that Bremner would be one of 17 Scottish players to be honoured for having won 50 or more caps.

51

Scotland Under-23s 2 Netherlands Under-23s 0 (AET; Netherlands win 4-3 on penalties) – 1976

24 March 1976
Easter Road, Edinburgh
European Championship quarter-final second leg
Attendance: 32,593

Scotland: Rough (Partick Thistle), Brownlie (Hibernian), Gray (Leeds), Jackson (Rangers), Miller (Aberdeen), Craig [C] (Newcastle United), Bremner (Hibernian), Pettigrew (Motherwell), Jordan (Leeds United), Smith (Kilmarnock), Johnstone (Rangers)

Holland: Schellekens (NEC), Meutstege [C] (Sparta Rotterdam), Lacroi (MVV), Balkestein (Sparta), Everse (Feyenoord), Kila (The Hague), Lubse (PSV Eindhoven), Hugo Hovenkamp (AZ 67), Kist (AZ 67), Nanninga (Roda JC), Van Deinsen (Go Ahead Eagles)

Referee: Klaus Ohmsen (West Germany)

Goals:
Johnstone (15), Jackson (33)

THIS WAS Scotland's last international at under-23 level, as later in the year the age range changed to under-21. It was also the first international match staged at Easter Road for 23 years since a B fixture against England that ended in a 2-2 draw.

Scotland went into the game 2-0 down from the first leg in Breda through goals from Van Deinsen and Kees Kist. With minutes of that game remaining, Dutch fans from behind Scotland's goal launched missiles at the Scots players. Willie Miller recalled hoping that the game might be abandoned. The Danish referee Bengt Nielsen later said the only reason he didn't abandon the game was that the bottles were plastic and not glass.

'I had a more personal reason to remember that game,' Miller wrote in his 1989 autobiography, 'for at one stage I thought it was going to be my last. Taking an opponent's elbow right on my Adam's apple. I thought at first I had swallowed my tongue as I struggled for breath. Possibly my injury was part of the price to be paid for having Kenny Burns as a team-mate, for earlier in the game he had made his presence felt, kicking all and sundry on the opposing side. It had to be me who suffered the backlash.'

Boss Willie Ormond said ahead of the game, 'All 16 players including the goalkeepers have practised taking penalties in case the tie goes on to a penalty decider. But I hope it won't come to that.'

The anticipated crowd was around 20,000, but on the night a crowd of 32,593 turned out. The *Glasgow Herald* wrote, 'The atmosphere was rapturous and affectionate.'

Scotland had wiped out the deficit within 33 minutes. After quarter of an hour Meutstege fouled Smith. Craig sent the free kick to the far post, where Derek Johnstone guided his header into the corner of the net. A corner from Gordon Smith was nodded on by Joe Jordan, where Johnstone touched it towards goal. The ball came back off the keeper where the permitted overage player, 29-year-old Colin Jackson, lying on the ground, swung a leg out and knocked it home.

It was harder for the Scots in the second half, but the chances were there to win the tie. Jordan twice rattled the crossbar, and both times Pettigrew failed to put away the rebounds. It was Jordan's first appearance in a Scotland shirt in 14 months.

Dickson of Queen of the South came on for Smith on 72 minutes as Ormond looked for more pace on the flanks.

Why Scotland couldn't find a winner was down to Harry Schellekens playing a blinder. 'I thought he was a brilliant goalkeeper,' Ormond said. 'He was in complete command of his goals. The way he came out for high balls and crosses stamps him as a world-class keeper.'

The tie, still level after extra time, went to penalties.

Miller scored first, while Nanninga made it 1-1. Jordan then had his kick saved by Schellekens. Substitute Henk van Rijnsoever put the Netherlands into the lead. Brownlie equalised, then Scotland got a lifeline when Wim Meutstege hit the crossbar. Frank Gray stepped up to put Scotland ahead at 3-2. Jan Van Deinsen levelled at 3-3. Tommy Craig, who had scored from the spot in the 4-0 win over Romania in December 1975, then had his penalty saved. Aad Kila stepped up to win the shoot-out for the Dutch.

Craig, who had scored seven out of seven penalties for Newcastle that season, was gutted by his miss. 'I was perfectly confident,' he told the *Evening Times*. 'But I didn't get enough behind it and the goalkeeper got it. That miss will live with me for a long time.'

By the time the match had ended at around ten o'clock, Edinburgh's pubs had shut.

'This defeat will go down along with all those other tales of bad luck upon which we cherish our illusions about a game which defies understanding,' wrote Ian Archer in the *Glasgow Herald*.

In the following days, the newspapers were scathing of the fact a match like this had to be decided on penalties. This was the international side's first experience of a shoot-out.

52

Scotland Win the Cannes Youth Tournament – 1976

THE FESTIVAL International de Football Junior de Cannes had been running since 1950. It was originally for club sides with previous winners, including AC Milan, Sheffield Wednesday and Chelsea.

In 1969 it became a tournament for international teams. Brazil had won four in a row from 1971 to 1974, with Mexico winning the 1975 edition.

Andy Roxburgh, the SFA's director of coaching, was in charge of Scotland who were drawn in Group B alongside Finland, Brazil and Italy. Group A consisted of France, Iran, Mexico and Holland. All the games were played at the Stade Pierre de Coubertin.

Finland were the first opponent on Wednesday, 14 April with a 5pm kick-off. Scotland's team was: Brand (Everton), Harvey (Hearts), Cooper (Aberdeen), Hay (Hearts), Dawson (Rangers), McGhie (Leeds United), Boyd (Rangers), Wark [C] (Ipswich Town), Dodds (Dundee United), Melrose (Partick Thistle), McCluskey (Celtic). Wark and McCluskey were replaced by Hannah (Celtic) and Carroll (Hibernian).

The Scottish team won 5-1, with the goals coming from Harvey, Dodds (two), Melrose and McGhie.

Two nights later, Scotland took on Brazil with the same starting 11. Melrose picked up an injury in the first half and was replaced by Robertson (Rangers), while Carroll again came on for McCluskey.

Scotland were unlucky not to win, with John Wark missing a penalty and Robertson hitting a post. The game ended goalless.

The final group game was with Italy on 18th April. Billy Thomson of Partick Thistle was in goal, while Hannah started instead of McCluskey. Brogan (Everton) replaced Hay, and McCluskey came on for Boyd in the second half. Two goals from Hannah gave the Scots a 2-1 win to top their group.

That meant they faced France, the winners of Group A, in the final. The night before, some of the Scotland side decided to sneak out of their camp to bring in some pizzas and soft drinks.

'It was probably one of the most bizarre, surreal and unbelievable incidents of my life,' George McCluskey said to his biographer Aidan Donaldson. As they stood in the pizzeria, they witnessed a yellow Citroën pulling up. Inside were 'some of the biggest rock stars in the world, and we ended up talking to them'.

It was members of the Rolling Stones who were staying in nearby Pégomas rehearsing for their upcoming European tour in support of their *Black and Blue* album. McCluskey said, 'Ronnie Wood asked us what we were doing, and our response was a mixture of "buying pizzas" and "playing football". Ronnie wanted to bring us to a party at their chateau, but all we wanted to do was to get back to the hotel with the pizzas and not get caught.'

The players did get caught, however, as McCluskey discovered that when he attempted to climb in the window he had clambered out of an hour earlier, it was Roxburgh's hands pulling him in. The Celtic youngster found himself on the substitutes' bench for the final.

The line-up was Brand, Harvey, Cooper, Hay, Dawson, Hannah, Wark (captain), McGhie, Carroll, Dodds and Melrose. Boyd and McCluskey replaced Hannah and Dodds during the second half.

'With about 20 minutes to go, [Andy Roxburgh] told me to get warmed up,' McCluskey recalled. 'I almost told him to get stuffed and that I should have been on from the start. But thankfully, I didn't. I went on the park, and the game changed.'

In the 73rd minute, McCluskey picked the ball up in midfield and went on a run to the byline. He cut the ball back, and Gordon Boyd scored from close range. It would prove to be the winner.

Billy McGhie won the Player of the Tournament award. 'I was proud of all 16 players in my squad,' Roxburgh said afterwards. 'Those boys who did not play in the different matches gave the others all the encouragement in the world, and it was great to see it.'

The win led the SFA to rethink its stance on sponsorship. In August, it announced a deal with Mackinlay's Old Scotch Whisky which would make an award for the football personality of the month. SFA president Rankin Grimshaw said, 'The success of our youth team at Cannes was most gratifying, but it cost the SFA a considerable sum. If we can get sponsors, we will take them. We must live with the present and not the past.'

53

Bruce Rioch

24 caps, 6 goals (1975–1978)

BRUCE RIOCH was born in Aldershot where his father, Jim, a regimental sergeant major with the Scots Guards, was stationed. Although Rioch grew up in England and never played for a Scottish club, he always saw himself as a Scot. His father was born in Kineff, Aberdeenshire and his mother was from Skye.

Moving around different Army barracks in England and Germany when he was young, Rioch had trials for England Schoolboys, but a spine injury prevented him from playing. Rioch began his career as a 14-year-old with Third Division Luton Town, turning professional in 1964. At 17 he went to Lilleshall for trials with the England youth team. This time, though, he wasn't picked. In 1969 he earned a move to Second Division Aston Villa. Rioch eventually made it to the English top flight with a transfer to Derby County in February 1974.

When Rioch began playing, the rules of international selection meant that he could only play for the country of his birth; however, a rule change allowed players to choose to represent the countries of their parents' birth. When this came in, Rioch was selected for Scotland by Tommy Docherty, who had been his club manager for a period at Aston Villa. However, Rioch declined his approach. 'I won't go into the reasons but can say categorically that I wasn't waiting for England to come calling,' he told *The Scotsman*. However, in 1977 Rioch said, 'Of course, at one time there was a question in my mind about playing for England, if I got the chance, but my preference was for Scotland, in any case, and when the dual-qualification rule came in, I jumped at the chance to play for Scotland.'

'A very talented player,' Docherty said of Rioch in 1994. 'Strong, quick, aggressive, good balance. And he was very adaptable. He could play it whatever way you wanted.'

In the 1974/75 season, under Dave Mackay, Derby won the First Division title. Rioch was ever-present, and Willie Ormond rewarded his performances as he gave him his international debut aged 27. 'Dave Mackay said, "How would you like to play for Scotland?" "I'd be delighted," I said. "Good. Ring a Mr Donald, as in Duck, and he'll tell you where to be." My debut was a friendly against Portugal at Hampden. Walking out of the tunnel, I heard a familiar voice, "Hullo, mucker!" It was my brother Ian. "Fancy a bite of my meat pie?" The game went well, and we won.'

Although Rioch only earned 24 caps, he was part of an exciting time for the national team. He played in the 1976 and 1977 wins over England and played a part in the successful 1978 World Cup qualifying campaign.

Of the win at Wembley, Rioch said to the *Daily Record* in 1996, 'I'll never forget it for as long as I live. I think I've still got the crossbar in my back garden somewhere. My abiding memory is of the fans. The victory meant the world to them and to every player on the pitch.'

Rioch was part of the 1978 World Cup squad in Argentina, despite being on the transfer list at Derby, then managed by Tommy Docherty. 'I think in that World Cup Ally MacLeod was too loyal,' Rioch said to *The Scotsman* in 2019. 'I was the beneficiary in that he picked me to play against Peru, but he shouldn't have done.'

'I've never had any regrets sticking with Don [Masson] and Bruce in midfield,' MacLeod said to Mike Wilson in his 1998 book *Don't Cry For Me Argentina*. 'Bruce was a great choice. He was a smashing bloke, very popular with the players, and if ever there was a problem, he would always come and have a chat with me.'

Rioch's last game for Scotland was in the 3-2 win over the Netherlands in Mendoza at those finals. 'I had a great view of

Archie Gemmill's wonder goal. Then when Johnny Rep lined up his shot, I thought, "He's too far out," but he wasn't. We were close, just not close enough.'

Jock Stein took over in the autumn of 1978, but he didn't find a place for Rioch in his Scotland sides. 'I was disappointed, but I accepted his decision. He didn't have to phone and tell me – he was the great Jock,' said Rioch.

54

The Wembley Invasion – 1977

SATURDAY, 4 June 1977 is one of the most infamous dates in Scottish football history. It's also one of the most joyous. Scotland hadn't won at Wembley since the famous victory in 1967. On their last visit, they had been thrashed 5-1, with Rangers' Stewart Kennedy becoming the latest Scottish goalkeeper to have his career defined by his performance in the match.

It was the weekend of Queen Elizabeth II's Silver Jubilee. The *Evening Times* reported, 'The biggest ever contingent of Scots fans showed up at Wembley today,' estimating their number as around 70,000.

By any observer's reckoning, Scotland outclassed the English side that day, with Danny McGrain being most people's man of the match.

England had been working on set pieces ahead of the game. Manager Don Revie and his assistant Les Cocker were both well aware of Gordon McQueen's aerial threat, having worked with him at Leeds United. On the training field, reserve goalkeeper Joe Corrigan, 6ft 4in, stood in for the 6ft 3in McQueen, with goalkeeper Ray Clemence and his defenders becoming well drilled in what to do if Scotland got a free kick around the box. But it would all be for nought.

In the 43rd minute, Phil Neal handled the ball down the left flank a few yards outside the English penalty box to concede a free kick. Asa Hartford chipped the ball into the danger zone, McQueen climbed higher than anyone else to send his header flying into the England net, putting Scotland one up.

After the game, Cocker remarked to his son Dave, 'When we were at Leeds, we told the players what to do and they did it, simple as that, but some of this lot, they don't seem to have a clue.' McQueen said that the Scottish training for set pieces consisted of the taker being told to aim for the biggest thing on the pitch – his head.

With an hour gone, Kenny Dalglish scrambled the ball over Ray Clemence's goal line to put Scotland 2-0 up. Mick Channon scored a consolation penalty three minutes from the end to make the scoreline more respectable. Scotland had won at Wembley and collected the British Home Championship as well.

Then came the pitch invasion.

'The Wembley fence is not yet up, so the fans have come over the barriers,' the BBC's John Motson said as he commented on the aftermath of the win. An 8ft fence was due to be erected before England's November game with Italy. 'Perhaps one shouldn't say anything other than critical about this because crowd invasions are one of the reasons why fences have gone up everywhere and indeed are going up at Wembley, and you're really divided between appreciating the delight of the Scottish fans but not wanting to see the ground pulled apart like this,' Motson continued.

At that moment, a crossbar gave way under the weight of Scots fans sitting on top of it. 'They've even knocked the goals down and broken the crossbar,' said Motson.

The man on the crossbar was 21-year-old Alec Torrance. In 1995 he spoke to the *Daily Record*, 'I was just carried away by the whole thing. I was ecstatic and ran cheering for the terraces when I saw everyone going on to the pitch. There were lots of people climbing the posts, and I just grabbed the net and hauled myself up. Just as I was inches from the top I heard the bar crack and went crashing to the ground. I'm not sure if it was the weight of my platform shoes that finally toppled the whole thing. We never meant any harm, everyone just sort of got caught up in the celebrations.'

In Howard Bass's official history of Wembley Stadium, he wrote, 'Then followed the most disgraceful scene ever to be held at Wembley. Fanatical hooligans invaded the pitch and, not content with deliberately damaging the turf, climbed on to the crossbar of one goal and exerted pressure until it split in two like matchwood. All right-minded Scots were sick with shame that day.' That final sentence is a stretch; you would have to speak to a significant number of Scots before you found a majority who felt shame at the antics of the fans that afternoon.

In his 1996 autobiography, Kenny Dalglish was keen to defend the Scots supporters, 'They were acting out of high spirits, not malice. Our supporters never wrecked the stadium, as some people wrote. The reason why the media coverage focused on the fans was that it took the pressure and spotlight off England's defeat. I don't condone people coming on the pitch, but no England player was threatened.'

Supporter Alex Burnett was 17 at the time. In 1999 he told *The Guardian*, 'It wasn't planned it was just instinctive. I wanted to run towards the centre circle, but I got to the goal and saw people climbing it. I jumped on to the netting, and then the goal just came crashing down as I was standing in the goalmouth doing a Highland fling. It was fantastic.'

'I was one of those caught out as the Wembley staff and police were simply overrun that day,' manager Ally MacLeod wrote in his autobiography. 'It was bedlam, and when I tried to get up the tunnel, a London bobby would not let me. I said, "I'm the Scotland manager." He said, "Yeah, right, and I'm Her Majesty the Queen." Don Revie saw this, and he said, "He really is the Scotland manager." So the policeman let me up the tunnel. When I got in our dressing room, there were four Tartan Army supporters there in the bath with Alan Rough.'

Head groundsman Don Gallacher told the *Sunday Mirror*, 'I was disgusted and heartbroken … they dug up my turf with their fingers.' He said he had never encountered anything like it in his 40 years as a groundsman, 'I almost wept when I saw what they were doing.' Gallacher's father had been born in Glasgow in 1881 and played for a time with Duntocher Hibs and Parkhead Juniors before moving to London.

The *Evening Times* wrote that the London police, good-humoured with the Scots in the lead-up, seemed woefully under strength to deal with the deluge of Scots fans on to the pitch. The police were at odds with the Wembley officials as, ironically, concern for the pitch led to a stadium official cancelling a senior policeman's orders to have 20 mounted horses clear the pitch. A police spokesman said it would have been done 'quickly and without hurting the pitch'. 'Cut the turf up?' Gallacher remembered replying when he was told by a policeman why the horses weren't going on. 'What do they think 30,000 nutcases are doing out there? Get the mounted police after these bastards.'

In his memoir, Gallacher recounted his horror as he watched Scots fans rampage across his turf, taking souvenirs from every inch of the ground, 'One woman, she must have been 50, wrapped in garish tartan, pushed two big lads over and snatched their souvenir from them for herself, it was a piece of goal net about as big as a scarf – that's how she wore it, on her head, and she danced with delight.'

On attempting to physically stop a supporter from lifting turf, Gallacher was told to go and find his own as there was plenty to go around. 'There ye are sonny, have a bit of Wembley to take home for the lads,' the groundsman recalled being told. 'They were absolutely, blissfully happy. I'd never seen such happiness.'

Len Went, the Wembley spokesman, said, 'Their disgraceful behaviour has destroyed a new £18,000 pitch.' He said it would cost £5,000 to repair the playing surface alone, as well as gates, fences and the greyhound track that surrounded the pitch. The greyhound track was cleared first for the race meeting two nights later.

Holes on the pitch ranged from several inches to 14ft in length. Some were 3in deep, some only skin deep. The grass from behind the goals, about 40 yards by 79 yards, was identified as being used to resurface the pitch area. Gallacher referred to the process of relaying the turf as 'a fair cow of a job'. Goalposts were sourced from Sweden, and the England-West Germany Schoolboy international on 18 June went ahead.

In the 2023 TV programme *Billy Connolly Does…*, the star, present at Wembley, said, 'It was amazing. I was pished. I was with a cartoonist from Scotland, and we both got shit-faced.'

When Billy arrived on the terraces, the Tartan Army welcomed him. 'This incredible cheer went up, and Billy stood there taking it all in,' cartoonist Malky McCormick told the *Sunday Mail* in 2002. 'He was wearing a ludicrous tammy and had spent most of the day in the pub, signing autographs and having his picture taken with fans.'

'We were watching it, and it was just amazing,' Connolly said. 'The fans emptied on to the park. People with kilts and platform shoes. Just nuts. Rod Stewart was there. He was leading the throng. And somebody stole his watch.'

'At the end, I wanted to go on the pitch with the rest of the fans,' singer Rod Stewart recalled, 'but I was there with my dad, who said, "No." I said to him, "Just try and stop me." When I got to the pitch, police were trying to stop the fans going on. I lifted my hat to show my face, and when the officer saw who it was, he said, "Oh, all right, go on then." All the supporters got me on their shoulders and lifted me up. I got my Cartier watch stolen.'

The culprit was caught and fined £150 in court. Stewart was later reunited with his watch, 'It turned up in Edinburgh about two months later.'

Gordon Strachan, then playing for Dundee, was also on the pitch. In an interview with the *Daily Telegraph* in 2013 he recalled, 'I was there as a supporter. I was there on my honeymoon. I was invited on the pitch by a policeman. Me, my wife Lesley and my best man were the only ones left on the terracing. He just looked at us and went, "On you go." So we went.'

A Scotland Yard spokesman said, 'The Scots arrived here in a boisterous but peaceable mood and remained in that state until they left.' Denis Howell, the Labour government's sports minister, said, 'The majority of people were not in a vindictive mood – rather in a mood of euphoria.'

The SFA later presented Wembley with new goalposts.

55

Santiago – 1977

IN JANUARY of 1977, the Scottish Football Association announced a three-game tour of South America in the hope and expectation that Scotland would qualify for the 1978 World Cup in Argentina. The itinerary would take in matches with Argentina and Brazil, opening with a game against Chile at the Estadio Nacional in Santiago. This particular match met with protests almost immediately.

The Scottish Trades Union Congress was one of the first organisations to condemn the plan publicly. James Kirkwood, the assistant general secretary, said his general council had written to the General and Municipal Workers' Union – to which the players belonged – asking for support in their campaign to have the SFA cancel the match.

Norman Buchan, Labour MP for West Renfrew and a member of the Chile Committee on Human Rights, asked the government to issue a statement expressing disapproval.

The shadow minister for sport, Hector Munro, the Conservative MP for Dumfries, said, 'It is really high time some politicians got off the back of the SFA. National sporting bodies are perfectly capable of deciding what countries to play.'

The stadium in Santiago was built in 1938 and hosted matches in the 1962 World Cup finals. The Andes were on one side, with the Pacific Ocean on the other, but the root of the issue was in its bloody role in Chile's recent past.

On 11 September 1973, armed forces staged a coup d'état. President Allende, Chile's democratically elected leader, died during an assault on the presidential palace, and a junta composed of three generals and an admiral, with General Augusto Pinochet as president, was installed.

The *Caravana de Muerte* (Caravan of Death) was a death squad that began rounding up tens of thousands, but with no space in the jails, the government needed other large public spaces to intern victims. The national stadium became the country's largest detention centre. Ten other stadiums were also used.

Hugo Lepe, a Chilean international footballer and trade unionist looking after players' rights, was interned there. Team captain Chamaco Valdés led a hunt for him supported by other players. After a month and a half, he found him, and Lepe was freed. Alfonso Reyes, the national team doctor, was also interned there, where he was tortured many times.

Adam Schesch, who was interned there for ten days, told *The Independent* in 1998 that he watched prisoners being organised into a line. 'Just before they led the one line out into the stadium, they would start the extractor fans in the changing rooms just to make some noise,' he said. 'The gunfire would last for 45 seconds, maybe a minute, and then there was no sound. Then someone would come back in and turn off the fans.'

The Pinochet government ended the stadium's use as a prison camp on 9 November 1973 in order for it to host football. Chile were due to play the Soviet Union in a World Cup qualifying match, the first leg in Moscow finishing goalless. The Soviets complained about the intended venue, so FIFA said it would investigate.

Prisoners were rounded up and taken underneath the stadium, being held at gunpoint and ordered to remain silent. Some prisoners, though, were left in the stands and watched the men from FIFA inspect the ground. 'We wanted to yell out and say, "Hey, we are here, look at us,"' Felipe Agüero, one of the prisoners, told the *New York Times* in 2015. 'But they seemed only interested in the condition of the grass.'

On 2 February 1977, SFA secretary Ernie Walker said, 'Having made enquiries of Her Majesty's Government and having considered the reply, the International and Selection Committee have decided unanimously to proceed with plans to have the Scottish international team play three international matches in Chile, Argentina and Brazil in preparation for our anticipated participation in the 1978 World Cup finals.'

A response came quickly from Alex Ferrie, divisional organiser of the Amalgamated Union of Engineering Workers, who described the SFA's decision as 'their usual pig-headed approach to things'. Ferrie said that they would be pressing the government to have the SFA reconsider.

On the same day, Edward Rolands, the minister of state at the Foreign Office, said in the House of Commons, in response to a question about Scotland going to Santiago, 'We were asked to give a political assessment, which we have done. There can be no question of government approval for such a visit.'

The SFA had admitted that the financial guarantee they had from the Argentine FA for the three matches to be played would not cover the expenses for the trip.

On 7 February, the executive committee of the Ross and Cromarty Constituency Labour Party wrote to the SFA asking them to reconsider saying that to play in the Estadio Nacional would 'shame Scotland'.

Norman Buchan, the Labour MP for Renfrew West, told a press conference at the House of Commons, 'It would be a dishonour for Scotland if this game goes on.'

Scottish groups of Amnesty International wrote to the SFA saying the decision was 'regrettable'.

In February, manager Willie Ormond went on a fact-finding tour of South America. On his return, he wouldn't be drawn into any political comments but remarked that the stadium in Santiago was 'a braw place'.

In March, Scotland's Labour Party Conference called on the government to ban the team from playing in Santiago.

In May, Alex Kitson, a national officer of the Transport and General Workers' Union, handed in a protest petition to the SFA. It contained 40,000 signatures.

In the House of Commons on 4 May, Dennis Canavan, the MP for West Stirlingshire, asked Edward Rowlands, 'As the

Scottish Football Association is using the threat of disciplinary action to force footballers to play in a stadium which has formerly been used as a concentration camp and which is stained with the blood of countless innocent victims, will my honourable friend demand that this match be stopped? If the SFA refuse to stop it, will he tell Willie Allan, the reactionary autocrat who runs the SFA, that there will be absolutely no government hospitality or official facilities at all during the whole of the SFA tour of South America?'

Rowlands stressed that the government were clear on their assessment.

The protests and appeals had no effect. The Scotland team flew first to London then to Recife, Rio de Janeiro and Buenos Aires before landing in Chile. Goalkeeper Bobby Clark recalled, 'Obvious signs of oppression were not apparent, and apart from our military escort to and from training, all was quiet.'

The Chilean FA had disbanded their team after failing to qualify for the 1978 World Cup finals. Their four-game qualification group had ended in March. They hastily put together a squad from five Santiago club sides. The majority of the team came from Unión Española, whose coach Luis Santibáñez was in charge of the national team.

Willie Ormond had resigned his post in May and Ally MacLeod was in charge. 'I'd say it's about the best team Scotland has had in 20 years,' MacLeod said before the match.

In the game itself Scotland had an excellent 90 minutes. Dalglish opened the scoring after 19 minutes with a shot from 15 yards. Eleven minutes later Chilean goalkeeper Adolfo Nef dropped a cross from Bruce Rioch behind him and Lou Macari lashed the ball into the roof of the net. Asa Hartford made it 3-0 when he hit a spectacular shot from 35 yards.

The terracing was three quarters empty, with 17,600 in an 85,000-capacity stadium, but the Chileans applauded the Scots team, particularly Willie Johnstone who turned right-back Juan Machuca inside out. 'When others came across to cover, he looked capable of beating the whole of Chile's defence on his own,' reported the *Evening Express*.

Rogelio Farías scored for Chile three minutes into the second half as the Scots suffered from complacency. But the three-goal cushion was back when Johnstone beat three men and played the ball back to Macari who hit the ball into the net. Julio Crisosto scored Chile's second on 70 minutes.

Ferenc Puskás, coach of Santiago club Colo-Colo, was in the crowd. 'If you play like that in Argentina next year you'll be among the top five nations,' he said afterwards.

56

Anfield – 1977

THE EUROPEAN World Cup qualifying Group 7 contained three teams – Scotland, Wales and Czechoslovakia – with only the winners reaching the 1978 finals in Argentina. Scotland had beaten Wales 1-0 in the group opener before a loss to Czechoslovakia. However, a 2-1 win over the Czechs at Hampden left Scotland requiring a victory over the Welsh in their final game to qualify. Wales, with one win and one defeat from their two games so far, needed a win to stay in contention.

Ninian Park in Cardiff was the original choice of venue for the match. However, the 1975 Safety of Sports Grounds Act saw the ground be deemed unsuitable, as South Glamorgan County Council could only provide a safety certificate for a 14,000 capacity. Wrexham's Racecourse Ground had a similar restriction imposed by Clywd County Council.[5]

Aston Villa were approached about Villa Park being used. In October of 1976, a friendly between Villa and Rangers was abandoned after 53 minutes when a riot broke out. Over 70 people were injured, with the two teams sprinting off the pitch as fans spilt on. Villa were naturally trepidatious about another influx of

---

5 Many retrospective accounts of why the match was played at Anfield state that Wales were ordered to play the match away from Cardiff due to crowd trouble in a game with Yugoslavia in May 1976. This is incorrect. The ban was imposed by UEFA, who ordered Wales to play all home matches in the 1978–1980 European Championship qualifiers on grounds at least 124 miles from Cardiff. Their home European qualifiers were all played at the Racecourse Ground, Wrexham, around 139 miles away from Cardiff.

supporters from north of the border. Birmingham police said they would not veto the match should Villa Park be selected.

At the end of August, Anfield was selected as the venue. Cardiff chairman Stefan Terlezski was furious, 'If it had been a rugby matter, there would have been debates in parliament, protests in the media, and the Welsh Office would have been called in,' he said. 'Because it is soccer, there have been no signs of any MP, Jim Callaghan the prime minister or Denis Howell intervening. The sooner Mr Howell loses the minister of sports title and looks after the water taps, the better.'

It would be the first full international at Anfield in 46 years since England beat Wales 3-1 in the British Home Championship on 18 November 1931.

Welsh FA secretary Trevor Morris said Anfield was designed to attain as much home advantage as possible for the Welsh players, 'Anfield is just as acceptable to many people from North Wales as Wrexham. They can easily get there in less than an hour.'

In the *Liverpool Echo*, Michael Charters anticipated an 'invasion of some 20,000 Scots in full battle order'. The Anfield Residents' Committee had contacted their local councillor with concerns, but a police spokesman assured residents that security arrangements would be put in place to ensure everyone's safety.

Both Ally MacLeod and Mike Smith, the Welsh boss, were happy with the venue. Wales planned to train at Wrexham, while MacLeod had booked hotel accommodation in the Wirral and would use Tranmere Rovers' Prenton Park to train.

In *The Observer*, Peter Corrigan wrote, 'I fear Wales have made a mistake in transferring the game to Anfield. They will surely make a great deal of money, and the game will be granted a suitable atmosphere. Yet the sort of hysterical atmosphere we can expect is more likely to stir the Scots than the Welsh.'

Trevor Morris said that Scots fans would not get more than their allocation, which at 12,000 was a quarter of the ground. Supporters made day trips to Wales to get tickets and even went to the headquarters of the Welsh FA in Wrexham to secure briefs.

Prices ranged from £1.50 to £5. Turnstiles opened at 4.30pm, three hours ahead of kick-off. BBC Scotland had the whole game live from 7.25pm; however, BBC Wales only had highlights at 9.55pm.

Scots fans who arrived in Liverpool without tickets tried everything they could think of to get some. Several even knocked on the door of former Liverpool boss Bill Shankly. 'I don't know where they got my address from,' Shankly said to the *Echo*, 'and I had no tickets to give them, but these fans are among the most loyal in the world.'

Trevor Morris wrote an address in the match programme, criticising the restrictions that led to Cardiff being ruled out as the venue. He stated that the Safety of Sports Ground Act was 'pushed through parliament without proper consultation with football and other sporting authorities'. However, he stressed the act was commendable and necessary, 'So rigid was the application of the guidelines by the local authority responsible for issuing the certificate that restrictions imposed made Cardiff out of the question.'

There was no realistic alternative but to play outside Wales, he wrote. It was 'absurd', he said, to have the game played in front of only 14,000 spectators.

The crowd was recorded as 50,850, although there's little doubt many without tickets managed to get in. The famous Kop was designated as a Welsh end, but by kick-off it was 90 per cent Scots.

'It became our home game,' recalled Joe Jordan in 2012. 'The Anfield crowd was dominated by Scots, and that was important for us. We knew we were playing a very good Welsh team, but seeing the number of fans we had and hearing them gave us the edge. I don't know how so many of them got tickets, but we took over Liverpool that night.'

'I'll never forget that night,' Lou Macari told the *Daily Record* in 2020. 'Coming out of the tunnel and seeing Anfield three-quarters full of Scottish supporters. From that moment onwards, I never felt we were going to lose. Afterwards, I'm sure the Welsh FA felt they'd made a big mistake taking it to Liverpool because the response from the Tartan Army was, "Let's get down there and make this our home game." Archie Macpherson summed it up perfectly in the commentary when he said, "You've never heard noise like this in all your life."'

'This was supposed to be Wales's home game,' Paul Fitzpatrick wrote in *The Guardian*, 'but the rueful look on the face of [Terry] Yorath, the Welsh captain, as he led his side out to noise that beat like fists on the eardrums said much.'

The turning point of the game was a wonderful save Alan Rough made from a John Toshack volley in the second half. Rough, yards off his line, leapt backwards and turned the goal-bound shot over the bar as Toshack sank to the ground in disbelief. Over the years, Rough has been reluctant to call it his greatest save, but speaking to Aidan Smith of *The Scotsman* in 2022 he said, 'The saves you remember are the most important, and the one from big Toshack was certainly that.'

'Scottish goalkeeping was a bit of a joke back then, but Rough had the game of his life,' Welsh midfielder Brian Flynn recalled.

With 12 minutes remaining, Scotland were awarded a penalty. A long throw from Willie Johnston went into the Welsh box, where Joe Jordan rose alongside Norwich City's David Jones, and a hand went up in the air. Referee Robert Wurst pointed to the spot; captain Don Masson took responsibility and fired the penalty home.

Much debate has raged since that award as to whose hand played the ball. Was it Jones? Or, as most Welsh people believe, was it actually Jordan?

In *The Guardian*, Paul Fitzpatrick wrote, 'It is hard to believe that if Jones had been a total innocent, he would have reacted in the meek way that he did. It is rare that a referee's decision is accepted with so much equanimity, even in a humdrum league game, let alone a World Cup match of such importance.'

'As far as I know, the ball did not touch me,' Jordan said directly after the match. 'I did not feel it and was surprised when the penalty was given.' Joe has remained tight-lipped since that day over the incident, accepting that Welsh people want to quiz him on it but feeling saying nothing is the best thing to do.

Mike Smith said afterwards, 'There's disagreement among my players as to why the kick was given, but the referee gave it for a foul.'

Searching for an equaliser, the Welsh left gaps at the back, and with three minutes remaining Scotland exposed them. Buchan was in acres of space on the right, and he put in a perfect cross for Kenny Dalglish, playing on his club's home ground, to leap and head into the net for 2-0. Scotland had done it; they had qualified for Argentina. Now the expectations had really begun.

As for the Welsh, due in no small part to that match, the FAW made a record profit of £60,000 in 1977.

57

Ally's Tartan Army – 1978

WITH WORLD Cup qualification achieved, there were now money-making opportunities to be had. A World Cup song, official or not, was a must. In 1974 the Scotland World Cup squad had a top-20 hit with 'Easy, Easy', written by Bill Martin and Phil Coulter. In 1978, however, the limelight was taken by just one man – comedian Andy Cameron.

In 2020 Andy told the *Shoot! The Breeze* podcast how the song 'Ally's Tartan Army' came about. 'It was a Rangers song, "Who's That Team We Call the Rangers",' he said. 'I had a fitba act at the time, and I was going round the clubs. Clem Dane had a wee record company called Moonbeam, and he said, "You should make a record and sell it round the clubs." So we went into Radio Clyde … and we did the words. I was writing bits and pieces, and Pete Shipton [the engineer] to his eternal credit – I got the line "England cannae dae it cos they didnae qualify" – and Pete Shipton says, "That's the hook. That'll sell the record."'

Once the record was released, Andy realised it was becoming more serious than just selling copies from a holdall around the clubs. 'There were phone calls, "WH Smith are taking it. Woolworths are taking it." All that sort of stuff. We got 2,000 made, and they went, in no time at all. It was incredible.'

The song first charted on 4 March 1978 at number 32. That was enough for Andy to get the call to appear on *Top of the Pops* alongside The Jam, Elkie Brooks and Kate Bush. After shaking off his surprise, he organised his father and his brothers to accompany him to the recording.

At the studio, Andy and his family sat backstage, waiting for his turn to go on. 'The door opens, and in comes Generation X. Billy Idol was their lead singer. He's six feet five to start with. He had an Oor Wullie haircut, and he had platform soles on, and I'm this size. I've got the Scotland jersey on, a tartan tammy, a tartan banner, and he's looking down at me. I looked up at him. He spoke first, and he went, "Who the fack are you?" And before I could say anything, my old man went, "Who are you fuckin' talkin' tae?" He's nearly got him up against the wall. But the thing that done me was: "That's mah boay!" I was 38 at the time!'

Two weeks later, the record was at number 13, and Andy was on *Top of the Pops* again, this time alongside Elvis Costello, Mud and Suzi Quatro. In all, it spent eight weeks on the chart, peaking at number six at the start of April and selling more than 300,000 copies.

The downside for Andy was that he had a tour lined up while the World Cup was on, and when the results didn't go the way Scotland wanted them, he still had to step onstage and entertain. On the night of the match with Iran, Andy's plea to management to go on before the match was ignored. So, after the shocking 1-1 draw, Andy took to the stage, 'Right at the start of my act, a really big fella – massive – stood up and shouted, "Wee man, tell all the jokes you want. But see if you sing that song, you are going oot that windae!"'

58

The Hampden Send-Off – 1978

ON THURSDAY, 25 May, the day that the Scotland squad flew out to Argentina to contest the 1978 World Cup, they first assembled at Hampden Park for a grand send-off.

Comedian Andy Cameron introduced the squad individually to the crowd from the back of an open-topped bus. Massed pipe bands played, and majorettes performed for the crowd. The SFA assured Scots fans that this was 'unique in world football'.

A victory parade before a ball had been kicked was certainly a novel idea.

'I got the credit for that, and it was nothing to do with me really,' Ally MacLeod said on the 1986 BBC documentary *Only a Game?* 'It was Ernie Walker one day said to me, "It would be a marvellous thing," he said, "if we had a send off at Hampden."'

'It wasn't a lap of honour anyway,' Walker said in the same documentary. 'It was arranged in conjunction with the police because we recognised that there was going to be tremendous problems and scenes from wherever the team left.'

'I said, "Aye, we're celebrating winning the World Cup before we've won it. Really, that's what you're doing,"' said MacLeod.

Tickets for the event were 50p for seating and 30p for a spot on the terracing. Proceeds would go to the restoration of Hampden Park. Doors opened at 5.45pm and around 30,000 fans turned up to wave the team off. 'I had more at Hampden for a nought a game than some teams have for games,' said MacLeod.

At 6.30pm the massed pipes and drums of ten of Scotland's best-known pipe bands, including Red Hackle Pipes and Drums,

Strathclyde Police Pipe Band and Milngavie Pipe Band, marched into the stadium. At 6.50pm Andy Cameron took to the mic. At 7pm the squad was introduced to the crowd, a guard of honour being formed by the girls of Merrylee Drum Majorettes and the Barmulloch Majorettes. Twenty minutes later came the Scotland players who saluted the crowd by running to each end of the ground. 'It was highly emotional – and thoroughly embarrassing,' MacLeod wrote in his autobiography. At 7.40pm came the farewell, when the team went around the ground twice on the bus, and fans had the opportunity to say goodbye and good luck.

A banner in the crowd read, 'Argentina. We came, we saw, we conquered.'

'What a tremendous send-off,' MacLeod said to the *Daily Mirror* on the night. 'Now we must win the World Cup for them.' The fact that MacLeod was ready and eager to provide outlandish statements should a journalist cast a shadow over him surely contributed to the beating he eventually took from fans and press alike a few weeks later.

Danny McGrain, injured and withdrawn from the squad, went to Hampden to see the team off. 'If we win the cup, the first player to touch it will be Danny McGrain,' the Scotland boss said. Topping even that statement, McLeod revealed, 'We even turned down an invitation to go to 10 Downing Street to show the World Cup to the prime minister first.'

'The event … must go down as one of the finest public relations exercises the game has seen anywhere,' MacLeod wrote in his autobiography.

'The send-off was terrific,' Archie Gemmill wrote in his autobiography, 'a once-in-a-lifetime experience and to some, it must have felt as if Scotland had already won the World Cup.'

Captain Bruce Rioch, however, said to *The Independent* in 1994, 'The send-off at Hampden – well, it was like celebrating before the medals are handed out.'

'It wasn't a celebration of winning the World Cup before we got to the place,' Ernie Walker said. 'People were saying I think that they were happy we were in the World Cup, and you know it was a wonderful evening. It was a wonderful gathering of family people and the patriotic night, etc. It wasn't meant to be boastful.'

MacLeod reflected on the occasion, 'Too many people, I'm afraid, read too much into that wonderful Thursday evening. Instead of simply saluting our achievement in reaching the finals when so many other great nations had failed, I suspect that the majority of the fans felt that we were making some kind of promise, celebrating in fact, before we had really kicked a ball.'

MacLeod felt that the event actually put extra pressure on the squad in Argentina and contributed to the depth of the bitterness fans felt once things went wrong in the tournament. The simple, practical reason for the event, MacLeod stated, was that without it, there would have been congestion at the team's hotel in Glasgow and at Prestwick Airport with fans trying to see the team off.

As it was, more than 4,000 fans were there to meet them at the airport.

On the way from Glasgow to Prestwick Airport, fans lined the route, waved flags, cheered, and stood outside their homes and on bridges. In particular, MacLeod recalled the moment when the team coach sat at traffic lights, a housewife waved at the bus from her living-room window, only to be quickly joined by her husband, naked and dripping wet straight out of the bath.

'I can look back and laugh now,' MacLeod said of the send-off in 1986, 'but I didn't like it at the time. Oh, I didn't like it at the time.'

59

Teófilo Cubillas

'It is a place to become a star or to fail before the world.'

Teófilo Cubillas speaking about the World Cup to the *Miami Herald*

THERE ARE names that resonate in Scottish football history because of the damage they've done to the national psyche. Teófilo Cubillas is one of them.

He was a player Scotland should have known all about before their first group game of the 1978 World Cup, but for some reason he seemed to take Ally MacLeod and the team by surprise.

Cubillas started his career with his local club Alianza Lima, at the age of 16. Within two years, he had been capped by the national team. He came to the attention of the world at the 1970 World Cup in Mexico.

Powerfully built, he combined speed with skill and forged an impressive striking partnership with Hugo Sotil. Cubillas scored a memorable winning goal in Peru's 3-2 victory over Bulgaria, then hit a double in the 3-0 win over Morocco and the consolation in a 3-1 defeat to West Germany. In the quarter-final he scored again in the 4-2 loss to eventual winners Brazil. His five goals had announced his arrival on the world stage.

In 1972 Cubillas won the South American Footballer of the Year award, making the move to Europe the following year with first a brief spell in Switzerland at Basel before moving to Portugal and joining Porto.

Scottish fans had a glimpse of him when his Porto team knocked Dundee United out of the 1975/76 UEFA Cup.

Cubillas was part of the Peru team which in 1975 won the Copa América. He scored in the 3-1 semi-final first-leg win over Brazil, and although he missed a penalty in the final, Peru beat Colombia 1-0.

Scotland's group at the 1978 World Cup finals – Peru, Iran and the Netherlands – was looked on most favourably. But the opposition spent very little time fearing the Scots.

'Tell Scotland that we are preparing for our first game against them more seriously than for any other,' Cubillas told the *Daily Mirror* in May of 1978. 'We know that if we can win this, they are on the way out.'

'Ally MacLeod would be a wise man not to underestimate Cubillas,' chief sportswriter Frank McGhee wrote in the *Mirror*. 'Don't say you weren't told.'

In ITV's preview show for the World Cup, Nottingham Forest's boss Brian Clough, who referred to Scotland as 'we', said, 'I don't want anybody stupid enough to underestimate Peru.' He implored MacLeod 'to get his priorities right'. Of the Scottish team, Clough said, 'I'm sick of seeing them sponsoring cars or rubbing somebody's T-shirts on their backsides.' Clough suggested that the players had one eye on the field and one eye off it.

MacLeod hadn't watched Peru in person, although he highlighted in his autobiography that neither had he seen Czechoslovakia before Scotland beat them to qualify. 'It is fair to point out,' MacLeod wrote, 'that Peru had never watched us – and no one criticised them for that.' Marcos Calderón, the Peruvian manager, did attempt to scout Scotland, travelling to Verona to watch MacLeod's team in action, only to find it was an Italy B vs Scottish League game.

The match on 3 June against Peru didn't start badly for Scotland; Joe Jordan put them in front with just under 20 minutes played. Just before half-time, Cubillas and Oblitas exchanged a series of passes ending in César Cueto scoring past Alan Rough for the equaliser.

With just over an hour gone, Scotland had a penalty when Bruce Rioch was brought down in the box. Don Masson wasn't as clinical as he was against Wales at Anfield, and his nonchalant kick was saved. That was it for Scotland.

Fifteen minutes later the Scots defence gave Cubillas all the room he needed to accept the ball around 25 yards out and whistle a right-footed shot past Rough. The first glimpse of it for Rough was as it came back out.

Ten minutes were remaining when Stuart Kennedy gave a free kick away just outside the box. Cubillas stepped up and pinged a right-footed shot into the net.

MacLeod felt that the defensive wall wasn't lined up properly. 'Of course, that had been Masson's job,' he wrote. MacLeod had substituted Don Masson five minutes earlier.

The 3-1 defeat went down as one of Scottish football's biggest disasters.

MacLeod wrote in his book that his midfielders forgot that they had to defend as well as attack, 'It was this surrender of the midfield, particularly to the elderly and rounded Teófilo Cubillas, which cost us dear.' Cubillas was 29 years old.

'Scotland fell for all the ruses,' David Lacey wrote in *The Guardian*, 'gladly bought each dummy and eagerly plunged in to tackle thin air for the last hour and a quarter as Cubillas dispatched the fearsomely fast Munante down the right and sent in Oblitas from the left.'

Calderón said he had played Guillermo La Rosa for two thirds of the match in order to wear the Scottish backs down and get them used to playing against a European-style striker. He then brought on the smaller and more skilful Hugo Sotil of Alianza Lima, who played a classically South American style of football. Calderón said this disoriented the Scottish defence for a quarter of an hour, the period in which Cubillas scored his two goals. Calderón said he would like to 'congratulate Scotland and Mr MacLeod on the team they presented to us'.

'Qualifying was looked upon as the ultimate achievement,' Lacey wrote. 'The rest – the perks, the commercials for cars, beer and the Co-Op, even the cup itself taken for granted.'

'Our main fault lay in not marking Cubillas,' MacLeod said directly after the game. 'Only a baby would leave Cubillas and Cueto unmarked,' Calderón said.

Before Peru's final group match against Iran, where Cubillas scored a hat-trick, New York Cosmos tabled a $1m bid for his services. Cubillas would play in America for Fort Lauderdale Strikers alongside George Best and Gerd Müller, appearing for Peru again in the 1982 World Cup. Calderón would die tragically in the 1987 Alianza Lima air disaster

60

Archie Gemmill's Goal Against the Netherlands – 1978

TO SAY Archie Gemmill's finish in Mendoza is the most famous goal in the history of Scottish football isn't overstating its significance. It's transcended its purpose as the winning goal in an ultimately fruitless final group game in the World Cup finals to become a cultural phenomenon. 'It was just an instinctive thing,' Gemmill said to *The Express* in 1998. 'There was nothing planned. I got past one defender, then another and just kept going.'

Scotland took on the Netherlands having lost to Peru and drawn with Iran, the two games most punters and pundits thought would have secured maximum points and rendered the clash with the 1974 runners-up simply a match to see who topped the group. Instead, Scotland needed a win to qualify – a victory by three goals.

Rob Rensenbrink put the Netherlands ahead from the penalty spot on 35 minutes after Stewart Kennedy had brought down Johnny Rep. The Bastia winger years later admitted to author Simon Kuper that he had dived, or performed a *Schwalbe* as the Dutch called it. 'Against Scotland in 1978, I let myself fall in the penalty area,' he replied when Kuper asked him if he had ever done a *Schwalbe*.

On the stroke of half-time, Kenny Dalglish equalised. Two minutes into the second half Graeme Souness was pulled down in the box and Gemmill converted the penalty to put Scotland in front.

In the 68th minute, Dalglish was tackled on the edge of the Dutch box, and the ball broke to Gemmill, who was around 15 yards from the right touchline. He first of all skipped past Wim Jansen before sending Ruud Krol flying the wrong way with a subtle shift to the right. Gemmill slipped the ball through Jan Poortvliet's legs as the PSV man fell to the turf. As Archie took another touch to control the ball, goalkeeper Jan Jongbloed committed himself and Gemmill lifted the ball over him and into the net. Gemmill wheeled away with his left fist clenched in a mixture of celebration and determination.

It was 3-1; Scotland now just needed one goal for an unlikely passage into the next round. Four minutes later, however, Rep let a shot fly from 30 yards, and the Netherlands were back to 3-2. The one-goal win wasn't enough and Scotland went out on goal difference.

Gemmill's goal became a cultural touchstone in Scotland, transcending football. It took on a prominent part of Danny Boyle's 1996 film *Trainspotting* as it plays on a TV screen as lead character Renton and his newly acquired partner Diane climax. 'It just fit so well,' screenwriter John Hodge said. 'We felt that Archie Gemmill's goal in the 1978 World Cup against Holland was ideal. It was a bit of fun, paid tribute to Irvine [Welsh]'s book, and the goal, as it came after two disastrous results, seemed to sum up Renton's journey well, even though Scotland were still knocked out of the tournament – so disaster, triumph and betrayal.'

Boyle said, 'I loved it. It's a funny piece of writing by John, a great moment of fun.'

The goal has also been turned into a dance more than once. In 2000 Andy Howitt took it to the Edinburgh Festival at Dynamic Earth. 'I was only 13 at the time [of the goal],' Howitt said, 'but I remember the balance and poise of the run and the way he punched the air afterwards.' Gemmill himself said, 'I think it is a bit strange, to be honest. It's flattering but very unusual, to say the least.' Titled 'Versus', a review in *The Stage* described it as more physical theatre than dance. In 2002 Alec Finlay put his version of the dance on the stage. He described the goal 'to be the most famous single movement event in my native culture'.

'You could have knocked me down with a feather duster a couple of years ago,' Gemmill wrote in his autobiography, 'when I learned that Andy Howitt, the Scottish Youth Dance company's artistic director, was getting 200 schoolchildren to Hampden Park to give a choreographed rendition of the goal, complete with feints, turns, shot and my celebratory punch in the air.'

In 2018, Archie Macpherson told the *Daily Record*, 'Archie's goal obscures almost any other in Scottish football history because of its marvellous spontaneity. It was school playground stuff. It was the perfect short story with a beginning, a middle and an end – the pick-up, the nutmeg … the wee swivel of his hips before he slid the ball over the diving goalkeeper.'

Gemmill described the goal himself when speaking to Sue Mott of the *Daily Telegraph* in 1996. 'We had a break down the left-hand side,' he began. 'Kenny Dalglish, I think it was, passed to me, and all of a sudden, I was on the edge of their penalty box. I beat a couple of men, and before I knew it, I was in front of the goalkeeper.' He told the *Aberdeen Evening Express* in 1998, 'I had a couple of breaks which took me in the clear, and I just finished. It all happens in a split second, and you can't explain why or how you did it.'

In 2002 the goal was included at number 51 in Channel Four's *100 Greatest Sporting Moments* show.

'If I had a fiver for every time I've been asked to describe the effort, I would be an extremely rich man today,' Gemmill wrote in his autobiography. 'But those few seconds on action have brought me something more satisfying than material wealth – the satisfaction of being able to lay claim to a little bit of fame for doing something with a certain panache. In total I touched the ball six times – all with my trusty left foot – in maybe as many seconds.'

61

Maradona Comes to Glasgow – 1979

ON A sunny day on 2 June 1979, in Glasgow's southside, Diego Maradona showed he had all the skills to go on to become football's biggest name.

'I did the commentary that day as I recollect,' Archie Macpherson told BBC Radio Scotland's *Sportsound* in 2020. 'He was unknown, he was just a name on a team sheet, but thereafter, watching him play, his style, his pace, control of the ball, we knew there was something special.'

Scotland lined up in a 4-4-2 of Rough (Wood 46), Burley, Hegarty, Hansen, Munro, Wark, Narey, Hartford (Gray 65), Graham, Dalglish, McGarvey.

Argentina set up in a 4-4-1-1 formation: Fillol, Olguin, Villaverde (Trossero 22), Passarella, Tarantini, Houseman (Outes 56), Gallego, Barbas, Valencia, Maradona, Luque.

St Mirren's Iain Munro made his debut in the match. 'I was at left-back and was grateful I didn't have to mark him [Maradona],' he told the *Daily Record* in 2008. 'I loved the experience but I couldn't get my family to video the game for me because Scottish Television was on strike and the BBC didn't show it. However, Argentinian TV showed it, and through a mate who worked for a TV production company in Glasgow, I managed to get a copy of it, complete with Argentinian commentary. It really was a one-off – no one else had a copy – but I made the mistake of mentioning it to Roughie, who played the first half, and that was the last I saw it. I kept phoning and asking for it back, and he kept putting me off. Eventually, he said, "Look, it was in the video recorder, and one of my daughters has taped *Snow White and the Seven Dwarfs* over it."'

BBC Scotland refused to pay the SFA £7,500 for the rights to show the game. The Argentinian camera crew were the only ones present, having done a deal with the SFA for an undisclosed fee. 'I think the TV companies have been getting football too cheap,' secretary Ernie Walker said. 'But those days are over.'

In the 31st minute, Maradona took Valencia's pass and left Arthur Graham, Paul Hegarty and Alan Hansen flailing behind him. He slipped the ball to Luque, who scored past Rough.

Graham told *The Times* in 2020, 'The pitch was dry and dusty but he could still control the ball with his first touch. He stole the show by always looking to take people on and he made good players look clumsy.'

Scotland were probably enjoying their best spell of the match when the visitors went one up, but by the time Luque scored a second on the hour mark it was all Argentina.

With 20 minutes left, Maradona collected a pass from José Valencia on the right-hand side of the six-yard box. As George Wood prepared for a chip, Maradona whipped the ball between the keeper and his left-hand post.

Maradona kept a diary of the tour for the Argentinian magazine *El Gráfico*. Of his goal, he wrote, 'The goalie stayed on his line, and the defenders came to close me down. I fooled them I was going to shoot high. The goalkeeper thought I was going to do that, and I kicked it slowly at the centre of the goal.'

Wood looked back on the goal, telling *The Independent* in 2008, 'It was unbelievable skill, executed with so much confidence.'

Denis Law called the goal the cheekiest goal ever scored at Hampden, 'Maradona has everything. There is no department of his game you can fault. He is strong, brave and skilful. He's an individual who works for the good of his team.'

In *The Guardian*, John Roberts wrote, 'Maradona's breathtaking virtuosity when playing for Argentina against Scotland … suggested that here, at last, was Pelé's worthy successor as the world's greatest player.'

'He was strong and pacy, and his movement was superb,' Frank McGarvey wrote of Maradona in his autobiography. 'His close control was sublime, and his awareness and vision were a joy to watch, even as an opponent. He remains the greatest player I have ever seen or played against.'

Paul Hegarty told the *Daily Record* in 2020, 'We didn't know an awful lot about him before the game. He was just a youngster of 18, and there was a bit of talk about this talented young lad in the papers before, but we had not seen anything of him.'

'We'd been preoccupied wondering if [Mario] Kempes would be there,' recalled John Wark. 'But then this little boy – just 18 – appears out of nowhere. We had no warning.'

'He was absolutely magnificent,' Hegarty said. 'I remember getting left in his wake. I was about 25 or 26 and had faced a fair few decent players by that stage. He was just a teenager but I went in to tackle him and he just bounced off me. I was thinking, "Hold on a minute here."'

'I couldn't believe how good he was,' said Wark. 'Everyone remembers the goal he scored against England in 1986 … the one where he beat about five players. Well, he had a run against us in 1979 that was even better. He must have gone by six or seven of us.'

Alan Hansen, two years into his Liverpool career, had been learning from his club colleague Phil Thompson a technique of taking small steps sideways and backwards before committing to a tackle. 'The first time I remember using it,' he wrote in his 1999 autobiography, 'was Diego Maradona's first game in Britain. It wasn't a great success. As Maradona ran towards me with the ball I took one small step one way, another step the other way – and by the time I was ready to make the next move, he was 20 yards past me. I would love to claim that I had hardly allowed him a kick, but I never got anywhere near him. He produced one of the greatest individual performances ever seen at Hampden.'

'I'd made my mind up early on that I was going to swap shirts with Maradona,' said Graham, who scored Scotland's 85th-minute consolation, 'and I made sure I was closest to him at the final whistle. I sold it in the 1980s, which I regret. I'd get a lot more for it now.'

'Arthur just beat me to it,' said Frank McGarvey, 'so I ended up with [Daniel] Passarella's shirt, which was covered in blood – mine.'

After the game, manager Jock Stein said to the *Sunday Post*, 'Everyone is talking about Maradona. After seeing him in Dublin on Wednesday, I said he was a wee bit special. But their best player, in my opinion, was big Luque. He was much more direct and dangerous.'

In his diary, Maradona wrote, 'Afterwards, the crowd started to scream "Argentina". I couldn't believe it. I took a good look at the stands to convince myself I was in Glasgow and not Buenos Aires. I don't think this has ever happened before. The opposition made a guard of honour to applaud us as we left the pitch, and the Scots in the stands gave us a standing ovation.'

Maradona spoke with reporters at the Sheraton Heights Hotel in New Jersey after Argentina had played New York Cosmos on 6 June. The match with Scotland, he said, was 'beautiful, because they let me play. There was no violence.'

'I celebrated my first goal in the blue and white of the first team,' Maradona wrote in his autobiography. 'We beat Scotland 3-1, and I felt I could beat the world.'

62

First to Have Names on Shirts – 1979

FOR THE friendly against Peru at Hampden in September 1979, Scotland became the first international team to play with each player's name on the back of their shirt.

The idea was Ernie Walker's, and he decided to keep it under wraps until the last minute. Only a handful of people at the SFA and at jersey manufacturers Umbro knew of the innovation until the players removed their tracksuit tops just before the start of the match.

The concept of putting players' names on the back of their shirts came from Bill Veeck, the owner of the baseball team Chicago White Sox, who introduced it in 1960.

The idea spread, and in American football, the American Football League – which later merged with the NFL in 1970 – added names to uniforms throughout the 1960s in order to give their players more publicity and make them easier to identify for television.

The practice became commonplace in the North American Soccer League, and this was where Walker got the idea from. 'Every reaction I have had from the public has been favourable,' the SFA secretary said after the game. 'Indeed, there does not seem to be a serious argument against it. After all, it makes it much easier for television audiences to identify players and I would think it is helpful to referees too.'

Scotland persevered with names on the back of their jerseys throughout the early 1980s, although on occasion the letters peeled. Oddly, other nations were slow to adopt the practice.

England didn't wear names on their jerseys until the European Championship finals of 1992. The USA in 1994 was the first World Cup finals to have names on the backs of shirts. Now, of course, it's common practice not only in international football but also at club level.

63

The Tories vs Hampden Park

BY THE 1970s, Scotland's national stadium was by any account looking worn and run down with barely adequate facilities. In 1972 with their centenary the following year, the SFA were looking for the government and Glasgow District Council to finance redevelopment work.

Several years later, Hector Munro, the minister for sport in Scotland, set up a working party under the Scottish Sports Council to see what could be done to modernise Hampden Park.

The Labour government agreed in 1978 to provide up to half the estimated cost, then put at £11m. The 1979 general election installed a Conservative government that was 'very ready to carry on and give its support to the agreed plan', said the new minister for sport in Scotland, Alex Fletcher.

In time, George Younger, the secretary of state for Scotland, would call the commitment a 'provisional offer'.

A new company, Hampden Park Ltd, was formed to move forward with the work. Peter Heatly, the British Empire (later Commonwealth) Games gold medallist diver, would be the chairman. It was anticipated that work would begin in the summer of 1980. The North Stand, 'a crumbling eyesore' in the words of Ernie Walker, would be the first to go.

Who would pay what share of the other half was a matter for debate between Glasgow District Council, Strathclyde Regional Council, the SFA, the Scottish Football League and Hampden's owners Queen's Park FC. The SFA and the SFL were unable to make a financial contribution other than to running costs. This made negotiations sticky as the councils were keen not to have taxpayers pick up the tab.

As the project grew, and as time wore on, the projected cost began to rise. The initial figure of £11m climbed to something more like £18m, meaning the government's share would be £9m. If the government couldn't foot half the bill, then the project couldn't go ahead.

In January 1980, Glasgow District Council reneged on its commitment to provide £1.13m. The reason, it said, was 'because of the effect of government spending cuts on essential services'. Hampden Park Ltd was insistent that the council had a legal obligation to the project. The Conservative South Aberdeen MP Iain Sproat said that the government could have a 'white elephant' on its hands and urged a rethink.

On 10 May 1980, Celtic and Rangers met in the Scottish Cup Final at Hampden. The game was settled in extra time as George McCluskey redirected a wild Danny McGrain shot into the net to give Celtic a 1-0 win. Within minutes of the final whistle, fans of both teams were on the pitch, and a mass battle ensued. Glasgow mounted police drew their riot batons for the first time since the 1926 general strike.

Two days later, the riot was debated in the House of Commons. Blame was pointed at the fans, the players, alcohol, alcohol sponsorship, lack of suitable fencing, the clubs, and religious bigotry. Alex Fletcher wanted both clubs banned from the Scottish Cup the following year.

It didn't take long, however, for someone to propose withdrawing government commitment to upgrading Hampden Park. 'Does not my right honourable friend agree that the activities of the hooligans on Saturday should now give himself and the government cause to rethink the funding of the new Hampden?' asked Bill Walker, the MP for Perth and East Perthshire. Walker suggested that with Glasgow District Council having dropped from the project, it would be 'wise' to see that all future matches are played in rotation around Scotland 'rather than remaining in one place where we know violence occurs'.

George Younger responded that the events at the final did have direct relevance to the decision on the renovation of Hampden Park.

On 7 June 1980, Fletcher went to Ibrox Stadium to see Jim Watt defend his world lightweight boxing championship against Howard Davis Jr. On his arrival, he was handed a letter by Rae Simpson, the Rangers chairman. The letter urged the government to postpone their final decision on Hampden funding to allow a secret ballot of Scotland's 38 league clubs. Simpson indicated several clubs had 'changed their attitude' towards a new Hampden.

Fletcher said that unless there was 'overwhelming support' from the clubs, the government would have 'no justification' to take any further action.

'Work is due to begin next week at the ground,' said Peter Heatly, 'so Rangers' statement could not have come at a worse time.'

Hours before contractors were due to begin demolition on 17 June, the government announced that they would not be giving grant aid to the project. The conclusion after the review was that the government would not be justified in putting resources into the Hampden project at a time when the priority concern was to contain public expenditure.

Ernie Walker could barely hide his disgust, 'It is evident that the SFA has made a serious error of judgement in assuming that because it was dealing with representatives of the government, it could expect to be treated honourably.' Only two weeks earlier, the government had written with confirmation of the grant money. Walker called it 'an act of betrayal'.

'There is little doubt that the prime minister herself [Margaret Thatcher] was personally responsible for terminating the government's commitment,' *The Guardian* wrote on its front page.

'I am glad my campaign has been successful,' Iain Sproat said. 'It is good for Scotland's economy because it means the money can be spent on something more important than this football ground.' Sproat, who had compiled the first *Cricketers' Who's Who* the previous year, had contacted Mrs Thatcher only a day after the government had given its assurances. 'I went direct to her and said, "It's a bad show to be telling nurses and teachers they can have no more money at the same time as doling out £10m for a football ground."'

The government said they would meet an 'appropriate share' of the money that had already been spent on the aborted project.

In Westminster, Western Isles MP Donald Stewart of the SNP asked what the government planned to do with the saved money. George Younger said that the balance of the money would be used to promote the regeneration of the west of Scotland. 'Waffle,' Stewart replied. 'The sum involved is another cut which will add to the savings of the Treasury at the expense of Scotland.'

The SFA insisted that internationals would not be played anywhere other than Hampden after MPs insisted that games should move around the country. The press suggested the match with Portugal in October would be moved. 'We will be damned if we will give up Hampden on the whims of politicians,' said Walker. It would be May 1990 before Scotland played a home international away from Hampden, taking on Egypt in a friendly at Pittodrie.

In late 1980 the SFA were looking for help from the business community to raise £20m to rebuild Hampden, with fears that due to being unable to afford the running costs, Queen's Park would look to sell the ground to developers. Walker, though, had no thoughts of asking the government for any further help. 'It has been something of a relief to finish with them,' he said to *The Guardian*. 'In many ways, we would have slept better if we had been dealing with the Mafia.' Work started in October 1981 on a more modest £2.2m renovation of Hampden.

In June 1982, the Hampden Appeal was set up. The SFA and Queen's Park donated £350,000 each, while the Scottish Sports Council, whose chairman was Peter Heatly, promised £250,000. It would be an ongoing commitment which would see the eventual redevelopment of Hampden Park.

64

Scotland Win the European Under-18 Championship – 1982

IN THE summer of 1982, Scotland's under-18 team set off for Finland to play in the finals of the European Under-18 Championship. They qualified by beating England 3-2 on aggregate in a play-off.

The Scottish Second Division player of the year, Clyde's Pat Nevin, had postponed taking his business study exams at Glasgow Tech to go on the trip. 'I said I couldn't go because my finals were at roughly the same time,' Nevin said to the BBC in 2017. 'Then we worked out that if we got to the final – which we probably wouldn't – my first exam was the next morning. So I said, "It'll probably be OK, we'll never reach the final."'

Also in the squad were Celtic's Paul McStay and Jim McInally, Heart of Midlothian's Gary Mackay and Dave Bowman, and Ally Dick of Tottenham Hotspur.

The young Scots first defeated Albania 3-0, with Nevin the man of the match. Turkey were then beaten 2-0, with Mackay and Nevin the scorers. That put Scotland top of the section with the final match against the Netherlands to come for a place in the semi-final. Coach Andy Roxburgh would give Nevin a free role to throw the Dutch team's marking off and pull their defenders around the penalty box.

A Marco van Basten goal put the Netherlands into the lead, but Gary McGinnis of Dundee United volleyed in from 12 yards to equalise. 'I sent Walter Smith to watch Holland in their second match so we knew what we were facing,' Roxburgh said in

2017. 'When Walter came back, he said, "We've no chance." We thought there's only one thing for it – usual Scottish mentality – we'll just have to fight. We go a goal down but we fight back in a positive way, we equalised and in fact we finished really strongly.'

'They were physically strong but I felt we were in no danger technically,' Nevin told the BBC in 2020. 'You could tell five or ten minutes in, "We can do them."'

The 1-1 draw was enough to put Scotland into the semi-finals and qualify for the World Youth Championship in Mexico in 1983.

Scotland's opponents in the last four in Lahti would be Poland, while Czechoslovakia would play Russia in the other semi.

Ally Dick scored twice in the first half to give Scotland a 2-0 win and a place in the final, with Nevin the man of the match and Paul McStay in command of the midfield.

'These youngsters have done a magnificent job for their country and have given me the proudest moment of my life,' Roxburgh said.

For the final at Helsinki's Olympic Stadium, around 100 Scots oil workers were in the crowd cheering the team on. John Philliben of Stirling Albion scored a minute before half-time to put the Scots into the lead in what was an 80-minute match.

After the interval, Nevin extended the advantage with what the *Glasgow Herald* referred to as 'the goal of the tournament'. He dribbled past three defenders before chipping over Jiri Krbeček in the Czech goal. Although Miroslav Miškuf pulled one back, Gary Mackay made it 3-1 with 16 minutes remaining with a rocket from the edge of the box.

An ecstatic Roxburgh said after the match, 'This was the most magnificent performance by a Scottish youth team I have ever known. Just think, we are now going to the World Championship in Mexico as champions of Europe.' Back home, national boss Jock Stein commented, 'I am absolutely delighted. This is a great tonic for everyone in the Scottish game.'

'It was a really difficult game,' Nevin said to the BBC in 2017. 'I can't remember the other goals, but I remember mine. We had a free kick outside the box, and the idea was someone was to pass to someone else who was to lay it off for someone else to shoot. The lads got utterly confused by it. The ball landed at my feet with four defenders just sprinting straight at me. I dribbled through and put the ball away to score. Anybody watching would have thought it was a technically organised piece of football, but it was nothing of the sort.'

He added in 2020, 'Roxy was good on unusual set pieces but we made a mess of it and the ball dropped to me. If there is one goal I'd love to have on video, it's that one. Just to see if it is as good as I think it was.'

In 2022 Nevin did get to see the goal again when he tracked down 40 seconds of footage from Czech TV as part of the BBC Scotland documentary *The Lost Final*. 'It is actually almost like a dream of something I kind of half-remembered. It's actually better. It's actually loads better,' he said.

Five of the squad – McStay, Nevin, McInally, Bowman and Mackay – went on to earn full caps for Scotland.

Scotland fans take to the pitch at Wembley in 1977.

The Corries – Roy Williamson, the writer of 'Flower of Scotland', and Ronnie Browne.

Scotland fans at Anfield in 1977 for the World Cup qualifier with Wales.

The Scotland squad wave to the crowd at Hampden in May 1978 before they leave for the World Cup in Argentina.

Hugh Allan, Jock Stein, Alex Ferguson and Brian Scott on the bench at Ninian Park, Cardiff on 10 September 1985.

Gary McAllister is disconsolate after missing a penalty in the European Championship match with England in June 1996.

Goalkeeper David Marshall and forward Leigh Griffiths leap in the air as the Scotland players celebrate qualifying for Euro 2020 as they beat Serbia on penalties.

The Scotland team ahead of the 2-0 win over Spain in March 2023.

John McGinn and Andy Robertson enjoy the win over Georgia in June 2023.

65

Scotland the Brave

FOR MANY years, the anthem played before Scotland games was 'God Save the Queen'. This never sat right with Scottish supporters, who frequently expressed their displeasure whenever it was played.

At the 1974 World Cup, manager Willie Ormond responded to criticism of supporters who booed and whistled 'God Save the Queen'. 'I don't blame the fans,' Ormond said. 'We're here representing Scotland, no one else.' In 1970, Scottish gold medallists in the Commonwealth Games stood on the podium to 'Scotland the Brave'.

The song had only been around for a couple of decades.

Glaswegian Cliff Hanley began his working life in journalism, originally a crime and court reporter with a small news agency on Glasgow's West Nile Street. He later worked for the *Daily Record*. Along with his musical partner Ian Gourlay, Hanley had developed a reputation for writing snappy songs for revues.

In 1950 Robert Wilson, a tenor opera singer who became one of the biggest names in light entertainment in Scotland, contacted Hanley with an old pipe tune thought to originate from around the 1890s. He asked if Hanley could write a new lyric for it. Wilson intended to sing the song in his solo spot at a revue show at Glasgow Empire Theatre in 1951.

Hanley duly wrote the lyrics, and Wilson suggested some changes, including the title line. As payment, Wilson offered Hanley £20 plus a royalty contract. 'Why bother about royalties?' Hanley recalled replying. 'The song might be all right for pantomime, but nobody will ever hear of it after that,' he told Wilson. 'This is going to be a big song. I know,' was Wilson's reply.

'Frankly, I knew he was daft,' Hanley said. 'The song struck me as pretty feeble. But if he wanted to force royalties on me, I could hardly complain.' Within a year, Hanley's share had risen to £200. 'That was the most profitable Saturday morning I ever spent,' Hanley said in 1983. 'Unfortunately you can't write two national anthems for the same country.'

The song became popular with audiences at the pantomime at the Alhambra Theatre in 1952/53. The first act of *Jack and the Beanstalk* ended with a rousing version of the song.

By 1981, with Scotland qualified for the 1982 World Cup in Spain, the thought of changing the anthem began to gather pace. Surveys were undertaken in national newspapers. Ahead of 'Scots Wha Hae' and the Corries' 'Flower of Scotland', 'Scotland the Brave' led the popular vote.

The Scottish Football Association made its choice and opted to have 'Scotland the Brave' replace 'God Save the Queen' in Spain.

The idea was that it would be in Scotland's interest to be identified by a uniquely Scottish tune and not the same anthem that both England and Northern Ireland would use. 'It was quite impossible to get unanimous agreement amongst Scots as to the most appropriate tune to meet football's requirements,' SFA secretary Ernie Walker said. 'But "Scotland the Brave" appeared to be the choice of the majority.'

It was played at Hampden for the first time before the March 1982 friendly with the Netherlands. The Scottish Office were unhappy with this departure from 'God Save the Queen' but acknowledged the selection was outwith its jurisdiction.

By 1990 the public mood had shifted towards 'Flower of Scotland' being played before national matches.

Hanley, a lifelong Partick Thistle supporter, suggested that 'Flower of Scotland' was a funeral dirge while his song was 'a nice cheery up-market song'. Hanley's lyrics, of course, were written for musical revue and had a touch of the tongue in cheek about them, while the Corries' song had resonated with audiences in folk clubs over the years and had recently been adopted by the Scottish rugby team.

The song, though, has never been completely replaced and still can be heard today.

66

The Toepoke – 1982

THE WORLD Cup match with Brazil on 18 June 1982 served up a glorious Scottish football moment that didn't so much create a new hero for Scots fans, more a beloved villain.

Scotland had opened their 1982 finals campaign with a 5-2 win over New Zealand, although what should have been a comfortable victory was tarnished slightly with the loss of two cheap second-half goals. All that was forgotten, however, as the Tartan Army joined up with Brazilian fans in Seville for the second group game.

Scotland's boss Jock Stein had already indicated to his team that this game wasn't one he expected them to win. They had done the business in the first match, and qualification for the second phase would go down to the final group game with the USSR, who had lost to Brazil in their opener. Anything they could do against Brazil would be a bonus.

So, when Scotland took the lead on 18 minutes, it was a surprise for the whole nation. Not that the goal was a fluke.

'The thing that really struck me is how good Jock Stein was,' South American football expert Tim Vickery said in 2022. 'And you see this in the goal because he's worked Brazil out. I love the 1982 [Brazil] side, but you can find lots of little flaws ... there are lots of problems. The key problem is that the full-backs don't want to defend ... and Jock Stein has seen this. The positioning of John Wark in this game; John Wark is a central midfielder who had a real goal threat. Where does Wark play? Wide right. Because they want to get him behind Júnior, the left-back, who doesn't really want to defend, and that's where the goal comes from. The whole thing is not luck. Scotland are playing to score a goal from that sector of the field. And that was Jock Stein who had spotted it.'

Graeme Souness sent a raking pass over to the right side, where Wark rose to meet the ball and headed it down several yards outside the Brazil penalty area. Dundee United's David Narey met the knockdown, took one touch and, as he ran on, smashed the ball high into the Brazil net to send Scotland a goal up.

Above the Estadio Benito Villamarín, a Scottish legend, was birthed. There in the BBC's commentary box was match summariser Jimmy Hill. 'In describing David's goal I ventured the opinion, "It might have been a toepoke," surmising it was the only way in which he could reach the ball to shoot,' wrote Hill in his 1998 autobiography. 'I went on to say, "It doesn't matter how he scored, Scotland are ahead of Brazil and perhaps on their way to victory." No one remembered that phrase when Brazil finally won 4-1.'

Hill has always contended that in his day – 359 league appearances for Brentford and Fulham between 1949 and 1961 – a toepoke was a skill. 'Of course I was aware that kids not blessed with footballing ability tended to kick with their toe rather than their instep,' he explained in his book. 'I wasn't accusing David of that, I merely believed he couldn't have reached the ball and shot so powerfully in any other way. Crestfallen, disappointed Scots wanted to believe otherwise and have never let me forget it.'

Among the most infuriated was Jock Stein. 'After that comment, the relationship between Stein and Hill was never the same,' Archie Macpherson wrote in his book *Action Replays*. 'Stein, in fact, was looking for blood and became unusually anti-English, unusual in the sense that he never wished to be seen to be stupidly nationalistic and did value their football. But on this occasion, he told me that if Hill approached him, he would chew him up.'

The *Sunday Mirror* reported in July 1982 that Hill interviewed Stein ahead of Scotland's vital match with the USSR, but the

BBC chose not to broadcast the exchange. According to the paper, Stein 'angrily challenged' Hill's description of the goal. 'If that had been an England goal, it would have been hailed as one of the great goals of the tournament,' Stein was reported as saying. A BBC spokesman told the newspaper, 'We don't screen every interview we film.'

The Scottish fans agreed to hate Hill from that day forward. A popular banner among Scottish fans read 'We Hate Jimmy Hill He's a Poof' and spawned a chant to go along with it. In the modern day, it would be widely condemned. But in that era it seemed an almost gentle insult. 'It was not only singularly inaccurate,' Macpherson wrote of the banner, 'but was to Jimmy simply an eccentric sign of endearment.'

Before Scotland's 1998 World Cup opener with Brazil, star striker Ronaldo spoke with the Scottish press about his memories of watching Narey score on television. 'Zico was my hero then – but that goal was one even he would have been proud of,' he said.

In 1998 the *Daily Record* revelled in discovering that after ten weeks of being available in Scotland, not a single copy of Jimmy's autobiography had been sold. However, on finding out that a book by Scottish fans which included a chapter mocking him was raising funds for a children's hospice, Hill sent them a cheque for £100. 'The Scots never believe me when I say how fond I am of the nation. This was a tangible way of showing it,' he admitted.

'David Narey will be one of the … names on my grave … on my tombstone,' Hill said in a BBC documentary about his career. 'Someone who the whole nation thought I was insulting. I was very pleased he scored.'

67

Scotland 3 Spain 1 – 1984

14 November 1984
Hampden Park
World Cup Qualifying European Group 7
Attendance: 74,324

Scotland: Leighton (Aberdeen), Nicol (Liverpool), Albiston (Manchester United), Souness [C] (Sampdoria), McLeish (Aberdeen), Miller (Aberdeen), Dalglish (Liverpool), McStay (Celtic), Johnston (Celtic), Bett (SK Lokeren), Cooper (Rangers)

Spain: Arconada [C] (Real Sociedad), Urquiaga (Athletic Bilbao), Goikoetxea (Athletic Bilbao), Maceda (Sporting Gijon), Camacho (Real Madrid), Victor (Barcelona), Urtubi (Athletic Bilbao) [Carrasco (Barcelona)], Senor (Real Zaragoza), Gordillo (Real Betis), Santillana (Real Madrid), Rincon (Real Betis) [Butragueno (Real Madrid)]

Referee: Adolf Prokop (Germany)

Goals:
Scotland – Johnston (33, 42), Dalglish (70)
Spain – Goikoetxea (65)

ALONG WITH groups one and five, Scotland's World Cup qualifying group had four teams. This meant that only the group winners qualified, while in the five-team groups, winners and runners-up went through.

The runners-up here would be looking at a two-legged play-off. Wales and Iceland were the other teams in Scotland's group, and the Scots had got off to a good start by defeating Iceland 3-0 at Hampden the previous month. A win against Spain would go a long way to claiming that top spot. 'We are not aiming at anything other than the number one spot,' manager Jock Stein told the press.

Of his team's make-up, Stein said, 'There's a bit of adventure and a bit of safeness. In every team you need players who can compete and players who can turn it on.' Spain, the 1984 European Championship runners-up, had defeated Wales 3-0, and Stein was cautious of the balance Scotland had to maintain between breaking down a tight defence and being caught on the break.

The team Stein selected was the same as in the 3-0 win over Iceland, the first time he had named an unchanged side since he became Scotland's manager in 1978. There were several youngsters selected; Steve Nicol was 22, Mo Johnston was 21, and Paul McStay had just turned 20. All three gave outstanding performances. Nicol, earning his third cap, 'tackled like a demon' according to the *Liverpool Echo*. The youngsters were backed by the more experienced players such as Willie Miller, Graeme Souness and Kenny Dalglish.

Souness had recently transferred from Liverpool to Italy's Sampdoria. Stein felt he had now become a more influential player due to his move. In Italy, he was now only playing on Sunday afternoons and not the frequent Saturday-Wednesday routine of English football. 'Graeme can now put more into his game for Scotland,' Stein said. 'He used to hold back a bit in the past.' In *The Guardian*, Patrick Barclay noted that Souness 'had a magnificent match. His passes ranged from the breathtakingly incisive to the simply intelligent; it's difficult to recall one that was wasted.'

The first goal came when Nicol met a Dalglish corner on the volley. Luis Arconada could only parry the ball, and Johnston dived headlong to divert it into the net. 'One of the few things I never managed to do in my career was score a goal for my country,'

Nicol said to *The Scotsman* in 2016. 'That night I thought I'd done it: my terrific left-foot shot was heading for the top corner. But Arconada saved it, and that wee bugger Johnston scored from the rebound.'

Just before the break, Miller, after breaking down a Spanish attack, found Bett on the right. Bett avoided a lunging challenge from Camacho to send over a cross which Johnston climbed to meet, sending a powerful header past Arconada. Johnston now had four goals from six internationals. 'A lively bugger, isn't he?' Stein said of his young striker afterwards.

Andoni Goikoetxea, the infamous 'Butcher of Bilbao', was unmarked in the six-yard box when Gordillo sent over a free kick. Leighton was in two minds about whether to stay on his line or go for the ball, and this allowed Goikoetxea to head into the net and bring Spain back into the game.

But five minutes later, Davie Cooper came forward and fed Nicol, who played the ball to Dalglish. Kenny cut inside and left two defenders floundering before beating Arconada with a left-footed shot.

'One of the greatest goals I've ever seen,' Alex McLeish said to the *Scotland on Sunday* in 2010. 'And a huge relief as well. Goikoetxea had made it 2-1 from a header, and I was thinking, "God, should I have been closer to him there? Was that my fault?" But we closed the door at the back after that. It was comfortable.' It was a goal that lived long in McLeish's memory, 'I can still see Kenny's goal now, him turning the player and rolling him and curling it in with his left foot, top corner. Magnificent. Those old Hampden goalposts, right up in the stanchion. It was wonderful to experience something like that.'

In his 1996 autobiography, Dalglish recalled his celebration, 'When I turned to run to the stand, my old man was sitting there in the front row. The look on his face was the same as mine: overjoyed.' The goal equalled Denis Law's 12-year-old record of 30 international goals for Scotland.

After the match, Stein revealed that Dalglish didn't train through the week, suffering from a knee injury. Stein emphasised that his years of managing Dalglish at club and country level allowed him to believe in the player, who, at 33, was winning his 96th cap. Remarkably Stein chose not to use Charlie Nicholas from the bench and allowed Dalglish to play all 90 minutes.

Stein said that the side didn't train much as a whole. 'We thought that Spain would out-gun us physically anyway,' he explained. Instead, the squad talked, and the man doing much of the talking was Stein's assistant Alex Ferguson.

'I was impressed by the pace of the Scots,' Spanish manager Miguel Muñoz said to the press. 'Particularly the forwards Johnston and Dalglish who forced our defenders into mistakes. I wasn't disappointed by the performance of our team, but it was a significant defeat.'

At the press conference at Hampden the next morning, Stein asserted that the Spanish had underestimated his side, 'They thought they could subdue the outside-left, and they didn't expect so much from Jim Bett. They thought Dalglish was very much on the wane and that we had defensive weaknesses they could capitalise on.

'This is undoubtedly the most satisfying night I have had since becoming manager.'

68

The Death of Jock Stein – 1985

Ahead of their final World Cup qualifying match with Wales in Cardiff on 10 September 1985, needing at least a draw to make the play-off, Scotland set up a training camp in Bristol. Assistant manager Alex Ferguson took training, while Stein worked with his goalkeepers.

Alan Rough (Scotland): You couldn't put your finger on it, but something was not right. Jock hated goalkeepers, and he enjoyed pushing us hard, but on that occasion, we didn't get the usual murderous routines. Jock always personally trained the goalkeepers; we had no specialised coaches back then. He would take us right to the pain barrier, we would be diving everywhere, but this time something wasn't right.

Steve Nicol (Scotland): At no stage in the two days leading up to the match do I remember thinking there might be something wrong with him.

Alastair Guthrie (journalist, *Aberdeen Evening Express*): He displayed no outward signs of strain or stress as he carried out his final training session as Scotland manager. He even rounded off his morning's exacting work by taking on Alan Rough at penalty kicks. The first sent the keeper the wrong way. How he enjoyed that one.

Gerry Francis (Bristol Rovers): I saw Jock Stein the day before he died down at Bristol when Scotland were training, and he looked dreadful.

Stein and Ferguson played pool to relax in the afternoon. Later, however, Ferguson felt that anxiety in Stein had begun to grow.

Alex Ferguson: Jock had a chest infection at that time, and I remember being in his room, and I said, 'Are you taking your tablets?' He said, 'Yeah, I'm fed up taking them.' He was coughing a bit, but you never think anything like that's going to happen.

Scotland's team doctor Professor Stewart Hillis was also Stein's physician. He knew Jock had a heart muscle defect and that those pills, diuretics – water tablets – were a vital part of his treatment to help remove excess fluid from his body. Because they made him use the toilet often, Stein refused to take them on the day of games.

Gordon Strachan (Scotland): I used to always be one of the last at the dinner table at Scotland camps, and I would speak to Jock, but he was not at his bubbly best then. I just took that to be the build-up to the game. Physically, he didn't look so well. I'd never seen him like that before. He was a bit grey. But he was perspiring. He's a big man, I know that, but it was just a thought that went in and out of my head very quickly. Jock's no' well today, and I came back to that thought later in the night when I sat down. Aye, he was'nae well.

Neville Southall (Wales): The Scotland fans behind my goal nicked every ball that went into the crowd during the warm-up. Eventually, I had none left and had to go into the tunnel and ask for more. Mr Stein overheard what I said and went out into the goalmouth with me to do something about it. All he did was make some gesture with his hands, and every ball that had been acquired by the supporters came flying back out to where we were standing. That was the measure of his standing. Jock was as good as there was in this game. Most of the managers I had known would have got the balls thrown at them if they had gone anywhere near the crowd. I have never seen anything like that before or since. He was a class act who had such an aura about him. I can't think of anybody else who could have taken control of a crowd like that. It was an incredible moment.

Alastair Guthrie: The fans showed their appreciation by spontaneously chanting his name as he made his way back to the players' tunnel. Jock also had a wave for them. It was to be his farewell gesture.

Stein's team talk focused on the threat of Wales's pair of world-class strikers, Mark Hughes and Ian Rush. However, Alan Hansen had left the squad to return to his club due to injury.

Alex Ferguson: Jock switched Nicol to right wing-back, with Maurice Malpas his counterpart on the left. We used [Richard] Gough against Rush, [Alex] McLeish on Hughes and [Willie] Miller as the free player at the back. I said, 'Get right into this Rush. He's a coward.' Now I don't believe that for a minute, but I was determined not to let our lads build those two up in their minds. I said of Hughes, 'He can't run. Get in front of him.' I underplayed Wales's most dangerous men to boost the morale of our own players.

Willie Miller (Scotland): The task was clear – we had to get something in Cardiff. But the worst thing happened.

Steve Nicol: Thirteen minutes in, and we found ourselves a goal down. Peter Nicholas took a heavy touch, and with the ball there to be won, I was pretty confident I could win the tackle. There was one problem. Roy Aitken had exactly the same thought. I was ready to make the challenge, but when I saw Roy also making a move, I hesitated, crucially, for a split second. In the end, neither of us made a proper tackle, and Peter was able to take another touch and quickly deliver a low cross for Hughes to give Wales an early lead.

Late in the half, goalkeeper Jim Leighton misjudged the flight of a lofted ball into the box from Kenny Jackett, leading to a panicked moment.

Brian Moore (commentating for ITV): Oh, Leighton's missed it. But he got it back in time. Leighton's concentration wavered for a moment. The bounce off his knees almost put Hughes in.

Ian St John (co-commentating alongside Moore): Mark Hughes had stopped running because he thought the goalkeeper was going to pick it up. Had he continued to move … he would have snapped that one up.

ITV presenter Jim Rosenthal and pundit Jimmy Greaves thought that the incident was down to Leighton opting to dribble the ball instead of catching it. The truth was more surprising.

Jim Leighton (Scotland): We were 1-0 down, and in 23 minutes my contact lens was knocked out of my left eye, meaning I could no longer judge distances or the flight of the ball. There were several close calls in the longest 23 minutes of my life.

Steve Nicol: At half-time, Jock was not a happy man, 'Sit down, all of you.' Gordon Strachan had replaced the suspended Graeme Souness in central midfield, but Jock was not overly impressed by his performance. He told him he was planning to bring on Davie Cooper in the second half as his replacement. Strach was not happy and tried to give as good as he got.

Gordon Strachan: I can remember him telling me at half-time that I would be coming off in the second half, allowing Davie Cooper to go on. That was how he wanted to play it, and I was ready to argue a little bit when Fergie said to me, 'Leave it alone. He's not well. Leave it.' And so I did, but none of us thought he was seriously ill.

Alex Ferguson: Gordon was upset, but there was nothing new in that.

When he entered the dressing room, Leighton made for the bathroom and called in physio Hugh Allan. He then revealed that he had lost a contact lens.

Steve Nicol: Then Alex began shouting at Jim Leighton. Talk about a noisy dressing room. When they were both done yelling, Alex asked Jock if he could have a word in private, and they went into the toilet area, out of sight from the players but not out of earshot. Jock was annoyed at Alex for not telling him his goalkeeper wore contact lenses! The trouble was Fergie didn't know Leighton wore contacts. Nobody did. Up until that point, Jim hadn't told a soul, not even his manager at Aberdeen.

Alex Ferguson: To say I found that dramatic is an understatement, considering that Leighton had been playing under me for seven years, and I never had the faintest inkling that he used contact lenses.

Jim Leighton: I was frightened to tell him the truth, for I'd kept the fact that I wore lenses a closely guarded secret. To make matters worse, I also had to confess that I had left my spare pair of lenses at home in Aberdeen.

Willie Miller: I had spent seven years with him at Aberdeen, and not once had I heard him talk about contact lenses or watched him put them in his eyes. Many a time, I had joked with Jim about his eyesight being deficient, but this was the first time that I had been proved right.

Leighton had to come off. However, substitute goalkeeper Alan Rough was nowhere to be seen.

Alan Rough: I was warming up with Davie Cooper, and we had been told we could not use the goals because a Welsh military marching band were walking up and down the pitch. So we had a wee competition to hit the ball across the breadth of the park and see how many hats we could knock off.

Another physio, Celtic's Brian Scott, was sent out to retrieve Rough.

Alan Rough: When he told me to come inside, I said, 'Nah, I'm not falling for that.' I was convinced it was a wind-up. Who would substitute a goalkeeper in such an important game?

Scott suggested Rough better take him seriously and quick. When the Hibernian goalkeeper arrived in the dressing room, the place was in an uproar.

Alan Rough: It was mayhem. Jock was shouting about contact lenses, and Fergie was shouting as well. The players were all sitting silent while Stein was shouting. He was still growling when he approached me. He just walked up to me and said, 'Right, you are on, you fat bastard.' The bell calling us back on the pitch rang, so I just put on my jersey and got on with it. That was the last time I ever spoke to him.

Alex Ferguson: We were soon grateful for the help that came from Rough. I was never a fan of his goalkeeping, but he is a very likeable person, and his laid-back attitude was perfect for the predicament we were in.

Steve Nicol: As we lined up in the Ninian Park tunnel, ready to go back out for the second half, I turned to Roughie and asked him what the fuck was going on. He simply laughed.

Graeme Souness (Scotland): Jock had asked me to come over from Italy, although I was suspended for that game, and when the players had gone back out, he turned to Fergie and me and said, 'Do you think we should make changes?' I remember finding it quite remarkable that Jock was asking us.

Jim Leighton: I didn't see any of the second half as I was sitting in our dressing room. I stayed where I was, listening to the roars of the crowd.

Sixteen minutes into the half Stein decided another change was needed. Davie Cooper was sent on in place of Gordon Strachan.

Gordon Strachan: Big Jock's got it spot on. I'm glad to say I was part of his last right decision. He's taken me off. It was the last big decision he ever made.

Davie Cooper (Scotland): Basically, he briefed me to have a real go down the Welsh right. I didn't feel any pressure knowing that I was the last throw of the dice. In fact, I was looking forward to going on.

With around nine minutes remaining, Scotland finally had the chance at an equaliser they had been waiting for.

David Speedie (Scotland): I tried to flick the ball over [David] Phillips's head and get a shot on goal, but he put his hands up, and the ball clearly struck them.

Steve Nicol: The arm wasn't overly outstretched, and the handball certainly wasn't deliberate. However, Dutch referee Jan Keizer pointed straight to the spot.

Graeme Sharp (Scotland): When the penalty came up that night in Wales, there was no doubt [Cooper] was taking it. It was a case of, 'I'll have it; I know what I'm doing.' It didn't faze him, even though it meant so much to Scotland as a nation. The pressure was immense. Only some people can take that on their shoulders.

Davie Cooper: It wasn't so much I picked up the ball. The other ten left it for me.

Jim Bett (Scotland): That moment probably summed Davie up for me. Most players would shy away from the responsibility of a penalty when so much was at stake, and he had not been long on the park, having started the game on the bench. But Davie was happy to take the penalty. He was just that type of guy. He was quiet, unassuming, but he had a lot of bottle.

Willie Miller: I knew when Davie stepped up, he was going to score. No problem.

Davie Cooper: I was always planning on hitting it low and left – generally a goalkeeper's weakest spot. It was not the best penalty I ever struck, and Neville Southall got quite a bit of glove on it but only succeeded in pushing the ball inside the post.

Jim Leighton: I didn't know Scotland had equalised until a member of the Ninian Park ground staff came into the dressing room to offer me a can of juice.

Stewart Hillis (Scotland team doctor): Near the end of the game, all the photographers were cramming around the Welsh bench at 1-0. Everything changed, though, when Cooper's penalty went in. The focus changed to our bench.

Mike England (Wales manager): A photographer had been bothering him all night, and in the end Jock got off the bench and dragged him away. Jock had asked him to move several times, but he refused, and in the end Jock physically did it.

Ernie Walker (SFA secretary): It would be grossly unfair to blame the photographer.

Andy Gray (Scotland): For all he was volatile, Jock was normally not a physical guy, so that was a sign of how worked up he was. How much the pressure was getting to him.

Alex Ferguson: He kept saying to me during the match, 'Keep your dignity at the end of the game.' I didn't know what he meant at the time, but I now believe he knew he was dying. That he was warning me against any public emotion.

With two minutes to go, the referee blew for a free kick. Stein mistook it for the final whistle and got up to acknowledge England. Instead, he collapsed into Allan. 'I'm away, Hugh,' he said.

Alex Ferguson: When he began to fall, I grabbed for him and shouted to Hughie Allan to do the same.

Mike England: He went forward a couple of yards, put his arm to his chest and fell to the floor.

Gordon Strachan: There was a bit of commotion, and then it all calmed down again. Then, next minute, there were a lot of people around. I looked over and thought, 'What's going on there?' And that was it. The words I remember were, 'Jock's no' well.' What? 'Jock's no' well.' I don't know who was saying it, but it's what I remember. 'Jock's no' well. There's something wrong with his heart.'

Allan and Ferguson supported Stein until paramedics arrived and carried him down the tunnel just as the final whistle blew. Television pictures briefly captured Stein's face as he was carried away. 'He was still conscious and telling people that he was OK, but clearly, the stress of the evening had got to him,' ITV reporter Martin Tyler said live on air.

Graeme Souness: Davie scored, and after that, I couldn't watch it any more, so I went into the bowels of the stadium to a bar. Then, with a couple of minutes to go, I go down to the tunnel, and I'm standing in the corridor; the tunnel is straight in front of me, the away dressing room is on the left-hand side, and slightly to the right are swing doors like an old American bar into the treatment room. All of a sudden, there's a stramash, and somebody is being carried up the tunnel on a stretcher.

Ernie Walker: I couldn't sit in the directors' box after Davie Cooper scored the penalty equaliser, and I made my way to the Ninian Park boardroom. Graeme Souness was suspended, and I met him on the landing, and he was in a bad state, as I was. I went in to pour a drink for both of us, but Graeme went out and saw on the TV that Jock had collapsed.

In the meantime, the final whistle had sounded, and the players began celebrating the point that carried them into the play-off for Mexico.

Willie Miller: At the final whistle, as captain for the night, I was leading the celebrations. Fergie came on to the pitch and urged me to keep the players out there and to milk the applause.

Maurice Malpas (Scotland): We knew quickly something was wrong. We were together on the pitch when one of the coaching staff told us. It was a long walk to the dressing room.

Mike Aitken (journalist, *The Scotsman*): The first message was simply that Stein was unwell and being cared for by the SFA's medical people as well as the Welsh FA's doctor, Graham Jones. There were also rumours an ambulance which had been called to whisk Stein to hospital couldn't get through the crowds.

Ernie Walker: I went down to the medical room. At first, it seemed Jock would be all right; he kept saying, 'It's this bloody cough,' because he had been troubled by a persistent cold.

Also in the room with Hillis were Graham Jones, SFA treasurer Bill Dickie, and Ernie Walker. David Will then arrived.

David Will (SFA president): He raised his eyes to the ceiling to signify exasperation. It was as if he was annoyed with himself for being ill and felt he should be with his players.

Graeme Souness: Then they got Jock on to a bed in the treatment room, and he's sitting on a bed with an oxygen mask on. There were people coming and going between these swing doors all the time, and I was just standing there, and it became evident this was a serious, serious problem for Jock.

Joey Jones (Wales): I saw him lying on the treatment table in the medical room with all these people trying to bring him around, but no one realised quite how serious it was at the time.

Willie Miller: By the time I got to the dressing room, all talking had stopped, and a general sense of foreboding pervaded the atmosphere.

Graeme Sharp: It was all quiet in the dressing room, but we were still not thinking that it was going to be fatal. The next thing was Jimmy Steele, Jock's close friend and the team masseur, coming into the dressing room in tears. We knew it was very bad then.

Roy Aitken (Scotland): Jim Steele came into the dressing room, and I knew just by looking at his face the worst had happened.

Richard Gough (Scotland): We were worried and concerned but no more than that. It all changed when I got into the dressing room. I saw our masseur, Jimmy Steele, in tears. At that moment, I knew. No one had to tell me Big Jock had gone.

Maurice Malpas: Steely was the one guy who could say anything he liked to Big Jock because they were so close. He was absolutely devastated.

Rodger Baillie (journalist, *Daily Record*): Alex Ferguson's head popped out of a door, and he dragged me over because I had phone numbers for Jock's family. The Welsh boss Mike England came over to me and said he hoped Jock was going to be OK and that arrangements were being made for an air ambulance to take him back to Glasgow. I squeezed out of a door and climbed a fence to get back to the press box. But by the time I had climbed back down into the area underneath the stand, it was clear that Jock had gone.

Ernie Walker: Then he died, the monitor screens told us, and nothing mattered after that. The game didn't matter, Mexico didn't matter. I had lost a friend, his family had lost a husband and father, and Scottish football lost much, much more.

Graeme Souness: Like everyone else who spent any time in his company, I was in awe of him, and I was in tears. I think it was Stewart Hillis who told me, 'He's away.' I think those were his exact words. When I went into the dressing room, it was just silence, like the game hadn't taken place and wasn't important. When we got the news that Jock had died, it was a pretty sombre place as you can imagine. There were tears.

Stewart Hillis: At 9.15[pm], Mr Stein collapsed as he turned to go back up the tunnel. He was taken to the medical room and examined. It was found he had had a heart attack which required emergency treatment, and a full resuscitation team was there. All the necessary resuscitation measures were initiated, and for 30 minutes, he had full heart massage. However, there was no spontaneous activity, and the procedure was terminated at 9.50[pm].

Steve Nicol: Alex came back into the dressing room and sat down near the door. 'Jock's dead.' Two words. That was it. I felt numb. We all did. How? Why?

Alex McLeish (Scotland): There wasn't a murmur. When we started asking, 'How?' and 'What happened?' Fergie was gone again. He couldn't say any more. From my memory of it all, I can't recall Alex saying anything else other than those two words, 'Jock's dead.'

Willie Miller: It was the sort of moment when you felt football didn't matter. It was such a sad end to a night that should have been joyous.

Gordon Strachan: It was awful, the emptiest feeling I've ever known and one that will stay with me and the rest of the players who were there as long as we live.

Word also began to spread to the Welsh dressing room, licking their wounds after going out of the World Cup.

Joey Jones: It was just sinking in, and the disappointment was immense, not just for us but for the fans as well. But the mood quickly changed when news of Stein's death filtered through to the dressing room. We had missed out on the chance of a World Cup place, but Jock Stein's death put it all into perspective for a lot of people.

David Phillips (Wales): It didn't seem appropriate to feel sorry for ourselves.

Neville Southall: I can't even remember how we heard, so great was the shock that greeted it. But somehow, within minutes of the final whistle, we learned that Jock Stein had died in the adjoining dressing room. After that, there was no bitterness or anger. Just numbness and a horrible, unyielding silence.

Ian Rush (Wales): I remember sitting in the dressing room when Mike England told us what happened to Jock Stein, and all we thought about was one of the greatest managers ever had died.

Mark Hughes (Wales): It was a very important game, but the death of Jock Stein meant events on the pitch paled into insignificance. It cast a cloud over everything. The game was put into perspective by the events after, and any hurt we felt for our own situation paled because of that. It actually helps you realise that there are things that are more important. You feel for people's family and friends when tragic things like that occur. It was a sad evening for everyone involved and for football in general.

Ronnie Cully (journalist, *Evening Times*): When the news finally filtered through to the press box some minutes later, grown men cried; openly and unashamedly.

Hugh McIlvanney (journalist, *The Observer*): We felt almost guilty about having allowed ourselves to be comforted by rumours.

Then, abruptly we knew for sure that the Big Man was dead, and for some of us, it was indeed as if our spirits, our very lives, had been burglarised.

Willie Miller: I could hear the fans outside chanting Jock's name, but as news of his death was spread, the noise died down.

David Will: As the president, I had to break the news to all his family, in Glasgow and his son who was in Switzerland. It was just awful. I was actually standing outside the door when he died, but I remember being in and out of the room. It was just a terrible experience – the worst experience I had ever had in football.

Jonny Owen (filmmaker): I can still remember the silence among the thousands as we walked from the ground, as though the very air around me had changed. My father and grandfather caught one another's eyes, as adults do when you're a boy. A slight shake of the head told me everything. It was the generation that showed little but everything by just the tiniest of things.

Gordon Strachan: I got dressed and went out through the deserted stand into the car park past little knots of fans from the Tartan Army who, like myself, were trying to understand how such a thing could have happened. Some of the fans were weeping.

Jim Bett: I remember being on the bus leaving the ground and seeing the fans milling about outside. By that time, they had heard the news, and they were just sitting on the kerbs or milling around in a daze. It was a strange journey back to the airport then home. I don't think anyone said more than a couple of words to each other.

Davie Cooper: The worst moment, and there were many bad ones, came when the coach left Ninian Park, and I asked myself what we were doing leaving when the gaffer was still there. Later that night, I thought back and briefly considered that I had just scored the most important goal of my career – and it meant nothing.

Alan Rough: There was a trail of supporters, and obviously news was beginning to filter out as we went along the road, and we saw fans greetin' at the kerbside. It was like a trail of anguish. And then, at the airport, we just sat there. That sort of victory would have been followed by champagne before the plane, champagne on the plane. But it was like a morgue. There is no other word.

Ronnie Robertson (Scotland fan): We came away from the match ecstatic that we had qualified for the World Cup. An hour later, we heard the news that Jock had died, and suddenly the success meant nothing to us. There were 16 of us on the bus from Cardiff to Fort William, and it was the longest journey of my life.

Jimmy Reid (trade unionist and author): Men wept, and I was unashamedly one. In a crowded hotel bar where Scots fans were staying overnight, an ordinary punter was granted a reverent silence for a most dignified toast to the memory of Jock.

Unnamed Scottish supporter (speaking on ITV News): I'm quite sure that every fan standing here the night would have wished Scotland got put oot the World Cup and Mr Stein was still with us.

Bad news in 1985 could take some time to travel, and while many were now engulfed in grief, some people were still oblivious to the tragedy.

Mike Peters (lead singer, The Alarm): I was in the players' lounge after the game, and Joe Jordan walked in. I had no idea what had happened after the game. There were no televisions everywhere like there are now. So I went up to Joe and said, 'Come on, Joe, admit you handled the ball in 1977.' He's never admitted to it, and he got really angry and aggressive with me. I said to him, 'Sorry, I was only joking.' Of course, he must have been very upset because he must have known what happened to Jock Stein, so that's why he went over the top.

Archie Macpherson (journalist): The son of Don Revie ran a hospitality company and invited me to speak at Cardiff Castle after the game. I headed up to the castle, unaware of what was going on back at the ground. But, as I was walking up the road, Scotland fans were approaching me, as I was, I suppose, a well-kent face. They were asking, 'What about Jock? What happened to him at the end?' I didn't know anything. We were having the main course at the meal when Revie's son quietly came up and told me, 'My father has been on the phone. Jock has died.' I just put a stop to the dinner but then instinctively gave an immediate elegy, extempore. I spoke about the man I knew. It is the most shocking thing that has ever happened to me. An eerie silence suddenly descended on us. In the baronial setting of a banqueting hall, it augmented the feeling that I had just intimated a royal death.

Stewart Hillis: It's bad to not be successful in a resuscitation attempt, it's even worse when it's someone that you know very well. We had what we needed. We had all the equipment. But it was a lost cause. The last thing Jock said to me was, 'It's a whole lot better now, Doc.' I'd known Jock for years. It was often said he had a heart attack in Cardiff, but he didn't have a heart attack as such. He had heart muscle disease. I still believe that had Jock taken his medication, he would not have died. But Jock was his own man.

Archie Macpherson: Without that medication, his lungs became flooded. Jock Stein effectively died of drowning that night.

At Edinburgh Airport's baggage reclaim area, a security guard called over the people milling around to ask them if they knew who owned the one unclaimed bag. There was no tag on it, but inside there was a letter. It was addressed to J. Stein Esq.

Mike Aitken: We'd all just dictated his obituaries, but only then did it become real. Jock was gone.

Alex Ferguson: I didn't shed a tear until I had flown from Cardiff to Glasgow and set out on the drive to Aberdeen. On the way up, I pulled into a layby and just broke down. I kept telling myself that I should have read the signs earlier. Jock was obviously not feeling well after half-time ... but typical of the man, he never said a word. When we scored our equaliser ... everyone else leaped off the bench to cheer except Jock, and it was then when I came to my seat and patted Jock on the head that I should have known. He just sat there motionless and I didn't read into that the meaning I should have because my thoughts were totally absorbed in a stupid game of football.

69

Only a Game? – 1986

PREMIERING ON BBC One Scotland on 28 April 1986, *Only a Game?* was an in-depth look at the history of the game in Scotland. It was packed with new interviews conducted by Roddy Forsyth and archive footage.

The series was written by William McIlvanney. The younger brother of sportswriter Hugh, who was featured as an interviewee, William was born in Kilmarnock in 1936. He became a schoolmaster, teaching at Irvine Royal Academy and Greenwood Academy, Dreghorn, where he served as deputy headmaster.

His 1975 novel *Docherty*, a portrait of a miner whose courage and endurance is tested during the Depression, won the Whitbread Novel Award. He then retired from teaching to devote himself to writing. However, he had stints as a presenter of a BBC books programme, a spell as a columnist for the newspaper *Scotland on Sunday*, and several periods as a teacher of creative writing at Scottish universities.

There was a launch at Hampden Park ahead of the premier of the first episode, where McIlvanney was joined by former Scottish internationals George Young, Tommy Gemmell, Jimmy Johnstone, Bob Reid, Bob McPhail, Denis Law and Tom Fagan.

Producer David Martin said, 'To illustrate the Scotland story, every archive in the land was searched for vivid footage of the national game.' The search went back to 1911.

The documentary was in five parts – The Player, The Manager, The Club, The Game and The Team – and cost

£70,000 to produce. In the *Daily Record*, Alex Cameron wrote, 'I have seen nothing better on Scottish sport in the last 25 years.'

The title came from a comment Jock Stein had made. Before his death in Cardiff in 1985, he had given his final interview to the BBC. Stein had said that when all is said and done, football is only a game.

In the show, Graeme Souness said in an interview recorded in September 1985, 'I'm a professional footballer who plays for money. I'm not ashamed of that. I've always been open about it. That's why I play football outside of Scotland. But I would still like to be player-manager of Rangers one day.' By the time the programme aired, Souness had been announced as Rangers' player-manager. He insisted there had been no contact with the club at the time he was interviewed, and it had been an impromptu comment.

Although initially shown only in Scotland, it was broadcast nationwide on BBC Two in August 1987.

In a review of the show for the *Lennox Herald*, Archie Fleming wrote, 'In a way it may be an epitaph for Scottish football for, whatever the optimistic talk of some of today's luminaries there's a feeling abroad that the glory days are gone.'

When McIlvanney passed away in 2015, Neil Cameron wrote in *The Herald* of *Only a Game?*, 'It has aged remarkably well, and the great and good of our game are all interviewed. However, it is McIlvanney who is the star, that wonderful voice of his could make the ordinary seem remarkable, and it was impossible not to allow every word to sink in.'

Despite BBC Scotland attempting an updated version in 2016, there has been nothing to touch the depth and detail that McIlvanney's documentary went into, before or since.

70

Only an Excuse? – 1986

FOLLOWING HOT on the heels of *Only a Game?* was the radio show *Only an Excuse?* Producer Philip Differ spoke to *The Herald* in 2014 about how the show came about. '*Only A Game?* was wonderful, but it lent itself to being sent up,' he said. '[William] McIlvanney is a poet, and he had lines like "The bleached bones of the Scottish game" and so forth on that programme. As parodists, it gave us a template from which to work, especially McIlvanney's voice.'

Differ took his idea to Colin Gilbert, who was at that time head of BBC Scotland's comedy unit, and told him he had an idea for a good parody. 'The name came out of the air like a flaming arrow … we would call it *Only An Excuse*, the *excuse* being to wallow in self-pity and moan about Scottish football,' he said.

The first episode appeared on Radio Scotland at 12.30pm on Sunday, 8 June 1986, several hours before Scotland took on West Germany in their second match at the Mexico World Cup. 'We first realised it was going to work when it took us all day to record because there were six of us crying with laughter when we read the script,' said Differ.

The cast was Jonathan Watson and Tony Roper, who were familiar to Radio Scotland listeners as part of the *Naked Radio* sketch show. The show featured take-offs of Alex Ferguson, Jim McLean, Mo Johnston, Jock Wallace, Danny McGrain and Kenny Dalglish, as well as Radio Clyde's Jimmy Sanderson.

'Nobody had ever heard of anything like it at the time – a comedy show totally about football – and it caused a ripple,' Differ said. 'We were chuffed.'

The show was repeated later that month, then again on New Year's Eve. A sequel, *A Tale of Two Seasons*, followed. The shows were then released on cassette in 1988, where they did great business. 'I'll never forget going into a record shop in Glasgow and seeing us in the indie charts,' Differ said in 2006. 'We were also on the shelf next to Ozzy Osbourne in the "O" section.' Fans were copying the tapes and sending them to relatives abroad as the show's popularity grew.

The next step was to take the show to live audiences, and their first stage show was at the Clyde Theatre in Clydebank in May 1990. The live shows got bigger and more frequent. In 1993 the show was at the Glasgow Pavilion and Paisley Town Hall before arriving at the Citizens Theatre. It proved popular among punters and those being sent up. 'I loved it,' Ally MacLeod said after attending a show. 'They even have a false nose when they take me off. If you can't laugh at yourself, something's wrong.'

By 1993 *Only an Excuse?* was muscling in on the Scottish Hogmanay slot that had been occupied by Rikki Fulton's *Scotch and Wry*. Differ said at the time, 'It's taken seven years to bring the show to television, possibly because no one realised the potential.'

In 1994 clips from *Only an Excuse?* were shown at the Royal Television Society awards in London and were the evening's big hit. That led to their 1994 World Cup Special being shown UK-wide. 'We are often asked why we don't do a weekly edition,' Tony Roper said to the *Daily Record*. 'Apart from the cost there's also the danger of doing *Only An Excuse?* so often that people get tired of it. So it's better that we only do a couple of shows each year.'

While Roper left the cast, Watson was joined by Alistair McGowan, Greg Hemphill, Lewis Macleod and Gordon Kennedy. The cast changed over the years, but Watson was the mainstay and added new impressions over the years to reflect Scottish football's ever-increasing cast of characters.

The show became a permanent fixture of New Year's Eve television, with football fans always debating its content, whether or not they felt it was top-drawer or past its best.

Watson's impressions of people like Graeme Souness, Alex Ferguson and Denis Law became the public's defining images of them. One in particular was Frank McAvennie, the five-times-capped former Celtic and West Ham striker, with his 'Where's the burdz?' catchphrase. 'Frank's a character who works really well,' Watson said in 1996. 'You don't need to know anything about football to find him funny.'

'There was so much warmth,' Watson said to journalist Hugh MacDonald as the show was coming to an end in 2020. 'I know it has come in for criticism over the years. That it wasn't as good as last year or whatever. But as an individual, I have only experienced warmth about the programme. That means a lot to me.'

71

Uruguay 0 Scotland 0 – 1986

World Cup finals, Group E
Estadio Neza 86, Neza
13 June 1986
Attendance: 20,000

Scotland: Leighton (Aberdeen), Gough (Dundee United), Miller (Aberdeen), Narey (Dundee United), Albiston (Manchester United), Strachan (Manchester United), Nicol (Liverpool) [Cooper (Rangers), 70], Aitken (Celtic), McStay (Celtic), Sharp (Everton), Sturrock (Dundee United) [Nicholas (Arsenal), 70]

Uruguay: Álvez (Peñarol), Diogo (Palmeiras), Acevedo (Defensor Sporting), Pereyra (Sao Paulo), Gutierrez (River Plate), Batista (Espanyol), Santin (Atlético Nacional Medellin), Francescoli (River Plate) [Alzamendi (River Plate), 84], Barrios (Olympiakos), Cabrera (Valencia), Ramos (Lens) [Saralegui (Peñarol), 70]

Referee: Joël Quiniou (France)

'What a shower of dirty bastards.'

Steve Nicol

'THAT WAS like no other World Cup game I've played in,' Gordon Strachan said in 1988. 'Scotland play with passion on these occasions, but we couldn't afford to that day in Neza because the priority was to remain cool at all costs. Uruguay had so much ability but forgot about it.'

Scotland went into their final group game of the 1986 World Cup with a chance of qualifying for the next stage despite losing their first two matches. A win would secure their passage to the last 16 as one of the four best third-placed countries. However, a draw would be sufficient for the Uruguayans.

Graeme Souness had come in for criticism for below-par performances in the games against Denmark and West Germany. 'I understand Graeme's had some criticism back home,' manager Alex Ferguson said to the press, 'but I've got to support my captain. We'll sort it out the right way.'

Squad member Alan Rough recalled in 2021 the tension that was apparent between the manager and captain, 'At nearly every meeting the players held with Alex – and Graeme was head of the players' committee, so there were plenty – they seemed to end up at each other's throats or get embroiled in shouting matches, frequently over what seemed like trivial matters.'

Ferguson omitted Souness from his team. 'It was a surprise because the match would have been right up his street,' said Arthur Albiston in 2020. 'He had played in two previous World Cups and had a wealth of experience in difficult European ties with Liverpool. He would have known exactly what was needed.'

Ferguson felt that three games in nine days in the heat of Mexico were a punishing schedule for anyone in central midfield. 'He's not the type to take things easy; he wants to be in the action all the time,' Ferguson said of Souness.

'I was never dropped in my entire career, and that was the last game I could have been dropped for,' Souness recalled for the *Lancashire Telegraph* in 2010. 'After that World Cup, I was going to be player-manager at Rangers, and if I left myself out, that was a different matter. It was disappointing, but I never blamed Fergie for it.'

Souness acknowledges he didn't play well in the previous two matches and states going into the tournament, he wasn't well, 'I was normally 13st, but I was 11st 2lb, and I had no power. I struggled with the altitude because it was 7,000ft.'

On the nights leading up to the match, Ferguson was only getting an hour's sleep. 'This is the most important game ever for me,' he told the *Daily Record*.

In the *Daily Record* on the morning of the game, Alex Cameron wrote, 'The French referee tonight, Joël Quiniou, must be a strong man. If he performs well, Scotland will drag a foot out of the grave and win.' This would be Quiniou's first match in the World Cup finals, although he had officiated at the 1984 Los Angeles Olympics and in the 1985 World Youth Championship. The 35-year-old contributed to one of the most sensational starts ever seen for a Scotland international.

The French journalist Didier Roustan spoke with Quiniou ahead of the game and asked him in what state of mind he approached the match. Quiniou replied that he would be sure to take his responsibilities seriously as he did not see himself allowing the players to act with impunity.

In the first minute of the match, Strachan was scythed by José Batista. Quiniou whistled, marched over to the Deportivo Español defender and pulled out a red card. With 56 seconds on the clock it was the fastest dismissal of any World Cup match. It shocked not only Batista but everyone else watching that day. Quiniou would later say that the decision led to him being nicknamed 'Lucky Luke', a French/Belgian cartoon character, a gunslinger in the old west who was famous as 'the man who shoots faster than his shadow'.

'This might sound daft,' Steve Nicol wrote in his autobiography, 'but the worst thing that could have happened to us was them having a man sent off so early.'

It was to Nicol that Scotland's best chance fell in the 18th minute. The Liverpool defender had plenty of time but didn't put enough power into his shot, and Fernando Álvez saved well. 'Instead of using the pace on the ball and just redirecting it, I tried to generate my own power. However, I hit it into the ground and that took the pace off the ball,' he said.

The Uruguayans had shown in their two previous matches that they were no strangers to roughhouse tactics, and so it continued. 'Their spoiling tactics – fouls, faking, time-wasting – seemed to mesmerise Scotland,' wrote journalist Patrick Barclay.

Uruguay's best chance came when Cabrera had a header saved by Leighton on 67 minutes.

Arthur Albiston spoke to Paul Forsyth of *The Times* in 2020. The years had not mellowed the former Manchester United man on the events of the day. 'They were brought up differently from us,' he said. 'They knew how to work the referee. They knew how to waste time, basically for 90 minutes. And our lads, especially the strikers, got lumps kicked out of them. Off the ball, it was just blatant: body checking, fouling, you name it. If you were down on the ground, they would move to help you up, but as they offered a hand, they would stand on your ankle. They were the most cynical team I ever played against.'

'These are not the sort of players who could ever be mistaken for cowards,' Hugh McIlvanney wrote of the Scotland side in *The Observer*, 'but they appeared to be shell-shocked rather than invigorated by the removal of Batista and played most of the rest of the match as if their minds and spirits had been chilled by dread of the monumental embarrassment implicit in failing when events, for once, seemed to be conspiring to see them through.'

Of the referee's performance, McIlvanney added, 'His courageous initial gesture definitely rendered him reluctant to deal harshly with the Uruguayans later.' That was an observation Quiniou confirmed to be true in his autobiography, writing that his one regret from the game was not the early dismissal but that it caused him to hesitate in sending a second Uruguayan off.

SFA president David Will said, 'What was happening in the Uruguay game was unreal. The things happening off the ball were totally unbelievable. I have never seen so much dirty play.'

At the post-match press conference, Uruguay's Omar Borrás, at 65 the oldest coach at the 1986 finals, said, 'The referee was a murderer.'

Alex Ferguson responded, 'I am sitting here wondering what the hell is going on. This conference is a complete shambles. I've listened to what Mr Borrás has said. He has no respect for other people's dignity. He is simply lying and cheating. If this is what happens then I am glad to be going home. I can't even shake their hands and wish Uruguay good luck.'

Bobby Charlton, there as a pundit, was nearby. 'We just shouldn't play these people again,' he said. 'It's simply not worth it. The way they go on has nothing to do with football, nothing to do with sport.' It would later be suggested Charlton was tapping up Ferguson to take over as Manchester United manager, which the Scot did later that year.

'That was no game of football out there today,' SFA secretary Ernie Walker said. 'There were ten cheats and cowards, the scum of world football. The TV audience back home could only have seen a quarter of what went on. If that is how they want to progress in this tournament it is not our way.'

Borrás's 'murderer' comment led to him being banned from the dugout at Uruguay's next match due to 'uncouth language'. Uruguay were also fined 25,000 Swiss francs (£7,000). Hermann Neuberger, chairman of the organising committee, said the behaviour of Uruguay's bench was unacceptable. He also noted that the referee was 'molested and threatened'.

The Uruguayans had actually been warned by letter about the behaviour on the bench after their first match with West Germany.

Sir Alf Ramsey, who infamously referred to the Argentinian team as 'animals' at the 1966 World Cup, called Uruguay's performance 'a shameful exhibition of the South American mentality to win at all costs'. He went on, 'I saw more butchery from Uruguay in 90 minutes than you'll ever see at Sainsbury's on a Saturday morning. It is monstrous that these savage men should qualify for the last 16. Apart from the brutality of their football they were play-acting, diving, feigning injury, time-wasting, spitting and pulling hair. No wonder the Scots refused to shake their hands at the end.'

72

Andy Roxburgh

Scotland manager (1986–1993)

WHEN THE 42-year-old Andy Roxburgh was appointed Scotland's new manager once Alex Ferguson's caretaker spell had finished after the Mexico World Cup, there were many 'Andy who?' remarks.

Some fans were baffled as to why a man with no notable playing record and no managerial experience at club level had been handed the national job.

It was certainly a surprise appointment. Manchester City manager Billy McNeill was believed to be the favourite, but the truth was that Roxburgh had been coaching with the SFA for several years; he was quoted by bookies as being a potential candidate to take over from Ally MacLeod in 1978, and he was highly rated by those in power at the SFA.

As a player, Roxburgh was a striker. Starting out with Queen's Park, he moved on to East Stirlingshire, then Partick Thistle. He had won the Second Division with Falkirk in 1969/70, scoring 17 times as he played up front alongside Alex Ferguson.

He joined Clydebank for the start of the 1972/73 season. The Bankies were run by his uncles, Jack and Charles Steedman. Roxburgh's early football education had been watching Jack in his days as a Junior player. By this time Roxburgh was the holder of an SFA coaching certificate, and he took on coaching duties at New Kilbowie.

Combining football with his profession as a schoolteacher, Roxburgh became the youngest headmaster in the Scottish education system when he was appointed to the role at Carlibar Primary in Barrhead at the age of 30.

In 1975, Roxburgh left both Clydebank and his teaching job to join the SFA, becoming the body's first director of coaching. Soon he had his first success as the Scottish professional youth team won the Cannes Youth Tournament. 'I'll tell you this,' Jack Steedman said to *Weekly News* at the time, 'Andrew will now go on to be one of the most important people in Scottish football for the next 20 years.'

He coached the under-18 side to European Championship glory in Finland in 1982, then was part of Jock Stein's backroom staff in Spain for the World Cup finals.

In 1983 wins over South Korea and Mexico took the young Scottish team to the quarter-final of the World Youth Championship in Mexico. They lost 1-0 to Poland.

On his appointment to the national job, the SFA president David Will remarked that Roxburgh knew more about the game than arguably anyone in Britain or even Europe. 'I was never a big-name player,' Roxburgh said. 'But the SFA have groomed me for ten years. I almost had to be picked up off the floor when I was told the job was mine, but football is in my blood, and I now hope to repay the SFA's faith in me.'

'Andy is a bigger name outside Scotland at the moment,' SFA secretary Ernie Walker said to the *Daily Record*. 'Top countries in Europe, such as Italy and Holland, often send for him because of his knowledge of the game.'

Roy Aitken also spoke up for Roxburgh on his appointment, 'The man has tremendous knowledge of the game at domestic and international level.' Aitken highlighted the fact that the best young players in Scotland over the years had all worked with Roxburgh, 'These lads are quality players who have Andy Roxburgh to thank for much of their progress.'

He developed strong relationships with players, Mo Johnston once saying he would 'run through a brick wall for Andy'. Paul McStay, who had played under him as a youth, said to *Shoot*! in 1987, 'I know my international colleagues are willing to sweat blood for Andy Roxburgh. He's given us all tremendous encouragement. He has ignored the flak around about himself to help the players.'

But Roxburgh also had his run-ins; Richard Gough, in particular, had a volatile relationship with him.

Gough famously scored a winner against Cyprus in the sixth minute of injury time, a length of time practically unheard of in 1989. 'It might have had something to do with Andy,' McStay said. 'He watches videos of all our opponents and couldn't help but notice how the Cypriots wasted time. He pointed it out to the ref and the UEFA observer before the game and it obviously did the trick.'

Roxburgh had success during his time as Scotland manager, qualifying for the 1990 World Cup as well as becoming the first manager to lead Scotland to the European Championship, in 1992.

73

Arthur Montford

'HELLO AND a very warm welcome.' This was Arthur Montford's regular introduction to *Scotsport* and encapsulated the comfortable feeling he engendered in his audience that allowed him to be part of Scottish football fans' enjoyment of the national game for decades. Born in Shawlands in 1929, Arthur's family moved to Greenock when he was young, leading to his lifetime allegiance to Greenock Morton.

Arthur went into journalism when he came out of the Army in 1949, where he had done his national service in Egypt. He began working at the *Coatbridge Leader*, where he met the Albion Rovers defender Jock Stein. The pair developed a long friendship. 'He was always aware of the problems involved with making a programme like *Scotsport*,' Montford said of Stein, 'and gave his full cooperation.'

Arthur's father, Sid, was a newspaperman, the Scottish sports correspondent for the *Belfast Telegraph* and *Ireland's Saturday Night*, writing under the name 'Angus Cathcart'. He had also worked on Glasgow's *Evening News* and the *Daily Record*.

Moving from print to television, Arthur was the first voice heard on STV when it went on air in 1957. 'We were based in Glasgow's Theatre Royal, and the telephone switchboard was set up right in the middle of the theatre foyer. But there was an exciting, electric atmosphere because we were entering a new world,' he recalled.

'Before I quit my newspaper job for television, Scotland's top footballers were, well – just names in the Hampden programme,'

Montford wrote in 1959's *Scottish Football Book*. 'But my, how television has changed THAT! Having interviewed and met enough international players to fill about three teams, I feel I know them just as well as I might know any other television personality. For take it from me, football players can be great TV stars.'

In his early broadcasting days, Arthur asked Carroll Levis, a noted Canadian talent scout, for advice, 'He [Levis] just told me, "Always be nice to the camera." He suggested never to say a word I might be sorry for.'

Montford moved to the sports desk and was promoted to editor in charge of all sporting events on STV.

It seems remarkable now, but at *Scotsport*, they negotiated with clubs on fees for games on an ad hoc basis, as Montford explained, 'We always agreed on what was a fair price; no haggling.' It was no different for internationals. 'We negotiated directly with the English FA,' Montford recalled. 'We once did a Scotland-England game from Wembley and ferried a film back up, processed it, edited it and showed it the same night and the rights for the game were £375 for 15 minutes of highlights. That was the early '60s when ITV weren't doing football.'

If you ask anyone who watched Arthur on television one thing about him, they would doubtless say his jacket.

'The sports jacket was, quite honestly, largely a myth,' Montford said to author Jeff Connor. 'I did have one or two light, cheery jackets but I felt it was part of the persona of *Scotsport*, bright, cheerful and just ordinary guys were doing this programme. We had fun.' Montford auctioned what he saw as his most outrageous jacket for Help the Aged. 'Some football nutter wanted to be wearing that,' he exclaimed, 'but it went to a good cause.'

Arthur's onscreen popularity was such that he succeeded Jimmy Reid as Rector of the University of Glasgow in 1974, a role he served until 1977. 'I was welcome at every ground in Scotland, which I always regarded as a great tribute to the professional work that I did. People could see that I loved the game,' he said.

Montford estimated that he did around 2,000 episodes of *Scotsport*, commentating on 400 matches. 'Scotland were qualifying for all those World Cups in the '70s and '80s,' he said, 'and that gave us many great programmes.'

Scotsport enjoyed one of its greatest successes on the night of one of Scotland's dismal failures. The 0-0 draw with Uruguay that saw Scotland eliminated from the 1986 World Cup was watched by an estimated two million viewers in Scotland, equalling the record set by Rikki Fulton's *Scotch and Wry*.

Arthur was once reprimanded by his then boss, an Englishman, for being 'blatantly partisan' in his commentary of a Scotland match. 'I was delighted to plead guilty to that,' he told the *Daily Record*. 'I also admitted that I wore a Scots rosette and sometimes had a tartan tie or scarf on at the matches.'

One of Montford's abiding memories was the aftermath of Scotland's win over Wales at Anfield in 1977, a match in which he uttered in commentary, 'I can hardly watch,' as Don Masson stepped up to take a penalty. He recalled, 'The dressing room was full of folk celebrating. In the middle of all this was Bill Shankly, the legendary Liverpool manager, standing there smiling and saying what a great night it had been. He just wanted to be part of the experience. It seemed to me to sum up what we Scots feel about football.'

Arthur retired from *Scotsport* after the 1989 Scottish Cup Final. In May 2010 he and his friend and fellow broadcaster Archie Macpherson were awarded the SPFA Special Merit award for services to football broadcasting and journalism. Arthur passed away in November 2014.

74

The U16 World Championship Final – 1989

THE THIRD FIFA U16 World Championship was the most prestigious tournament ever held in Scotland at that time.

The Scotland squad was selected over a year by Craig Brown, national coach Andy Roxburgh and senior staff coach Ross Mathie, who had been Brown's assistant at Clyde before joining the SFA's technical development department in the early 1980s.

Brown recalled in 2009, 'Expense was no object in making sure our players were as well prepared as possible, and that meant regular get-togethers at Largs. We even played 14 games against various opponents.'

SFA secretary Ernie Walker told Brown he must be sure the Scots team were successful. 'Ernie was top-class,' Brown said in 2019, 'but he had an aggressive and abrasive style at times. Ernie gave us the authority to do what we wanted. We were granted special permission to demand the boys were taken out of their clubs for as many international get-togethers as possible.'

The opening day of the tournament saw double-headers in Glasgow, Aberdeen, Dundee and Edinburgh, with Pelé in attendance at Hampden Park. Admission prices of £3, £2 and £1 were the same for all matches, which were 40 minutes each way. However, attendances were unimpressive, with Hampden hosting only 6,500 fans for Scotland's match, a 0-0 draw with Ghana. The matches had a combined attendance of 17,000.

Attendances, though, picked up as the tournament progressed, with television coverage attracting interest and the weather being favourable. There was a crowd of 9,000 at Motherwell's Fir Park for Scotland's second match, a 3-0 win over Cuba, with Bahrain beating Ghana in the second game. 'I was always convinced that when the word got round our people would come and support the tournament,' David Findlay, the SFA official in overall charge of the tournament, said. A 1-1 draw with Bahrain took both teams through to the knockout stages.

In the quarter-final at Pittodrie, Scotland faced East Germany in front of a crowd of 10,200. A goal by Dundee United's John Lindsay in injury time was enough to settle the tie.

Paul Dickov, who was in Scotland's squad for the tournament, said to the *Sunday Post* in 2019, 'We had loads of good players in the group, we were playing in front of patriotic crowds, and everyone believed in each other. Put those ingredients together and you have a team who thought we could win every game.'

In the semi-final, Scotland were up against European champions Portugal at Tynecastle.

'We know nothing about Scotland,' Portuguese coach Carlos Queiroz said before the game. 'Technically, I would think we will be better. But we know it will be a very hard game.'

Scottish fans turned up in numbers. A crowd of 29,000 saw the game, with 5,000 locked out. The kick-off was delayed for 40 minutes to let the supporters in. The police and FIFA officials made the decision to open the terracing perimeter gate to relieve congestion. The game was played only two months after the Hillsborough tragedy.

The crowd saw an end-to-end match with both sides having great chances. The only goal came in the 54th minute when Lindsay sent in a corner. Nuno Fonseca, in the Portugal goal, came for the ball and missed it. Brian O'Neil climbed above the defence and headed into the net.

Portugal, whose team included Luís Figo and Abel Xavier, came back, but Arsenal's James Will made several crucial saves to prevent an equaliser.

The noise from the crowd at the end lives long in the memory of those who were there. 'We had to do two laps of honour before the crowd would disperse,' Brown recalled. 'The police told the players to go out again because the fans just wouldn't leave the stadium.'

Full-back Tom McMillan spoke to the *Daily Record* in 2019, 'We felt we had a good squad, but we underestimated the scale of the tournament and the way it would capture people's interest in the country. We didn't expect to reach the final. We'd just come back from the European Championship and hadn't done so well. But we were well organised, and Craig Brown spent a lot of time with us on the coaching field.'

In the other semi-final, Bahrain, who had knocked out Brazil and had become favourites of the Scottish crowds, lost 1-0 to Saudi Arabia, who had previously eliminated favourites Nigeria.

The final was played at Hampden Park on 24 June 1989, with the match live on STV. The weather delivered a glorious sunny day, and a crowd of 51,674 came along.

Scotland took the lead after only seven minutes. A grounded Jim Beattie managed to push the ball out to Dickov on the left. The Arsenal man put a cross into Ian Downie, who sent a brilliant header past Mohamed Al-Deayea in the Saudi goal.

It was 2-0 after 26 minutes when Dickov pounced on the ball after Adnan Abdulshkor slipped and chipped his shot just inside the far post.

Saudi Arabia came back into the game on 51 minutes when a short free kick was played to Sulaiman Al-Reshoudi, who lashed a 20-yard drive into the net.

Scotland should have gone further ahead when they were awarded a penalty. O'Neil, though, shot tamely, and Al-Deayea, who would go on to win 178 full caps, saved easily.

With 66 minutes gone it was 2-2; Waleed Al-Terair took a pass from Al-Reshoudi and shot past Will.

The Saudis, with obvious talent on display, at the same time played the most cynical football the tournament had seen. Dickov and Gary Bollan were repeated victims of heavy tackling, which referee Juan Pablo Escobar López of Guatemala was slow to clamp down on. Abdullah Al-Hamdi was finally sent off seven minutes from the end after a kick at O'Neil.

The game went into extra time, and when there were no further goals it went to a penalty shoot-out. Both Dickov and Al-Shamrani missed from the first five kicks. O'Neil missed the sixth, leaving Saleem Al-Alawi to score, giving Saudi Arabia a 5-4 win.

Rumours persisted that the Saudi team were older than 16. The *Sunday Post*'s Doug Baillie wrote that they had plenty of 'old heads on old shoulders'. In *The Observer*, Glenn Gibbons wrote, 'An extremely mature-looking and certainly very powerful Saudi Arabia simply outplayed a team of Scottish teenagers whose defeat in this final of the FIFA Under-16 World Youth Championship could not have been more honourable.' In the *Glasgow Herald*, Ian Paul wrote similarly, saying the Scottish loss was a moral victory, 'The Scots looked behaved and played like young lads under 17 years of age. Many of their opponents looked, played and behaved like men of some considerable maturity and experience.'

'It was so bad, it was a joke to us,' Dickov said in 2019. 'Hampden Park was heaving because our run had really captured the imagination of the entire country. The line among the lads, though, was that the crowd would be way higher because the main stand was full of the Saudis' wives and kids. We were boys up against men, and everyone knew it, which is a serious handicap in terms of strength and power, let alone experience.'

Carlos Queiroz had objected publicly to the ages of some of the Saudi players after Portugal's first group game, while the Nigeria coach Sebastian Brodrick made a private objection to FIFA on the same subject after their quarter-final defeat.

Ernie Walker claimed years afterwards that he had been told the Saudi players were overage. Walker spoke to the *Record* in 2009, 'It was a fantastic tournament, but like everyone, my primary recollection is how the Scottish boys were cheated out of the final. It was an appalling thing to happen. It was a problem that was identified pretty early on by everyone involved, including the media. I mean, it was so obvious – the Saudi keeper looked like Peter Shilton.'

O'Neil, Dickov and Andy McLaren were the only three members of the Scotland squad who went on to win full caps.

75

Flower of Scotland

ANOTHER SONG sits alongside 'Scotland the Brave' as the country's unofficial national anthem. Similarly, it was written a lot more recently than many people assume.

Roy Williamson, who had a skiffle group, and Ronnie Browne, who had started folk singing, met in 1955 as students at Edinburgh College of Art. A few years later, when both were at teacher training college, they formed the Corrie Folk Trio alongside architect Bill Smith before being joined by Belfast-born singer Paddie Bell.

In 1963 they had their big break when they appeared for 26 weeks on TV as the anchor link on a folk programme called *Hoot'nanny Show*. Williamson and Browne, who were by now art teachers, quit their jobs and performed music full-time.

Bell left the line-up in 1963, with Smith departing in 1966, leaving Williamson and Browne to carry on as the Corries, the name being Scots for hillside indentations.

Williamson wrote 'Flower of Scotland' as a 'private and personal' statement around 1966. It was stored away for two years before Browne persuaded him to include it in the Corries' shows. It was played in public for the first time on 28 February 1968, at Ruthven Barracks, in Badenoch, for the television programme *Songs of the Jacobite Risings*.

'It's based on the Battle of Bannockburn and the spirit of the men who fought and won our independence from a tyrannical English king,' Browne said in 2014. When they changed the arrangement from a bouzouki and a bodhran to two guitars, the song became the Corries' anthem. It began to resonate with their live audiences, the group often performed it a second time to satisfy demand.

'I had no idea what I was starting,' Williamson once said of the song. 'In fact, I didn't even think it was good enough to sing. But it was the people themselves who decided what was to happen.'

'Nobody at the time expected it would be such a success,' Browne wrote in *The Independent* in 1990. 'But as the years passed, it came to be a popular anthem, a true folk song, adopted by people all over Scotland and Scotsmen all over the world.'

The song started to have a life outside of the clubs and halls the Corries played in as the Scots public embraced it at large.

'In the year 1974, "Flower of Scotland" caught on with the wider public,' Ronnie Browne wrote in his autobiography. 'More and more we would catch glimpses of it in television dramas, usually as some drunken Scotsman leaving a bar and singing, "Oh Flower of Scotland, na nya na nyaaaaa, na nya na nyaaaaa." They had learned the first line but hadn't quite got the hang of the second.'

Williamson and Browne both played rugby at college, Williamson also played for Edinburgh Wanderers while Browne played for Boroughmuir, so it was fitting that rugby was the first sport to embrace the song.

In the summer of 1974, the British Lions rugby team toured South Africa. The tour, in which the Lions went unbeaten, was infamous for on-pitch violence, but the visitors' 'one in all in' approach on the field was rooted in bonding by song. They would all sing on the bus on the way to a game. Billy Steele, a winger from Langholm, was their choirmaster. 'Billy started singing an arousing song,' captain Willie John McBride said in 1996. 'That really is when "Flower of Scotland" came to prominence.'

When the team bus arrived at the Loftus Versfeld Stadium in Pretoria for the second Test match, the team were only halfway through the song. The bus stopped and the doors opened. 'There were hundreds of people all there waiting for us,' remembered Steele, 'and nobody moved a muscle. They all sat there and sang right until the end of that song. The togetherness was incredible. There was not an attempt from anyone to stand up.'

When the team won the 1974 Sports Personality of the Year Team of the Year award, they sang 'Flower of Scotland' at the ceremony. 'Having that coverage internationally was a godsend,' said Browne. The Corries released the song as a single in February 1975.

The Scottish National Party said the song was 'an inspiration to the Scottish nation'. However, the duo weren't keen to associate with their cause. In 1976 Williamson said, 'We're not on a crusade for the SNP or anybody else. "Flower of Scotland" is nationalistic, not political and it reflects how I felt the week I wrote it. It's a personal song.'

Football wasn't far behind rugby in adopting it as a terracing anthem. The song was passionately sung by Scots fans at Anfield during the 2-0 World Cup qualifying win over Wales in 1977.

Both football and rugby made moves to introduce the song as a replacement for 'God Save the Queen' in 1989. Scotland's rugby players felt that the booing of 'God Save the Queen' generated from the crowd was embarrassing, particularly as their patron was Princess Anne. The players spoke to the Scottish Rugby Union and suggested 'Flower of Scotland' be played instead.

In his autobiography, Browne wrote, 'Bill Hogg, then the secretary of the SRU, explained that for the past two seasons' internationals, the team had adopted the habit of singing "Flower of Scotland" under their breath when "God Save the Queen" was being played before kick-off. They had grown tired of this surreptitious practice and wanted "Flower of Scotland" to be played as their anthem. Could they have permission to do so?' Browne didn't hesitate.

It was played for the first time in their game with Fiji in October 1989, while the SFA approved 'Flower of Scotland' to be played before the World Cup qualifier with Norway in November.

The song really resonated on 17 March 1990 when it was played before Scotland's Grand Slam win over England at Murrayfield. The lyrics were printed in the match programme. The Corries were due to lead the singing, but Roy Williamson was too ill to attend. 'Crucially and indisputably, it had an unnerving effect on the English,' captain David Sole wrote in his autobiography.

'The real panic was when "Flower of Scotland" was played, and their guys knew the words,' England centre Simon Halliday told Tom English for his book *The Grudge*. 'Previous years, they didn't sing anything. I had a little look across at them, and they were absolutely screaming it out.' Scotland went on to win 13-7 to clinch the Grand Slam.

Later that month, 'Flower of Scotland' was played again at Hampden before the friendly with Argentina. The SFA, however, stuck with 'Scotland the Brave' for Scotland's three games in Italy at the 1990 World Cup.

Roy Williamson died in August 1990. Ronnie Browne has continued to represent the song; in 1996, he was invited to Vienna to lead the singing of 'Flower of Scotland' before the Austria v Scotland World Cup qualifier.

In recent years it has been sung before internationals by Julie Fowlis and Amy Macdonald. 'I have absolutely loved singing "Flower of Scotland" before the games,' Macdonald said in 2012. 'I don't get nervous singing any of my own songs, only with "Flower of Scotland". But the buzz you get after doing it is certainly worth it.'

76

Juan Cayasso – 1990

SCOTLAND'S 1990 World Cup finals group looked typical of what supporters had grown accustomed to. There was Brazil, again, as in 1974 and 1982, and the Scots would probably lose to them. There was Sweden, the team Scotland would surely be fighting for second place with, but it was a game fans knew the team could win. Then there were the minnows, Costa Rica, the unknown quantity, the team the Scots were expected to beat – and beat well – but also, as the past had shown us, the side that could derail their whole tournament.

Ahead of the 1982 finals, when assessing New Zealand, manager Jock Stein had said he didn't like the idea of playing them first, as the 'rabbits', as Stein referred to the weakest side in each group, always had one good game in them, and it was usually the first.

Manager Andy Roxburgh was known to be thorough, and he did his homework on Costa Rica. Assistant manager Craig Brown had come back from a scouting mission with the identity of their main weakness – goalkeeper Gabelo Conejo. 'He was a flapper, put him under pressure,' Brown told the team. The feeling was that he didn't come for crosses, so put plenty in, and Alan McInally would put him under pressure.

'We'd watched pictures of him before, and he never really came out towards the edge of his box, but that day he came for every single cross,' Murdo McLeod told Simon Hart for his book *World in Motion*. 'That's the only game in my career I won't speak about,' McInally said to *The Times* in 2020.

Costa Rica's coach was Yugoslav Bora Milutinović, who had taken Mexico to the quarter-finals of the 1986 World Cup. His game plan for Costa Rica was to defend first and counterattack second.

Four minutes into the second half, with the game still goalless, striker Claudio Jara produced a sublime back-heel at the edge of the box. The element of surprise caught out the Scottish defence and, suddenly, Costa Rica had a one-on-one with Jim Leighton. The man with the chance was Juan Cayasso.

'I don't know if I remember it because I always see it on video people play,' Cayasso said to *The Herald* in 2018. 'But I could never be prepared for that moment. My team-mate Claudio Jara knocked the ball to me – we call it a taquito here. I was close to him, I step back and when he does the taquito I read it. At first, I'm like, "Oh," I'm frightened. But then I have to react, it's at my foot, Jimmy is out. Then it hits his belly and goes over him. I turn around and look at the referee, and he's going to the centre of the field. First I'm frightened, then I don't believe it, then, "Yes, goal." I had gone faraway in that moment. My mind was all about Costa Rica.'

Alex McLeish explained the moment to Simon Hart. 'Somebody allows this guy to come inside here,' he said. 'He shouldn't be letting him come inside. Force him out there. It's too easy. Stewart McKimmie got dragged in. I've been done as well there. A little bit of good movement from Cayasso – he was a good player – and he drifted off me as I watched the ball.'

Cayasso told Hart, 'You can see it on TV, and I'm still surprised when I look at it – see how I go to the corner and then turn around and give a smile. I know I'll never smile in that way again. A lot of sensations went through my mind. I couldn't believe it was happening. After the match, I remember people jumping around and celebrating, and I was in a corner. I was just sitting there trying to figure out what had happened.'

Scotland had 19 goal attempts to Costa Rica's four and 14 corners to three. 'We had so many chances. All we needed was for one to go into the net,' said Roxburgh.

In his book *All Played Out*, Pete Davies memorably described his colleague Hugh McIlvanney watching the proceedings, 'McIlvanney jerked and jumped at each lost chance in his chair, his face a kaleidoscope of rage and despair over the wretched fate of having to follow his unbelievable team.'

The win gave the Costa Ricans confidence. In their second game Costa Rica lost to Brazil, but only 1-0. Scotland beat Sweden 2-1. The fact that Costa Rica went on to defeat Sweden in the last group game and qualify for the next round did nothing to lessen the embarrassment that existed in Scotland due to the defeat. 'It was not difficult to play against teams like those because they are so predictable,' Cayasso said of the wins over Scotland and Sweden to the *Boston Globe* in 2001.

'I live in San Diego now and often visit Costa Rica, which is a beautiful country,' Richard Gough, who was substituted at half-time, said to journalist Ewing Grahame in 2020. 'A few years back, a friend there asked me if I'd like to meet Cayasso, and I agreed. We stayed in touch. Juan is now the sports minister for his region.'

77

Ally McCoist

61 caps, 19 goals (1986–1998)

ALLY MCCOIST initially began playing in midfield as a teenager with St Johnstone. He moved up front alongside John Brogan, and his form was such that in 1981 English First Division Sunderland took him down south.

After nine goals in 65 games with the Roker Park club, Rangers brought the 20-year-old back to Scotland in 1983.

Despite scoring regularly for Rangers, McCoist didn't make his Scotland debut until April 1986 in a 0-0 draw with the Netherlands under Alex Ferguson. There was a lack of opportunities at the time for players around McCoist's age. The under-21 side had played only twice in 1985, and there were no under-21 internationals between May 1985 and September 1986. 'Perhaps a B squad would be a good idea,' McCoist said to *Scottish Football Today*.

He wasn't part of Ferguson's plans for the World Cup that summer in Mexico, and it was only when Andy Roxburgh took charge that McCoist became a regular pick for the national team.

'Playing for Scotland was everything I expected it to be and more,' McCoist wrote in his autobiography. 'It's every schoolboy's fantasy to turn out for their country, and I think the ultimate dream of every youngster to pull on the Scotland number nine jersey. Now I was actually doing that. It felt great.'

His first goals came in a 2-0 friendly win over Hungary in September 1987. He followed that up with a goal and a booking against Belgium the following month.

McCoist noted in his autobiography that Graeme Souness, his manager at Rangers from 1986 to 1991, wasn't keen on him playing for his country. 'He definitely tried to sway me away from the national squad,' McCoist wrote. 'I'd come back from an international where I'd played well on the Wednesday and find myself dropped for our game on the Saturday. He reasoned that I'd left my legs in the country in midweek.'

In the World Cup qualifying campaign for Italy 1990, McCoist played a major role, contributing to the 2-0 win over France in March 1989 and scoring the winner against Cyprus in April.

Going into the final qualifier with Norway in November 1989, Scotland needed only a draw to progress. With a minute to go before half-time, Maurice Malpas headed the ball upfield, and Ally was off his mark. McCoist reached it ahead of Tottenham keeper Erik Thorstvedt and lobbed the ball over his head from the edge of the box. As the ball nestled in the net, McCoist was off and running again, this time in jubilation. 'The Hampden Roar had actually started before the ball was in the net,' McCoist remembered. A late Norwegian equaliser wasn't enough to stop Scotland from qualifying.

At the World Cup finals, despite McCoist and Mo Johnston being a successful front pairing for Rangers, McCoist was on the bench for the games against Costa Rica and Sweden, with Johnston partnering Alan McInally and Robert Fleck respectively.

For the last game, a 1-0 defeat to Brazil, McCoist started, but overall he found Italy 1990 a negative experience.

For the 1992 European Championship qualifying campaign McCoist was again vital, scoring important goals along the way. He set up debutant John Robertson for the first and hit the winner against Romania in September 1990 in front of only 12,801 fans at Hampden. There was a penalty miss in the 2-1 win over Switzerland in October, but he scored the Scots' goal in the 1-1 draw with Bulgaria in November.

On 11 September 1991 Scotland were 2-0 down to Switzerland in Bern. 'We had paid the home team too much respect,' assistant manager Craig Brown said. Gordon Durie pulled a goal back then McCoist notched the equaliser.

In the final qualifier in November, McCoist hit the fourth in a 4-0 win over San Marino. When Romania could only draw 1-1 with Bulgaria a week later, Scotland's qualification was confirmed.

At the finals in Sweden, McCoist wore the squad number five, as Roxburgh, heading off any dispute over which player wanted what number, settled on a number-by-caps system to allocate players their number, except the two goalkeepers, who had numbers one and 12, respectively.

'I have never been with an international set-up which felt so much like a club team,' McCoist wrote, 'and Andy Roxburgh and Craig Brown take all the credit for that.' Scotland went out with three good performances but only one win. 'I felt I played my part in three performances that earned Scotland a lot of praise, and I was delighted with that.'

One of the biggest setbacks in McCoist's career was the leg break he suffered in Scotland's 5-0 defeat against Portugal in Lisbon in 1993. It kept him out of the game for 18 months.

His return to the national team was in August 1995 at home to Greece, coming off the bench with 19 minutes remaining. 'Ally was thrilled,' Craig Brown wrote in his autobiography, 'because he had missed 15 internationals as a result of his injury. Within 60 seconds, he had headed a terrific goal from a John Collins cross.'

For the 1996 European Championship in England, McCoist missed the 0-0 draw with the Netherlands but appeared as a second-half substitute in the 2-0 defeat to the hosts.

Going into the last game against Switzerland, Scotland needed a win while hoping the Netherlands lost to England, with a five-goal swing in Scotland's favour across the two matches.

In the 37th minute at Villa Park, McCoist received Gary McAllister's pass and fired home an unstoppable 25-yarder. It was his 19th and final goal for Scotland. 'We never thought in a hundred million years that he was going to have a shot from 25 yards,' Swiss defender Ramon Vega told the *Glasgow Times* in 2022. 'As a defender, you were like, "What? What is he doing here?" I didn't even know he had the power to do that and I'll be honest with you, I think he was surprised himself.'

Patrick Kluivert's consolation in the Dutch's 4-1 defeat to England meant that they pipped Scotland for the runners-up slot.

McCoist's last two caps came in the autumn of 1998 as a Kilmarnock player.

Like Kenny Dalglish before him, McCoist's face was always a picture of joy when he scored. Also, like Dalglish, he had criticism from some fans that his international form didn't match that at club level. However, McCoist's 19 goals for his country see him fifth on the all-time scorers list, with only John McGinn looking like he might overtake him from the current crop.

78

Scotland Under-21s 4 Germany Under-21s 3 – 1992

24 March 1992
Pittodrie Stadium, Aberdeen
European Championship quarter-final second leg
Attendance: 22,500

Scotland: Watt (Aberdeen), McLaren (Hearts), Wright (Aberdeen), Lambert (St Mirren), Smith (Aberdeen), Fulton (Celtic) [Rae (Millwall), 59], Jess (Aberdeen) [Gemmill (Nottingham Forest), 45], O'Donnell (Motherwell), Creaney (Celtic), McKinnon (Dundee United), Ferguson (Dundee United)

Germany: Klos (Borrusia Dortmund), Paßlack (Bayer Uerdingen), Stadler (Borrusia Mönchengladbach), Wörns (Bayer Leverkusen), Schmäler (Stuttgart), Kranz (1. FC Kaiserslautern), Haber (1. FC Kaiserslautern), Franck (Borrusia Dortmund) [Baumann (1. FC Köln), 77], Herrlich (Bayer Leverkusen), Poschner (Borrusia Dortmund), Scholl (Karlsruher SC)

Referee: Joaquin Velazquez (Spain)

Goals:
Scotland – McKinnon (42), Creaney (68), Lambert (78), Rae (87)
Germany – Kranz (9), Scholl (40), Herrlich (59)

SCOTLAND HAD topped qualifying Group 2 with two wins over Romania and Switzerland, and one victory over Bulgaria. It set them up with a quarter-final against Germany.

In the first leg in Bochum, Scotland came away with a 1-1 draw thanks to Gerry Creaney's 30th-minute goal. Aberdeen's Michael Watt in goal was the star performer, making a series of saves.

In the second leg Germany were in front after only nine minutes when Markus Kranz swept the ball past Watt from 15 yards. Two minutes later, Phil O'Donnell hit a post. Watt tipped over a long-range shot from Thomas Franck to keep the deficit to one.

With five minutes of the first half remaining, Mehmet Scholl got through the Scots' defence and buried the ball for 2-0. Two minutes later after a free kick from Steve Fulton, the ball broke inside the six-yard box for Ray McKinnon to fire home.

Scot Gemmill replaced Eoin Jess at half-time. Early in the second half Duncan Ferguson was hauled down by Christian Wörns, but the referee appeared to see nothing.

Germany made it 3-1 on the night on 59 minutes when Heiko Herrlich scored. It looked like the young Scots were out, as with the Germans having three away goals, Scotland now required three to go through.

Nine minutes later Creaney scored to make it 3-2, then with 13 minutes left Paul Lambert scored to equalise. With Scotland now only requiring one goal, it finally came when Alex Rae chipped Stefan Klos from 25 yards for the winner with three minutes remaining.

Lambert recalled the game in 1998, saying it was, 'One of the best nights of my career. We found ourselves 3-1 down. All of a sudden we clicked and Gerry Creaney hauled us back into it. Then I had the kind of chance I like – an open goal from three yards – and we were level. The place was bedlam and the Germans were a bit shell-shocked. There was a real feeling we'd get a winner and Alex Rae duly obliged with a fantastic goal to set Pittodrie alight, and I had some fun when I arrived at Dortmund by reminding Stefan Klos, Heiko Herrlich and Steffen Freund – all of whom played in the game – about that night.'

Rae also made sure Klos didn't forget that evening. 'Somebody gave me a photo of the goal when I was at Ibrox,' Rae, who played for Rangers from 2004 to 2006, said to the *Evening Times* in 2011, 'and it was only then that I realised I had been playing against Stefan. Of course, I made sure I took the picture into the dressing room to show him.'

In the semi-final, Scotland drew 0-0 with Sweden at Pittodrie in the first leg, only to lose 1-0 in the second leg in Örebro.

79

The Gentleman's Agreement – 1992

IN THE early 1980s, Andy Roxburgh, then working for the SFA, spoke with the young Watford player John Barnes.

'I actually approached Barnes to get him to play for Scotland long before England picked him,' Roxburgh told the *Daily Record* in December 1992. 'But Graham Taylor, then Watford manager, told me, "No way."' Barnes was born in Jamaica, so as a Commonwealth citizen he had the choice to represent any of the home nations.

In his autobiography, Barnes wrote, 'Maybe if Scotland had asked me before England, I would have represented Scotland. I would have tried as hard for Scotland as England. Was I more patriotic for England than I would have been for Scotland? No. To keep everyone happy throughout my international career, I always said that my only choice was England because England is where I settled, but that wasn't true.'

The gentleman's agreement between Scottish and English bosses that Commonwealth players must live in the given country would have made the move a non-starter in any case.

It was only in 1971 that players could also represent not only the country of their birth but also the countries of their parents' birth.

In the mid-1980s the British associations formulated the agreement that players could opt to play for the country of their birth, the country of their parents or, if they were born outside the UK and held a British passport, the country of their choice.

In December 1992 there was another change to the agreement, and it would allow Scotland to cap players if one grandparent had been born in the country.

SFA chief executive Jim Farry said, 'The possibility of players born in England or abroad being eligible for us because they have Scots grandparents has been discussed, and looks like being approved. It's very possible the home countries will reach agreement on a new rule before Christmas, and this will widen our choice.'

FIFA had no problems as their ruling was that the nationality of a player's parents or grandparents would qualify them for a country; it was only the agreement between the home nations that prevented the grandparent rule from being used.

The four nations all agreed. The decision came after a plea from Northern Ireland, feeling that the Republic of Ireland had an advantage as, for years, they had accepted a grandparent as a qualification for eligibility.

In 1991, Nigel Spackman, born in Hampshire, had been selected for a Scotland squad against Russia as his grandfather had been born in Edinburgh. However, after a complaint by England, the Rangers player was removed from the squad.

'So long as there's a bloodline, I'm for the change,' Roxburgh, by then the team manager, said. 'There is no doubt Scotland, being a small country, has been disadvantaged.'

Players who were capped for Scotland thanks to a grandparent include Neil Sullivan in 1997, Kris Commons in 2008 and Ché Adams in 2021.

When Craig Brown called up goalkeeper Sullivan, who went on to win 28 caps, he came in for criticism. 'I am as patriotic as the next Scot,' Brown said, 'and if it was left to me, it would be the player being born here or having Scottish parents. That is my personal opinion. But the grandparent rule has been adopted by all four British associations, and it is my job to find the best eligible players for Scotland.'

80

Portugal 5 Scotland 0 – 1993

28 April 1993
Estádio da Luz, Lisbon
World Cup qualifying Group 1
Attendance: 28,000

Portugal: Baía (Porto), Xavier (Estrela da Amadora), Jorge Costa (Porto), Rui Costa (Benfica) [Veloso (Benfica) 53], Couto (Porto), Oceano (Real Sociedad), Barros (AS Monaco), Sousa (Benfica), Semedo (Porto), Futre [C] (Benfica), Cadete (Sporting CP) [Domingos (Porto) 80]

Scotland: Goram (Rangers), Gough [C] (Rangers), McInally (Dundee United), McPherson (Rangers), McKimmie (Aberdeen), Levein (Hearts) [Nevin (Tranmere Rovers), 60], McStay (Celtic), McCoist (Rangers), Collins (Celtic) [Durrant (Rangers), 85), Gallacher (Blackburn Rovers), McCall (Rangers)

Referee: Sandor Pillai (Hungary)

Goals:
Barros (5, 70), Cadete (45, 72), Futre (67)

FOR THE qualifying campaign for the 1994 World Cup in the USA, Scotland were handed another tough group. It contained Italy, Switzerland and Portugal, with Estonia and Malta seen as the minnows.

By the time the away match with Portugal rolled around in April 1993, Scotland were third with four points from four matches, six behind the Swiss and the Italians, who had both played two games more.

After the 3-1 defeat to Switzerland, goalkeeper Andy Goram had clean sheets in his last three Scotland games – 0-0 draws with Portugal and Italy and a 3-0 win over Malta. 'He's really established himself as first-class,' Scotland boss Andy Roxburgh said.

Unfortunately, Lisbon was Goram's worst night in a Scotland shirt.

In his pre-match team talks in his days as boss at Liverpool, Bill Shankly would write off the opposition. 'They're all cissies, or they've got pink eyes,' Scottish defender Ron Yeats recalled. 'There's always something wrong with them.' In Lisbon, Roxburgh was doing his own version of Shankly's psychology, deriding the Portuguese team. 'They were crap, he told us,' wrote Richard Gough in his autobiography. 'They were running scared. They were afraid of us.' Gough wasn't buying it and dismissed it as nonsense.

Scotland were behind after five minutes when Paulo Sousa sent a through pass for Rui Barros to fire past Goram.

But Scotland did have chances. In the 24th minute Kevin Gallacher was played in by Paul McStay and slotted the ball home but was ruled offside, although TV pictures suggested he was onside. McPherson headed over the bar from five yards out when Vítor Baía parried an Ally McCoist header.

In the minutes before half-time, Barros put Paulo Futre through. His shot was mis-hit but fell for Jorge Cadete, who rifled home.

Midway through the second half, things got worse as Portugal scored three times between the 67th and 72nd minutes. Craig Levein, who was doing an effective marking job on Futre, was withdrawn for Pat Nevin in an attempt by Roxburgh to save the game. In the *Daily Telegraph*, William Johnson wrote, 'Within two minutes Futre had been transformed from an insignificant role to that of arch destroyer.' Futre scored the third and set up the fourth and fifth.

There was also a horror injury to deal with. Oceano nipped in ahead of McCoist as the Rangers striker teed up a shot, but

McCoist's shin met with the Real Sociedad defender's knee. McCoist should have been stretchered off but no stretchers were available. Dr Stewart Hillis and physio Hugh Allen carried him from the pitch. The injury turned out to be a broken leg which kept him out of football for six months, and the national team for over two years.

Roxburgh claimed the result was a freak, but the press were in agreement it was a dreadful performance all over the pitch, with only Stuart McCall in midfield getting pass marks. 'We were a spent force,' Roxburgh claimed, saying the defeat was like a boxer who had one fight too many.

'Not since the 7-0 defeat by Uruguay in Basel in 1954 have Scotland been so humiliated in a World Cup tie,' wrote Alex Cameron in the *Daily Record*.

'It was the worst night I had ever known in my career,' Richard Gough wrote. The game was Gough's 61st and final cap. Dave McPherson and Jim McInally had also played their last games for their country.

The relationship between Gough and Roxburgh had always been frosty. Gough didn't take to the former Clydebank and Falkirk striker as international manager from early on, comparing him unfavourably to his former international bosses, Jock Stein and Alex Ferguson. Gough quickly became frustrated with Roxburgh's need for team meetings, and what Gough felt was Roxburgh's habit of playing players out of their best positions.

Roxburgh would appoint Gough his captain, although the defender felt that was to make up for the manager telling the press he was fit for a match with Switzerland in 1991 when the Scottish medical team acknowledged he had a thigh injury. The fallout from that incident had Gough and Roxburgh arguing in the baggage waiting hall of Glasgow Airport in front of journalists and Customs staff.

In the aftermath of the Portugal game, Gough saw Roxburgh's comments to the media of 'A team died' as suggesting he was finished with the national side. He was left out for the next international, and although he was captain, Gough said Roxburgh hadn't informed him.

Their relationship by now had broken down completely, and Gough decided he couldn't play for Roxburgh any longer. In his book, published in September 1993, Gough wrote that he and 'a lot of players' felt that the team was run badly. 'We talk all the time about the shambles it all is,' he added.

Roxburgh was asked about Gough's comments by Michael Grant and Rob Robertson for their 2011 book *The Management*. 'I wouldn't even give it the time of day,' Roxburgh said. 'If things go wrong, some people go quiet, and other people start to say, "It wis'nae me, it was him." I don't bear grudges. I understand players being disappointed, supporters and the media too. If you don't deliver, people won't be happy with you.'

There were eight changes for the next match just over two weeks later away to Estonia, Colin Hendry winning the first of his 51 caps, as Scotland won 3-0.

Two days before the return with Estonia, Gough announced his international retirement, saying, 'I cannot continue playing for a manager I don't respect.' He said he would reconsider if a new manager were appointed. The timing, days before an important international, didn't go down well with anyone.

Roxburgh announced his resignation as manager, after the 1-1 draw with Switzerland in September 1993 confirmed that Scotland wouldn't qualify for USA 1994. 'How will history remember me?' Roxburgh said. 'I suppose they'll be happy to say he was a trier.'

81

The SFA vs Duncan Ferguson – 1994

DUNCAN FERGUSON made his debut for Scotland as a Dundee United player in the 1-0 friendly win over the United States in May 1992.

A £4m transfer to Rangers in July 1993 made him the most expensive player in Britain.

By the time Rangers played a league match at Ibrox with Raith Rovers on 16 April 1994, Ferguson had four caps for his country. A scissor kick against Germany at Ibrox in 1993, which was saved by Andreas Köpke, was the closest he had come to scoring.

As the 22-year-old Ferguson jostled for the ball with Raith defender Jock McStay, the pair pulled at each other. Referee Kenny Clark, a lawyer by profession, awarded a free kick to Raith and turned away to point in the direction of the kick. At that moment, Ferguson leaned in and head-butted McStay, who went down to the ground holding his face. Clark didn't witness the offence, so took no action. Ferguson remained on the field to score the third in Rangers' 4-0 win, his first goal for the club in 14 appearances.

Referee supervisor Mike Delaney criticised Clark in his report saying he was only 15 yards away and should have ordered Ferguson off.

Ferguson had been in trouble off the field previously, with three convictions for assault, and indeed was seven months into a year-long probation. Newspapers made headlines from the incident, and it was featured on *Scotsport* the following day.

On 4 May 1994 Ferguson was formally charged with assault. The SFA were keen to be seen cleaning up football, so were eager to discipline Ferguson. It was thought that with a court case pending, the SFA would hold its disciplinary over until legal proceedings had been resolved. But the SFA bureaucracy waits for no one. SFA chief executive Jim Farry said, 'The SFA is quite clear on this. It is a football matter. Let other people deal with their side of things.'

Jim McInally, Ferguson's former Dundee United and Scotland colleague, spoke to Alan Pattullo for his book *In Search of Duncan Ferguson*. He recalled Ferguson being out carousing with senior pros on Scotland's North American tour of 1992, where the striker won his first two caps. 'People like Farry had made up their mind about him there and then,' McInally said. 'They had him down as a headcase. But he was led astray a bit.'

The SFA handed Ferguson a 12-match ban. It was the biggest-ever ban for a single incident.

Donald Findlay QC criticised the SFA, saying they were 'wrong, acted unfairly and contrary to the player's wider interests since he is an accused person'.

The SFA cited precedent and a High Court ruling from 1984. Christopher Bernardi, an amateur player, faced a disciplinary committee ahead of a court appearance.

Rangers appealed, which allowed Ferguson, having served one game of the ban already, to play in the 1994 Scottish Cup Final defeat to his old club Dundee United.

Ferguson's lawyers fought his 12-match SFA-imposed ban, concerned that it would be prejudicial to his criminal trial. The SFA appeals committee decided to postpone the hearing pending the outcome of criminal proceedings.

In October, Ferguson joined Everton on loan. The move was an instant success. Fans took to him straight away and the Toffees moved away from their perilous position near the foot of the Premier League table to achieve safety.

In December of 1994, Ferguson earned his fifth cap in Athens for a European Championship qualifier where Scotland lost 1-0 to Greece. Craig Brown told Pattullo he recalled Farry treating

Ferguson as a 'non-person'. Brown himself was supportive of Duncan and keen to have him included in national squads.

Adjournments meant the trial was held over until May of 1995. Ferguson was found guilty only days before he would win the FA Cup with Everton.

Despite Everton chairman Peter Johnson writing a letter outlining the good work Duncan had been doing visiting children's hospitals and coaching youngsters, Sheriff Eccles was not inclined to sentence Ferguson to community service. In October 1995, Ferguson was sent to prison for three months. He went to Barlinnie and served half of that sentence. While inside, Everton continued to pay his wages.

With the court case concluded, the SFA could now go back to imposing its ban. It was now Everton who would lose Ferguson for the remaining 11 games of his ban. Everton suggested the SFA were running a 'witch hunt' against their player.

'There was a suggestion at the time that the football authorities had hung him out to dry,' Farry said to Pattullo in 2009. 'Not at all. In fact, quite the reverse was the case. Stringent efforts were made that it was retained within football.'

The Goodison Park club took the case to the Court of Session in Edinburgh. In February 1996, Lord Macfadyen decreed that because Ferguson had not been punished during the game itself, the SFA appeals committee could not impose a ban.

Craig Brown was set on including Ferguson in his Euro '96 squad. While Duncan had never really impressed in his Scotland appearances thus far, his bustling style and 6ft 3in frame were looked at as an option for the national team.

Ferguson pulled out of more squads with injury than stayed in them. He made his seventh and final Scotland appearance in the 0-0 draw with Estonia in the rearranged World Cup qualifier in Monaco. 'Subconsciously, his presence affected our style of play,' said Brown. 'There was a tendency to thump the ball up to him. It wasn't deliberate, it wasn't planned. It was a case of "There's big Duncan; let's send it high."'

In September 1997 Ferguson sent a brief letter to the SFA saying he didn't wish to be considered for the foreseeable future.

He always felt he had no backing from the SFA and, now, happy in his club career, he wanted no more to do with them.

After Farry left the SFA in 1999, it was hoped that Ferguson could be enticed back. He was adamant that he wouldn't return. It was a long-standing sore for Ferguson, and he couldn't be persuaded.

When Berti Vogts took over as Scotland manager, he went to see Everton play with a view to including him in the squad. 'I spoke to him and asked him why he did not want to play for Scotland,' Vogts told Pattullo. 'He told me he had a lot of problems with the SFA. The SFA, he said, did nothing for him.'

82

Gary McAllister's Penalty Miss – 1996

THE 1996 European Championship threw up the group match all Scotland fans wanted – England at Wembley. It would be the first time the sides had played against each other since England's 2-0 win at Hampden in May 1989.

Neither side had established dominance in the first half, which ended goalless, then with seven minutes gone of the second half Gary Neville crossed for Alan Shearer to head England in front.

In the 77th minute Gordon Durie ran across Tony Adams, only for the Arsenal man to pull him down. Scotland had a penalty and a way back into the match. 'It was an experienced striker's penalty,' Gary McAllister said in 1999.

'My first thought was that we had worked so hard to get a lead that, if we lost it so quickly, Scotland would have the edge,' England goalkeeper David Seaman wrote in his autobiography *Safe Hands*. 'I knew their penalty taker was Gary McAllister and that he normally puts them away. He had not taken one against me, but I had seen him take them against other keepers, and he had put them both sides, so there was no clue there.'

Seaman's plan was to watch the run-up, not the ball, just until the taker struck it, 'It is the best way of judging where he is going to place the ball, and it has worked pretty well for me.'

McAllister was confident. He had scored two penalties for Leeds United that season in 3-1 wins over Coventry City and Manchester United. He had also scored two penalties for Scotland previously, both in 1992, the first in a friendly against Canada and the second in a European Championship match against CIS.

McAllister put the ball down, began his run-up and just as he was about to connect with the ball, it moved. Like Tommy Walker in 1936, the ball had blown off its spot. Unlike Walker, McAllister didn't notice and took the kick.

'Whether he had teed it up so much it shifted as his foot went towards it, I don't know,' wrote Seaman, 'but he still managed a good strike on it. I guessed right, and I remember thinking as I was diving to my right, "I can't get my hands to this," but by moving my elbow, I got just enough on it to deflect the ball up and past the bar. It came off me at a strange angle, but probably the only one that would have seen it go to safety.'

Only 59 seconds after Seaman's save, Paul Gascoigne scored at the other end to give England a 2-0 win.

'You get little gusts at Wembley, even on such a sultry day,' McAllister said to journalist Patrick Barclay in 1999. 'So I suppose one of those must have done it. It was too late for me to stop, and, anyway, I struck the ball well enough – just a shade too low. I'd decided to put it in the middle of the goal and, as Seaman dived, it hit his trailing elbow and went over.'

But someone else wanted to take credit for the kick not going in. Uri Geller was a magician, illusionist and self-proclaimed psychic, most famous for bending spoons. Magician and sceptic James Randi once described him as 'a man maintaining a Wizard of Oz facade' who 'lives on the brink of exposure every minute'.

To *The Independent* in 2020, Geller said, 'I was approached by some British … well I won't mention who they were. But some very high-ranking, powered British people who were slightly concerned – you know, although England always beats Scotland most of the time – but they were concerned. They said, "Let's take Uri Geller, put him in a helicopter and let him fly around Wembley during the match," because they believed in my powers. When I heard Gary McAllister was going for the penalty, I said, "No way! I'm going to move the ball!" So when he started running towards the ball, I simply screamed out, "One, two, three, MOVE!" And lo and behold, the ball moved.'

Geller came to believe he had done something unethical. He later said, 'I feel so bad about it now. I love Scotland and the Scottish people. I promise that if Scotland ever plays England again, this time I will be on Scotland's side.'

McAllister's Scotland career didn't get the end his service should have allowed. A key reason Scotland qualified for the World Cup finals in France in 1998 was his nerveless penalty in Belarus, ensuring a 1-0 win in June 1997. He had to miss the tournament due to a long-term knee injury.

His return to the team came at Celtic Park at the end of March 1999 as Scotland took on the Czech Republic. Scotland struggled against a stronger side, and several spectators took their frustrations out on the captain. 'For the first time in my career, I felt pressure from outside affecting my game,' McAllister told Barclay. 'I'd never suffered from doubts – and never have since – but out there, it was almost surreal. Looking back, I realise it wasn't the whole crowd, and people have told me it was only a minority. But to me, it sounded like a hundred thousand.'

In the 63rd minute, McAllister was substituted. 'I decided there and then that I didn't need the aggravation any more. It was the culmination of a lot of things – a general lack of appreciation, a long campaign by the tabloids to get younger guys in midfield. The same sort of thing happened to other people in the past. Paul McStay, for instance, was hounded out in the end after a fine career.'

McAllister felt that being captain was part of the problem. He was the public face of the team, and each time he was in front of the press he was asked to justify his presence in the team, something he didn't feel he needed to do. 'The Czech game was the final straw. I'd always been used to geeing people up, but that night, in my first game back, I needed a wee bit of help and understanding myself. Instead, I got aggravation. It was time to quit.'

'I met him recently, and he said he was sorry,' McAllister said of Geller to the *Sunday Telegraph* in 2002. 'I said it was OK – I'd always blamed the wind.'

83

Estonia Fail to Arrive – 1996

THE WORLD Cup qualifying Group 4 match at the Kadriorg Stadium in Tallinn was scheduled to start at 6.45pm local time on 9 October 1996.

The Scottish party had seen the floodlights and knew that they were not up to the standard required. The problem was one set of lights to the left of the stand, which emitted a low-level glare.

FIFA commissioner Jean-Marie Gantenbein initially disagreed, but after a late-night fax from Jim Farry, the SFA chief executive, to Sepp Blatter, general secretary of FIFA, citing regulations and articles, Gantenbein came around to the Scots' way of thinking. A ruling was made that the kick-off time would be brought forward to 1pm.

Scotland arrived at the ground for the new kick-off time, went on to the pitch for a pre-match warm-up, and then, in the dressing room, manager Craig Brown went through the formation and tactics. 'He made us prepare for it properly,' said striker John McGinlay.

However, the Estonian team were still adhering to the original kick-off time and remained at their training camp, 50 miles away, eating a pre-match meal.

At 1pm the Serbian referee Miroslav Radoman blew his whistle to start the game. Billy Dodds, who was making his debut, played the ball forward to captain John Collins who walked it into the Estonian half, then Radoman blew his whistle to end the game. It had lasted for three seconds.

The Tartan Army, as ever, looked on the bright side, singing, 'One team in Tallinn, there's only one team in Tallinn' and coming on to the park for a kickabout once the farce had ended.

The Estonian team turned up 90 minutes before the original kick-off time.

Estonia's Icelandic manager Teitur Thordarson said, 'I feel terrible. It was too late for us to change the time when we were told. We were looking forward to playing Scotland; we were ready for the match, and the players were fit.'

Keith Cooper, a FIFA spokesman, indicated that the match would be awarded to Scotland, 'FIFA's regulations state that if one team does not report for a match, it shall be considered as having lost, and the three points shall be awarded to their opponents with a score of 3-0.'

Estonia appealed, supported by group rivals Sweden and Austria, and the game was ordered to be replayed. 'Thus the team that had complied with FIFA rules appeared to be penalised, while the team that didn't had a second chance,' wrote Craig Brown in his autobiography.

Blatter said, 'The decision to replay the match has been taken in a sporting spirit as Estonia had wanted to play the game and did not voluntarily refuse to play. The point was that they did not have enough time to reorganise the arrangements after receiving a fax from FIFA at nine o'clock in the morning, and this was taken into account by FIFA.'

There was actually precedent for the situation. For the November 1973 World Cup qualifier in Santiago, the Soviet Union boycotted their match against Chile due to their opposition to the coup that overthrew Marxist Chilean President Salvador Allende.

FIFA disqualified the Soviets but required that even with no opponents, the Chileans had to score a goal in order to progress. Their players waved to supporters and then passed the ball down the field nine times before scoring into the unguarded net, giving them a 1-0 victory. The 'game' lasted for 19 seconds.

Gary McAllister was now required to serve his one-match suspension in the next match, which was against Sweden, as the Estonia fixture would no longer count.

Estonian FA vice-president Aiva Pholack said, 'Scotland have been very unsporting and unfair – they have been bloody-minded and they have bullied a small country. I also think they leaned on the officials – I don't think they wanted this game to go ahead from the start.'

'I was appalled by claims we were afraid to play as we had six players unfit,' Brown said to the *Daily Record*. 'We have six players unfit for every game.'

Although Brown said after the match that all players would receive a cap, the SFA agreed that those who had been selected would not be formally credited with an international appearance. Nevertheless, they would receive the normal appearance fee.

The match was replayed in February 1997 in Monaco, where an uninspired Scotland were held to a 0-0 draw.

84

Julie Fleeting

121 caps, 116 goals (1996–2015)

THROUGHOUT JULIE Fleeting's career, the women's game evolved – and she was at the centre of the changes. She excelled at the top level as the game rose from being a hobby to becoming a viable option for young girls to make a career.

The daughter of Jim Fleeting, who played for Ayr United in the 1970s and 80s, Julie began her football career at the age of nine, playing with a boys' club, until the age of 12 when rules said she had to play with an all-girls team. She joined Prestwick Girls, which later became Ayr United Ladies. 'It was the first time I'd come across girls who shared the same hobby,' she said in 2008.

Her exceptional talent was quickly recognised by her country. She was called up to the Scotland under-16 team at the age of 14, while her senior debut came against Wales in 1996 when she was only 15. She also played hockey for her school and excelled at basketball, being selected for both the Ayrshire and West District under-15 girls' teams.

At 16, Julie was part of the Scotland team who played three games in Brazil, and although they lost all three heavily, she believed it was an educational experience. 'It was a brilliant opportunity,' she told the *Daily Record*, 'the standard of women's football over there is very good.'

In May 1998, Fleeting scored the equaliser as Scotland drew 1-1 with the Czech Republic in their penultimate qualifying match for the 1999 FIFA Women's World Cup. It meant that Scotland, playing at the B level and unable to qualify directly, had to beat Lithuania at Scotstoun Stadium a week later by 17 clear goals in order to make a play-off. Going into injury time, Scotland were 16-0 up. Just as the referee was about to blow the final whistle, Fleeting headed the 17th. Scotland lost a two-legged play-off with Spain.

After completing a BEd in physical education at Moray House in Edinburgh, at the age of 21, she moved to the US to join San Diego Spirit, becoming the first Scottish woman to play in the professional WUSA league. Her team-mates nicknamed her 'Shrek' after the Scottish-accented Disney character. 'I'm glad that one hasn't stuck,' she said to *The Californian* in 2003.

Spirit coach Omid Namazi described her as the closest thing they had to a complete player. 'She does everything well. She can hold the ball, she can get by people on the dribbles, she has an excellent shot with both feet. There's really no weakness to her game. It's just been a joy to watch her.'

In 2003, by now the captain of her country, Fleeting had moved back to Scotland with Ross County Ladies. She signed for Arsenal in 2004 and was voted as the FA Women's Players' Player of the Year the following year.

Fleeting scored 130 goals in 141 appearances for Arsenal. Vic Akers, who signed her, told Arseblog, 'She was in the top echelons of all the forwards I managed.'

In an unusual arrangement, Fleeting, who had a full-time job as a PE teacher in Scotland, flew to England every Sunday to play with the team but never trained with them. 'I know she felt a bit strange doing that,' Akers said, 'but it was the only way we could get her to play for us, and we were prepared to do it.'

During the Euro 2009 qualifiers, Fleeting hit her 100th goal, against Slovakia, on 27 October 2007 and won her 100th cap against Denmark four days later. She was awarded the MBE for services to women's football in 2008. Brief spells in Scotland with Kilwinning Ladies, Celtic Ladies and Glasgow City wound down her playing career.

Julie played her final Scotland international in a 4-0 win over Northern Ireland in February 2015, three and a half years after her previous appearance.

85

Hugh McIlvanney

ONE OF the most erudite commentators on Scottish football over the years was the late Hugh McIlvanney. He was respected by managers, players and fellow journalists alike and remains the benchmark for many of today's sports reporters. In fact, many felt he was the best sportswriter of his era, and Scottish football was richer for his having reported on it for many years.

McIlvanney had done some sports reporting for his first newspaper, the *Kilmarnock Standard*, but as he told Donald Trelford in 1993, 'The fear of ending up as a fitba writer in Scotland was considerable.' It was his editor at *The Scotsman*, Alistair Dunnett – McIlvanney described him as 'a rather exceptional man' – who asked Hugh to write about sport and convinced him it was a worthwhile pursuit. Writing not only on football but also notably on boxing and horse racing, McIlvanney set a standard few others could match.

The journalist and author Paul Howard said in 2020 of McIlvanney, 'You could give him the same 12 words as the rest of us, and he could do something more extraordinary than we could even dream of doing with those 12 words.'

'I've never met anyone with the command of the English language Hugh had,' Alex Ferguson once said. 'I've probably met people without knowing the stretch of their intelligence but McIlvanney's was there every week in the papers.'

In 30 years of writing for *The Observer* and 23 years with the *Sunday Times*, McIlvanney would say that from time to time, he was plagued by doubts if sports writing was a proper job for a grown-up, adding, 'But I am comforted by the thought that in writing about sport, it is usually easier to deal in an acceptable form of truth than it is in other forms of journalism.'

McIlvanney was regarded as a football man by those who knew the sport. He was close not only to Ferguson but to those other giants of Scottish football management, Bill Shankly, Jock Stein and Matt Busby.

On the Sunday after Stein's tragic death, McIlvanney began his tribute to him with the words, 'The larcenous nature of death, its habit of breaking in on us when we are least prepared and stealing the irreplaceable, has seldom been more sickeningly experienced than at Ninian Park in Cardiff on Tuesday night.'

In the pages of the *Sunday Times* in 1994 McIlvanney also eulogised Sir Matt Busby, writing, 'If Busby had stood dressed for the pit, and somebody alongside him in the room had worn ermine, there would have been no difficulty about deciding who was special. Granting him a knighthood did not elevate him. It raised, however briefly, the whole dubious phenomenon of the honours system.'

In 1997 McIlvanney wrote and presented *The Football Men*, a three-part programme for BBC's *Arena* documentary series on Stein, Shankly and Busby. 'Their daily experiences, whether of politics, sectarianism, work or football, had a great intensity about them,' he said to the *Liverpool Echo*. 'Life in that tiny corner of Scotland taught them about being in a place of pressure and coming through it without losing self-respect. It equipped them to understand the need for mutual tolerance and in their careers shaped them as moral men who put the emphasis on family.'

In the series, he described Shankly's appeal, 'In 60s Liverpool Bill Shankly's ability to be ordinary and magical at the same time – the messiah next door – made him irresistible.'

McIlvanney was there in Argentina to witness and report on the Scottish disasters at the 1978 World Cup. 'If there is ever a World Cup for self-destructiveness, few nations will have the nerve to challenge the Scots,' he wrote shortly after Willie Johnstone had been sent home for use of a banned substance. 'It seems astonishing that the race have never produced a kamikaze pilot, but perhaps the explanation is that all the volunteers insisted on attacking sewage farms.'

For his 1999 autobiography, Ferguson went to Hugh to write the book with him, working on the project together over 18 months. Ferguson, a man who put fear into generations of footballers, told of the discussion they had during the writing when Ferguson insisted that Robert Burns was a greater writer than William Shakespeare. 'Don't be so fucking stupid' was McIlvanney's reply.

86

Tom Boyd

72 caps, 1 goal (1990–2001)

TOM BOYD'S debut came in September 1990 in a European Championship qualifier at home to Romania, when he came on as a substitute for Bobby Connor. The following month Boyd started against Switzerland at Hampden.

In 1991 Boyd captained Motherwell to a famous Scottish Cup win, his last game for the club before making the move to Chelsea. At Stamford Bridge he played alongside future Scotland manager Steve Clarke. He made his debut in the First Division against Wimbledon in August 1991, but by February 1992 he was heading back across the border to join Celtic in a swap deal with Tony Cascarino.

Boyd was part of the Scotland squad travelling to Sweden for the 1992 European Championship. By the time he got on the pitch, Scotland had been eliminated from the tournament after losses to the Netherlands and Germany. Boyd, though, played his part in the 3-0 win over the CIS, beginning the move that led to Brian McClair scoring Scotland's second.

At the European Championship in 1996, Boyd played all three of Scotland's games. 'We've come down here with the attitude of thinking we can win the whole thing,' Boyd said to the *Daily Record* after Scotland's backs-to-the-wall performance in drawing 0-0 with the Netherlands. Of course, it wasn't to be as Scotland failed to qualify from the group.

Boyd played in all the qualifying matches in the campaign to reach the 1998 World Cup finals, scoring his only international goal along the way in a 2-0 win over Estonia at Rugby Park in March 1997. With the 2-0 win over Latvia, Scotland qualified for France. The result was earned on the occasion of Boyd's 50th cap. 'Doing it at Celtic Park as well has ensured it will be a day I will never forget,' he said.

Scotland opened the 1998 World Cup with a group match against holders Brazil. It was remembered for all the wrong reasons for Boyd.

Scotland had gone a goal down after four minutes but had levelled the game through a John Collins penalty. In the second half, Dunga played a ball into the penalty area which fell to Cafu, who hit a shot from just outside the six-yard box. Jim Leighton parried the ball but it came off the in-rushing Boyd and went into the Scotland net.

'Of course it was devastating at the time,' Boyd said to the *Daily Record* in 2013. 'And I get reminded of it from time to time when anniversaries of the game come up, but I've never really been too hard on myself about it because there was nothing I could have done to avoid it. If I had been short with a pass-back or something, I could blame myself, but what happened was just bad luck, plain and simple.'

Scotland closed the tournament out with a devastating 3-0 defeat to Morocco.

'We were close to getting a draw against Brazil in the first match,' said Boyd, 'and I think, with the level of performances in those two games, we went out and underestimated Morocco. That was a big mistake because they were a good side, and we simply didn't turn up. We lost 3-0, and the defeat could have been heavier. It was a sickening way to end the tournament. That was the major disappointment for me, not scoring the own goal against Brazil.'

Boyd's last appearance for Scotland was in a 2-0 World Cup qualifying loss to Belgium in September 2001.

With 72 caps, Boyd sits seventh on the list of all-time capped players.

87

Jim Leighton

91 caps, 42 clean sheets (1982–1998)

JIM LEIGHTON'S Scotland career lasted three days short of 16 years and included several highs and lows.

Beginning his career with Dalry Thistle, Leighton benefitted from working there with ex-Denmark and Rangers goalkeeper Erik Sørensen, who 'made it his business to lick my skinny 17-year-old frame into shape', Leighton wrote in his autobiography *In the Firing Line*. 'And he showed no mercy.'

The Ayrshire Juniors system was a tough place to learn the goalkeeper's trade, but Leighton benefitted from the environment. Scout Bobby Calder spotted him and Leighton was soon off to join Aberdeen.

Bobby Clark, the incumbent in goal at Pittodrie, developed a serious problem with his back, and Leighton became the regular choice from the 1980/81 season. Showing up well for Scotland's under-21s, Jim was taken to the 1982 World Cup in Spain as an uncapped player. Although he didn't appear in the finals, he made his international debut in Scotland's first game after Spain, keeping a clean sheet in a 2-0 win over East Germany at Hampden.

George Wood, who Leighton had superseded in the race to replace Rough, told *Match Weekly* he believed Leighton could be the first choice for ten years. 'He's very agile and quick around the box,' Wood said. 'He also handles really well – in the air and on the ground – and he wants to catch everything.'

Scotland didn't make it through to the European Championship of 1984, but Leighton played in all six World

Cup qualifiers and the two play-off matches that saw Scotland reach Mexico in 1986.

Leighton played in all three matches – defeats to Denmark and West Germany and a goalless draw with Uruguay, which hurt most. 'I could hardly believe that some members of our squad were actually quite happy about our failure,' he said about the dressing room after the last group game. 'All they were interested in was going on holiday. I wanted to bang their heads against the wall until they shed tears like the ones in my eyes.'

Leighton, now a Manchester United player, played in seven of the qualifiers for Italy 1990. Going into the last qualifier at Hampden against Norway, Scotland needed just a point to secure their place. It was one of the more disappointing nights of Leighton's international career.

Scotland were leading thanks to an Ally McCoist goal going into injury time. Erland Johnsen of Bayern Munich then struck a shot from around 40 yards out. Leighton reflected, 'I was convinced the ball was heading past the post when it suddenly took a tremendous bend. I've never seen anything like it before or since, for it must have moved in the air a good four yards before leaving me looking badly at fault as it went into the net.' The final whistle sounded moments later, however, and Scotland were through to their fifth World Cup finals in a row. Twenty years later Leighton went on to the Norwegian TV show *Golden Goal* alongside Johnsen to recreate the goal.

By the time the finals came around, Leighton had lost his first-team place at Manchester United. Leighton had a poor performance in the 1990 FA Cup Final as United drew 3-3 with Crystal Palace, and manager Alex Ferguson dropped him for the replay.

It strengthened Leighton's resolve to do well for his country, but a 1-0 loss to Costa Rica was the worst start possible. Scotland rallied and beat Sweden 2-1, meaning a draw with Brazil in the third group game could take them through to the knockout stages. There were only eight minutes remaining when Leighton failed to deal with a shot from Alemão, and Müller followed up to score. 'It was a goalkeeping error that had opened the door for

Brazil,' Leighton wrote, 'and it took me a long time to get over it.' Leighton memorably kicked his goalpost in frustration.

Returning to his club, Leighton played only once in the 1990/91 season, against Fourth Division Halifax in the League Cup. Andy Goram, who had made his debut in 1985, had now emerged as a top-class goalkeeper and Scotland's first choice. 'Rivalry doesn't really exist between us,' Leighton said in 1990. 'It's only the newspapers that suggest otherwise.' In 1991 Goram said similarly, 'Jim and I were not rivals in any sense. We became good friends, and he was always passing on tips.'

At this point, the 32-year-old Leighton could have called time on his career, at international level at least, but he didn't give up. There were loan spells at Arsenal and Reading before effectively restarting his career at Dundee.

'I suppose I'm a stubborn so-and-so,' Leighton told author and podcaster Ally Begg in 2022. 'There were so many people writing me off. I was desperate to prove people wrong.' Moving to Hibs, Leighton felt wanted for the first time in years, and within months he was back in a Scotland jersey.

Having missed 28 internationals, Leighton returned to the side for the World Cup qualifier against Malta on 17 November 1993, where on his 59th appearance he kept a clean sheet in a 2-0 win.

Between that date and the 1996 European Championship, Leighton played 16 internationals to Goram's eight, but it was the Rangers man who played all three matches in the tournament in England.

Leighton was the regular choice, though, for the 1998 World Cup qualifiers and played in all three games at the finals in France.

Leighton's final cap was at the age of 40 on 10 October 1998, in a 3-2 win over Estonia. His total of 91 caps is currently second only to Kenny Dalglish's record of 102.

88

Berti Vogts

Scotland manager 2002–2004

A LACKLUSTRE 2-1 win over Latvia in October 2001 confirmed what Scotland fans had known for some time: the team hadn't done enough to qualify for the 2002 World Cup. Scotland failed to reach two major tournaments in a row for the first time in 30 years, and manager Craig Brown's tenure was at an end.

The SFA now felt the time was right to appoint a foreign manager for the first time in the nation's history.

A three-man shortlist was drawn up by SFA chief executive David Taylor. The list included Italian Nevio Scala and Frenchman Philippe Troussier, then in charge of Japan, and German Berti Vogts.

Vogts's only club was Borussia Mönchengladbach, where he played from 1965 to 1979, winning 96 caps for West Germany along the way. During his playing career he acquired the nickname 'Der Terrier' due to his persistent ankle-biting of opponents, proving his worth to his team by preventing the opposition's most dangerous player from excelling.

The greatest example of this was the 1974 World Cup Final, when detailed to nullify Johan Cruyff; he was so effective that Cruyff dropped into defence and spent much of the match in his own half. 'Good but very unfair' was how Cruyff described Vogts's game.

'Thousands of footballers were much more talented than me,' Vogts once said. 'But I was more driven.'

He had played against Scotland four times, in the pair of World Cup qualifiers in 1969 and in friendlies in 1973 and 1974.

Vogts was assistant to Franz Beckenbauer with West Germany for four years and was Beckenbauer's handpicked successor, taking over just after they had won the 1990 World Cup. The East and West had unified, strengthening the pool of players Vogts had at his disposal.

In eight years, he took Germany to two European Championship finals, losing in 1992 to Denmark and beating the Czech Republic at Wembley in 1996.

In that time Vogts managed against Scotland twice, a 2-0 victory in Euro '92 and a 1-0 friendly win at Ibrox in 1993.

For that friendly Vogts turned up in Glasgow with a bottle of champagne for each member of Scotland's squad who had been at the European Championship in Sweden as a thank you for beating the CIS, which enabled Germany to reach the semi-finals. 'I've never seen a weak Scottish team yet,' he said before the game as Andy Roxburgh fielded a largely inexperienced side that featured three debutants.

In 1998 Vogts left the Germany job after two uninspiring autumn friendlies. The writing was on the wall in July when the Germans fell to their worst defeat in 30 years, the 3-0 loss to Croatia in the 1998 World Cup quarter-final.

Vogts took two years out of management before spending six months at Bayer Leverkusen and five months as boss of Kuwait.

On 15 February 2002 the SFA unveiled Vogts as Scotland's new coach. Vogts, the first foreigner to hold the post, officially took charge on 1 March. He was handed a four-year contract worth more than £2m.

One of Vogts's first actions was to speak with Paul Lambert to ask him to reconsider his decision to retire from international football. Vogts was familiar with Lambert due to the midfielder's season with Borussia Dortmund.

Lambert's recall to the Scotland team under Craig Brown for games against Latvia and Estonia in October 1996, 16 months after his previous cap, was down to a phone call Vogts made. 'Berti told me he had seen Paul play three times for Dortmund and that he had been outstanding each time,' Brown told the press at the time.

While Lambert was happy to return, Vogts also tried unsuccessfully to get Gary McAllister and Duncan Ferguson to change their minds about their own international retirements.

The first match in Vogts's reign was a Paris friendly against France. Scotland went down to a crushing 5-0 defeat to a strong French side. 'It was an experience for the players,' Vogts said afterwards.

Defeats in friendlies to Nigeria, South Korea, South Africa and Denmark followed. The only win Vogts enjoyed in his first six months in charge was a 4-0 triumph over the Hong Kong League, which the SFA deemed a full international.

His first competitive game was the Euro qualifier away to the Faroe Islands, ranked 163rd in the world. Down 2-0 after 12 minutes, it was a disconsolate Scotland team heading into the dressing room at half-time.

Barry Ferguson said that Vogts had nothing to say, 'I think he was just taken aback.' But there were strong personalities in the team. 'Lambo [Paul Lambert], the most senior player in the squad, stood up and had a bang at everybody,' said Ferguson, 'Which I quite liked. That got me fired up. There were a few ding-dongs in terms of players having a go at each other and that was the best thing that could have happened.'

Second-half goals from Lambert and Ferguson gave Scotland a face-saving draw.

One qualifier in, the talk had already begun in the press and among the support over whether Vogts should go.

A win against Iceland followed, and despite some defeats and dispiriting draws in friendlies along the way, Vogts's reputation improved as he guided Scotland to a European Championship play-off where they met the Netherlands. A 1-0 win in the first leg was eclipsed by a 6-0 defeat in the second leg.

More friendly defeats followed, including a 4-0 hammering by Wales. 'They [the press] complained that Craig didn't bring young players through,' defender Christian Dailly said to *The Independent*. 'When Berti did experiment, they jumped on him because we weren't winning friendlies.' By the time the World Cup qualifiers began in September 2004, Vogts knew he was on borrowed time.

A 0-0 draw at home to Slovenia wasn't the best start, and it was only to get worse.

The 1-0 defeat to Norway in October was Scotland's first home defeat in World Cup qualifying since a loss to Wales in 1985, which in itself was the first since Poland's 2-1 win in October 1965. James McFadden stopped a net-bound Claus Lundekvam header with his hand. He was sent off, and Steffen Iversen netted the penalty.

The 1-1 draw away to Moldova on 13 October 2004 was Vogts's last match in charge. He resigned on Monday, 1 November, he said, 'with great reluctance'. His statement spoke of the warmth he experienced from the people of Scotland. At the same time, he also stated, 'I must say that the major factor in this decision has been the disgraceful abuse I have suffered, especially of late.' These supporters, Vogts claimed, had been influenced by the 'unacceptable power of the tabloid press'.

In his 32 games in charge Vogts oversaw nine wins, seven draws and 16 defeats, using 64 players in total, a number not suggesting consistency.

Despite Vogts's poor record as manager, it's only fair to look at some of his successes. He wasn't afraid to blood new talent. Gary Caldwell, James McFadden, Darren Fletcher and David Marshall were all aged only 19 when Vogts handed them their full debuts. Craig Gordon and Andy Webster were aged 21.

Vogts, who'll never be looked on with much affection by the Scottish support, remains the only foreigner to manage the Scottish team.

89

Scotland 1 Netherlands 0 – 2003

15 November 2003
Hampden Park, Glasgow
European Championship play-off first leg
Attendance: 50,670

Scotland: Douglas (Celtic), McNamara (Celtic), Naysmith (Everton), Pressley (Hearts), Wilkie (Dundee), Ferguson [C] (Blackburn Rovers), Fletcher (Manchester United), Dailly (West Ham United), Dickov (Leicester City) [Miller (Wolves), 65], McFadden (Everton) [Hutchison (West Ham United), 89], McCann (Southampton) [Pearson (Motherwell), 70]

Holland: Van der Sar (Fulham), Ooijer (PSV Eindhoven), Stam (Lazio), De Boer [C] (Galatasaray), Van Bronckhorst (Barcelona) [Seedorf (Milan), 46], Cocu (Barcelona), Van der Meijde (Inter Milan), Davids (Juventus) [Van der Vaart (Ajax), 61], Van Nistelrooy (Manchester United), Kluivert (Barcelona) [Makaay (Bayern Munich), 77], Overmars (Barcelona)

Referee: Terje Hauge (Norway)

Goal:
McFadden (21)

'I think the Dutch are there for the taking. I don't see why we should fear them.'

James McFadden

ON THE last day of Euro 2004 qualifying in Group 5, Lithuania were only one point behind Scotland, and while a draw at Hampden would suffice, it was a huge relief when Darren Fletcher cracked in his first goal for his country to seal second place.

The runners-up spot meant a two-legged play-off against the Netherlands. It wasn't a tie in which Scotland were much fancied. The Dutch, though, had missed out on a spot at the 2002 World Cup, drawing with and losing to the Republic of Ireland in their qualifying group. 'Because of what happened against Ireland, there will not be even half a per cent underestimating Scotland,' winger Marc Overmars said to *The Guardian*. Overmars felt the big pitch at Hampden would suit their technical abilities.

The Dutch were managed by Dick Advocaat, who had spent three years in charge at Rangers.

Berti Vogts's team had a trio of youngsters who would go on to become the mainstays of Scotland's team for several years. Nineteen-year-old Darren Fletcher, 'the biggest young talent in the United Kingdom' according to Vogts, was winning his third cap, while James McFadden, who had moved from Motherwell to Everton only months earlier, was winning his eighth cap at the age of 20. On the bench was Kenny Miller, who had six caps.

There were also players in their early and mid-20s, such as Gary Naysmith, Lee Wilkie and Barry Ferguson. It all added up to optimism for the future. 'I have to cultivate the youngsters,' Vogts said to *The Guardian*. 'We have to be patient, but it suddenly looks very positive.'

Vogts's pre-match instructions to his team were to close them down, play 'Scottish-style' football and put pressure on their defence and midfield. Nullify the midfield was the key, said Vogts. He invoked his own performance in the 1974 World Cup Final against the Netherlands, where his West German side came from an early goal down to win 2-1. 'I had to do a job against Johan Cruyff, and my boys have to do their jobs now,' he said.

Qualifying for the finals in Portugal would, Vogts said, be a bigger achievement for him than winning Euro '96 as manager of Germany.

Fletcher, a club-mate of Dutch striker Ruud van Nistelrooy at Manchester United, said he relished playing against players of that calibre. 'In a few years, he could be our playmaker,' Vogts said of Fletcher.

In the 21st minute Scotland forced what would be their only corner of the match. Holland would win 11. McFadden's kick was headed straight back out to him by Patrick Kluivert. He collected the ball and touched it outside to his left. He gave a left-footed pass to Fletcher, then ran inside the box. Fletcher immediately gave him the ball back with a deft back-heel. McFadden took two quick touches to make himself more room, then hit a shot that lifted him up off the turf. It hit Frank de Boer and flew into the net. Hampden erupted.

The Netherlands fought hard for an equaliser, which wouldn't come. They had 20 shots on Rab Douglas's goal, with 12 on target. Scotland defended in a pack and Christian Dailly, earning his 50th cap – the 24th Scottish player to reach the milestone – was the man of the match.

Paul Lambert, the captain, then out injured, called the win 'arguably the greatest result in the history of Scottish football'.

There was a second leg to come, and it would only have been the most positive Scotland fan who thought the team had one foot in the finals. At best the win ensured that Scotland could be competitive in the second leg in Amsterdam four days later.

Unfortunately, the Netherlands carried on where they had left off in looking for goals. Wesley Sneijder pulled the strings and Van Nistelrooy benefitted as the Dutch went 3-0 up after 34 minutes, eventually winning 6-0 with the Old Trafford man netting a hat-trick.

'I've spoken with [Manchester United's Welsh winger] Ryan Giggs,' Fletcher said, 'and he admits that he'd be really disappointed if he never made it to a championship. But I look around me, and I know I'll be playing in a major finals with Scotland at some stage.'

90

James McFadden from 35 Yards – 2007

SCOTLAND'S WIN over France at Hampden in October 2006 was as well earned as it was unlikely; France had been beaten just once in 40 previous qualifiers, and the return match in Paris on 12 September 2007 was where they would get their revenge. Scotland doing the double over the World Cup runners-up was seen as unlikely.

That the scoreline stayed at 0-0 for so long was often down to the Scottish defence and, in particular, goalkeeper Craig Gordon. He made two great saves in the 54th minute from Franck Ribéry and two minutes later from Nicolas Anelka.

In the 64th minute Gordon cleared the ball upfield. It dropped in midfield to James McFadden, who was facing his own goal. With space around him, he had time and room to turn and take a touch. He looked up and hit the ball for the French goal. Barry Ferguson had started to run and was looking for a pass. 'I shouted, "What the fuck are you doing?"' Ferguson said after the game. 'When I saw he was going to try his luck from that distance, I was giving him pelters.' The ball swerved slightly and although goalkeeper Mickaël Landreau got a palm to it, the shot flew into the net.

In *The Guardian*'s minute-by-minute report, Scott Murray wrote, 'Landreau should have done better, as his hand bends back like a damp sheet of A3 paper.'

The goal gave Scotland a famous 1-0 win.

French boss Raymond Domenech said, 'Instead of looking for faults in our defence or goalkeeper, why not give a little congratulations to McFadden for the way he struck the ball at the goal. No one expected him to hit the ball from that distance. He got the ball and struck it so quickly, so cleanly, that before we knew it, the ball was in the back of the net. The ball was going straight until it got to goal, and it swerved at the last minute. Mickaël did well to get a hand to it because it was a marvellous strike, one of the best I have seen.'

When asked by *The Scotsman* how he did it, McFadden said, 'I don't know, it was just one of those things. You just do it and think about it later. I got a touch and a turn, and there was nobody there, so I thought I may as well have a go.'

Scotland flew back to Glasgow after the game and landed in the early hours. McFadden went straight home to his parents. In the kind of tale the *Daily Record* are often fond of, the newspaper reported McFadden's mum Anne-Marie as saying, 'All he wanted was a roll and Lorne sausage and a cup of tea. That's just the kind of boy James is. I'd been out and bought a bottle of champagne for him, but he didn't want a glass.' Anne-Marie was, of course, naturally delighted, 'I always try to give James as much support as I can. It's a great feeling to see your son's dreams come true.'

The *Record* also canvassed several Scottish celebrities, many of whom didn't even watch the game, and included a quote from Janette Krankie, who said, 'It was fandabidozi.'

'People obviously talk about the Paris goal but you know what, up until I was about 14 I didn't have a lot of power,' McFadden said to the *Daily Record* in 2020. 'I didn't have a powerful shot as I got older either. As a kid I found it hard to get the ball off the ground. So I didn't take too many shots from a distance. I'd always try to use my dribbling instead. I wouldn't even try long-range passes. From corners, I struggled to get purchase on the ball until I gradually mastered my technique.'

Archie Gemmill, the scorer of another iconic goal for Scotland, was asked for comment. 'His goal was better than mine when you consider what was at stake,' Archie told the *Evening*

Standard. 'Three points were hanging on it, and that makes it a very important goal. It was a wonderful moment of magic.'

To *The Herald* in 2018, McFadden said, 'I hate talking about the goal I scored against France because it meant nothing – we never qualified.'

91

Scotland 1 Italy 2 – 2007

17 November 2007
Hampden Park
European Championship qualifying Group B
Attendance: 51,301

Scotland: Gordon (Sunderland), Hutton (Rangers), Naysmith (Sheffield United), McManus (Celtic), Weir (Rangers), Ferguson [C] (Rangers), Fletcher (Manchester United), McCulloch (Rangers) [Boyd (Rangers), 90+2], McFadden (Everton), Hartley (Celtic), Brown (Celtic) [Miller (Derby County), 74]

Italy: Buffon (Juventus), Panucci (Roma), Cannavaro [C] (Real Madrid), Barzagli (Palermo), Zambrotta (Barcelona), Camoranesi (Juventus) [Chiellini (Juventus), 83], Gattuso (Milan) [De Rossi (Roma), 87], Pirlo (Milan), Di Natale (Udinese) [Iaquinta (Juventus), 68], Toni (Bayern Munich), Abrosini (Milan)

Referee: Manuel Enrique Mejuto González (Langreo, Spain)

Goals:
Scotland – Ferguson (65)
Italy – Toni (2), Panucci (90)

'We battered them.'

Alex McLeish

THE DRAW for Group B hadn't been kind to Scotland. They were placed alongside World Cup holders Italy, runners-up France and quarter-finalists Ukraine. The seven-team group was completed by Georgia, Lithuania and the Faroe Islands.

Scotland went into the penultimate group match against Georgia away on top of the group with 24 points, one ahead of Italy and two more than France, meaning four more points would take them through. But a 2-0 defeat to Georgia left Scotland needing a win in the final match against Italy. A draw might be enough, but only if France lost in their last game against Ukraine.

In the *Daily Telegraph*, Alan Hansen wrote that qualification would be 'an achievement unparalleled in the country's history'. Italy had never won in Scotland previously, with a defeat in 1965 and two subsequent draws.

There was a real cup final build-up to the match. There was no club football the week before, so the focus was on this game. 'I'm used to Rangers fans saying "good luck" and certain other fans not being quite as complimentary,' Barry Ferguson said. 'But this time, everyone you meet is right up for it. It's something I've never experienced before.' The 5pm kick-off time did much to put those watching the games in pubs around the country into a party spirit.

Every hotel room in Glasgow – over 17,000 – was booked in advance for the weekend, the match was expected to generate around £6.6m for the local economy, and the landlords' association expected to sell an extra five million pints.

The rain came down all day, but the fans were in great voice as, before the match, the public address system played The Proclaimers' 'I'm Gonna Be (500 Miles)' alongside a montage of famous Scottish wins.

'I've urged the players not to fear failure and to play their hearts out,' manager Alex McLeish said ahead of the game.

Ten of Italy's starting line-up were World Cup winners.

Scotland were caught napping early on. Gianluca Zambrotta took a throw-in, and Antonio Di Natale spun and cut the ball back for Luca Toni, who stabbed the ball into the roof of the net. Italy were one up after only 73 seconds.

The crowd shook off their shock to get behind their team, and they almost had an equaliser to cheer when Lee McCulloch hit a shot that appeared to be blocked by the arm of Zambrotta. The referee ignored the Scottish appeals for a penalty.

On 65 minutes Alan Hutton ran 60 yards with the ball and only Zambrotta's desperate lunge could stop him on the edge of the box. McFadden took the free kick, which pierced the wall, the ball dropping to McCulloch, who hit a right-footed shot that Gianluigi Buffon blocked. Barry Ferguson immediately latched on to the ball and scrambled it over the line from around two yards.

Growing up, Ferguson had an Italy shirt and idolised Italian striker Roberto Baggio. He was the captain for the 26th time in his 43rd international and the goal was his third for his country.

Italy looked to be tiring, and the belief in the crowd transferred to the pitch and vice versa. Kenny Miller, on as a substitute, had a good chance after an exchange of passes with McFadden, but he shot wide.

In injury time, as Hutton attempted to mop up in the left-back position, he was bundled over by Giorgio Chiellini. The referee blew for a foul and thoughts quickly turned to getting the ball upfield for one last chance. But to everyone's astonishment, the free kick was awarded against Hutton.

Andrea Pirlo swung the kick into the box, where Christian Panucci headed past Gordon. Scotland had lost. 'After all the hard work, we've been robbed,' said McFadden.

Dejected Scotland players sat in the dressing room until they were told to get back out and receive the ovation the fans were insisting they deserved. 'It put a lump in the throat,' Darren Fletcher said. 'They respected we were in a tough group and they have respected what we achieved.'

'We gave some of the big teams a fright,' McLeish said, 'and this group of players have got years ahead of them.'

92

Boozegate – 2009

GEORGE BURLEY was a regular at full-back in the successful Ipswich Town team of the late 1970s and early 80s under Bobby Robson. His performances won him 11 caps for Scotland between 1979 and 1982.

Going into management, he began at Ayr United in 1991, moving south to Colchester United three years later, where he stayed for only a few months. He took over at Ipswich, where he enjoyed the most success of his managerial career, taking them into Europe with a fifth-place finish in the Premier League in 2000/01. A couple of seasons at Derby County followed before what looked like becoming a successful time at Hearts until he fell out with owner Vladimir Romanov a few months into the 2005/06 season. His next appointment was in December 2005 at Southampton in the Championship, leaving them in 13th position to take charge of Scotland in early 2008.

Burley's spell in charge of the national team didn't contain many memorable matches. He oversaw three wins – two 2-1 victories over Iceland and a 2-0 win over Macedonia. His legacy would turn out to be the unimaginatively named 'Boozegate', a lack of professionalism, discipline and respect in the Scotland squad that the tabloids lapped up.

On 28 March 2009 Scotland lost 3-0 to a strong Netherlands team in a World Cup qualifier in Amsterdam. Nine of the Dutch starting line-up would start the 2010 World Cup Final.

The Scotland squad flew home after the match and returned to the Cameron House Hotel on the shores of Loch Lomond at

4am. There was another qualifier to be played four days later against Iceland at Hampden.

Food was made available for the players, and, despite it being the middle of the night, they were allowed to have a few drinks.

Steven Pressley was one of Burley's coaches, having developed a good relationship with him during their time at Hearts. The Elgin-born defender, still a Celtic player at the time, had won 32 caps between 2000 and 2006.

After getting some hours of sleep, Pressley came downstairs to meet his family. 'When I arrived in the bar area it was maybe nine o'clock in the morning and I saw Barry [Ferguson] sitting there with Allan McGregor,' he told journalist Keith Jackson.

Ferguson, 45 times capped, was the captain, having been appointed by Berti Vogts, while his club-mate at Rangers, McGregor, had just earned his fourth cap in goal.

Pressley said he and two members of staff helped the players to their rooms, but then swiftly returned to the bar, 'At that point I think it became public knowledge they were in a seriously bad way.'

There were tensions within the Scotland camp, which Pressley acknowledged. 'The truth is I was never accepted by the Rangers players in the squad,' he said in 2018. 'At that time, it wasn't a brilliant squad in terms of unity. There was a definite Rangers-Celtic divide. No doubt about it.'

On his podcast *Fergie Time* in 2019, Ferguson said that he felt neither Pressley nor assistant manager Terry Butcher, who played with Burley at Ipswich, were the correct appointments, 'Pressley was still a player, and Terry Butcher was an awesome football player, but he was England captain. Whether it's right or wrong, that's my opinion.'

Soon there were rumours that Celtic's Scott Brown, as well as some other players, were also present. Brown, it was suggested, only went to bed 20 minutes before Pressley discovered the players. 'Scott wasn't there when I walked in on them,' Pressley said. 'There was a rumour he had shaved off Allan McGregor's hair, and maybe he did, but all I know is, when I went there, Scott was in his room.'

The press soon got hold of the story, and the legend of Boozegate was splashed across the back pages.

After the headlines, there was a game to be played. Ferguson and McGregor, who had both played 90 minutes against the Netherlands, were named as substitutes. Burley had initially wanted to send the pair home but reportedly bowed to pressure within the squad to keep them with the party.

Burley told the BBC in 2014, 'The last thing I said to the whole squad was, "Right, we've been in the news, make sure you don't do anything wrong, go out there, win the game and act in a totally professional manner."'

Ross McCormack and Steven Fletcher scored the goals that gave Scotland a 2-1 win, but the result was largely forgotten. Sat on the bench, with press photographers training their cameras on them, both Ferguson and McGregor made V-signs. The childish gestures only exacerbated the situation, and the inevitable happened – both players were told they would no longer be selected for their country.

An SFA report cleared Scott Brown, Gary Teale, Alan Hutton and Steven Whittaker, who had all gone to their rooms when the bar staff suggested they should, around 8am, leaving Ferguson and McGregor as the only two players to be punished.

Back at Ibrox, boss Walter Smith was not impressed and the two players were fined two weeks' wages, while Ferguson was stripped of the captaincy and was later sold to Birmingham City. Ferguson acknowledged that the incident was responsible for ending not only his Scotland career but also his time at Rangers.

Burley was sacked by Scotland in November 2009. His successor Craig Levein contacted both players and asked them to return. McGregor was back in the Scotland team in August 2010, going on to win a total of 42 caps. Ferguson discussed the offer with Mick Oliver, who was Levein's head of scouting, as well as former team-mates and his family. In the end he opted to focus on his club career. 'It would just have been a media circus. I didn't think it was fair on the guys in the squad,' he said.

'Players will judge whether or not they let themselves down,' Burley said in November 2009. 'It was an accumulation of things, but in general they know it's important when you represent your country that you act in the right manner.'

'It was my own stupid mistake,' said Ferguson. 'Let's be honest. There's no one else I can sit here and blame. It was nothing to do [with] the management team. I'm the one who took the punishment for being an absolute twat.'

93

4-6-0 – 2010

FOR THE Euro 2012 Group I qualifier against the Czech Republic in Prague on 8 October 2010, Scotland manager Craig Levein had one thing on his mind: don't lose. To this end, he sent the team out in a formation that shocked fans and pundits, lining up in a 4-6-0 system.

The headline here – no striker – might not sound unusual now; the false nine is a well-regarded system employed by the likes of Barcelona, Liverpool and Manchester City. That plan works by a centre-forward moving towards the ball in deeper positions from a high starting position, often dropping to receive centrally. The main intention is to get on the ball away from the opposition centre-backs, therefore drawing players out of position and creating gaps in the back line. The Levein version worked by sitting deep with the back four protected by six midfielders.

Kenny Miller, set to earn his 50th cap, was dropped to the bench despite scoring in the last qualifier, a 2-1 win over Lithuania. Queens Park Rangers forward Jamie Mackie made his debut out wide. Rangers striker Steven Naismith was also in a wide role.

Roman Hubník scored for the Czechs on 69 minutes. Levein brought on Miller and Chris Iwleumo as 76th-minute substitutes, changing to a 4-4-2 system. It couldn't prevent the Czechs from claiming their first win in the group.

'I've got no regrets about the way we went about it at all,' Levein said directly after the match. 'The game plan was never to come here and attack and open the game up, it was to sit in, to defend, to protect our centre-backs.'

Levein didn't rule out using the formation again, 'It's difficult to say the game plan worked when we didn't get something from the match. But I was happy that for long spells of the game, exactly what I was looking for occurred.'

Levein's assistant Peter Houston vigorously defended the formation, saying, 'If I'm being brutally honest, Scottish football fans probably need to get used to the fact that this is the way our teams will go about trying to get results. When you're playing top sides that's what you need to do.'

One of the things wrong with that statement was that no one particularly regarded the Czech Republic as a top side. In their previous match they had lost at home to Lithuania, and they were only ten places above Scotland in the FIFA rankings.

Scotland failed to qualify from the group, which Spain won, with the Czech Republic second.

In 2013, Bleacher Report called Levein's system 'the most ridiculous formation ever played'.

'I honestly didn't realise at that time that it was such a significant moment and that everyone was going to talk about that system for as long as they have,' Levein said to *The Scotsman* in 2020. 'Look, I didn't invent that formation. It was used by managers before that game and has been used since. I have no problems being criticised because it didn't work the way I intended, but I just have to laugh that I'm the one who is always associated with it.'

Levein took over the Scotland job in early 2010, leaving after defeats to Wales and Belgium in World Cup qualifiers in October 2012.

He explained his thinking behind 4-6-0, 'As a centre-back, playing against a striker who is much deeper, it is really difficult because you don't know when to push out or sit in, and I was hoping to catch them by surprise and maybe sneak a goal on the counterattack.'

Levein had seen the system used successfully when he watched Rubin Kazan hold Barcelona to a 1-1 draw at the end of

September 2010. He knew from watching the Czechs previously that their full-backs advanced regularly, and as they moved forward with seven players, there was a chance Scotland could exploit the spaces left at the back.

'The logic was sound. I thought it could work. It didn't, and I take full responsibility for that, but how many times have Scotland gone abroad and been beaten 1-0, 2-0, 3-0?'

Levein revealed that one of his players leaked the team through his agent, leading to the outcry ahead of the match.

The system ended up being Levein's legacy as Scotland boss. 'I wouldn't swap any of it,' he said to *The Times* in 2013, 'even the kicking I got towards the end. It's all character-building, and I was hugely proud to be national team manager.'

94

Professor Stewart Hillis

Scotland team doctor (1982–2010)

PROFESSOR STEWART Hillis was the official team doctor for 228 full internationals from 1982 to 2010 and 54 under-21 matches from 1976 to 1982, serving under nine permanent managers.

Hillis was a professor of cardiovascular and exercise medicine at the University of Glasgow, vice-chairman of the medical committee of UEFA, and a medical advisor to FIFA.

After graduating from the University of Glasgow in 1967, Hillis became a consultant cardiologist there in 1977, developing BSc and masters courses in sports medicine.

Hillis served his local club, Clydebank, for 27 years, joining in 1970. He put in place a lot of forward-thinking practices that seemed quirky at the time but are now commonplace. In the 1976/77 season he hooked Bankies players to a device that recorded their heart performances, lung capacity and recovery power. 'This is another example of how progressive Clydebank are,' he told the *Scottish Daily Express*. 'By wiring up these players, we get their exact physical capabilities and can plan training schedules accordingly. It's a subject I'm particularly interested in, but for so long, it has scarcely been touched upon by football clubs.' His wages at Kilbowie Park were a turkey from the club every Christmas.

In June 1995, having been recently appointed to UEFA's committee, he feared he had jeopardised his position when during Scotland's friendly with Japan in Hiroshima he ran on to the pitch to remonstrate with the referee after a nasty foul by Akira Narahashi on Rab McKinnon. The Colombian official, Armando Pérez Hoyos, refused to allow him to treat the injured Motherwell player and sent him off. McKinnon was then dropped twice by the stretcher team who carried him off. Craig Brown saw the act as an example of Hillis's paramount concern for his players' welfare.

Moving on to work with Rangers in 1998/99, his time at Ibrox was defined by one unfortunate signing. Romanian international Daniel Prodan arrived from Atlético Madrid for £2.2m but wouldn't play a first-team game due to a knee injury. Rangers owner Sir David Murray was so fixed on rushing the deal through that Hillis was not given enough time to perform his usual assessments. 'Mr Murray said to me, "There's a press conference in 45 minutes,"' Hillis later told *The Herald*. Hillis took the blame publicly and always held himself responsible, but it would later turn out that medical forms sent to Rangers had been falsified.

'He was great company and was hugely respected in his job,' Gordon Strachan said. 'There's nothing more you can ask of your team doctor but the "Prof" always lit up the room with his personality. As a player you loved having him around and as a manager you could always rely on his advice.'

The worst incident Hillis had to deal with in his time as Scotland's doctor was the night Jock Stein passed away. The two worst player incidents he dealt with were the broken leg Ally McCoist suffered during a World Cup qualifying defeat to Portugal in Lisbon in 1993 and the knee ligament damage which effectively finished John Kennedy's career 11 years later. McCoist had been in intense pain on the flight home until Hillis pulled out some liquid anaesthetic. 'That was the time when I managed to find two bottles of Beaujolais in my medical case,' he said to *The Herald*.

Campbell Ogilvie, president of the SFA at the time of Hillis's death, said, 'He was a medic of the highest standards and we are all fortunate he brought those standards to the Scottish FA during his time as international team doctor and medical director and adviser.'

If Professor Hillis has a lasting legacy, it is in convincing the SFA to set up the Sports Medicine Centre inside the refurbished Hampden Park, the first of its kind in a national stadium.

His successor Dr John MacLean stepped down from the job as Scotland team doctor in 2021 after 229 full internationals. 'Professor Stewart Hillis was my mentor for much of the last 40 years and I miss him every single day,' he told the *Daily Mail*. 'He passed away just the day before the opening ceremony of the Glasgow Commonwealth Games in 2014 and I owe everything in football to Stewart.'

95

Scotland 2 England 2 – 2017

10 June 2017
Hampden Park
World Cup qualifying Group F
Attendance: 48,520

Scotland: Gordon (Celtic), Tierney (Celtic), Robertson (Hull City), Berra (Hearts), Mulgrew (Blackburn Rovers), Morrison (West Bromwich Albion) [McArthur (Crystal Palace), 46], Armstrong (Celtic), Brown [C] (Celtic), Griffiths (Celtic), Snodgrass (West Ham United) [Fraser (AFC Bournemouth), 67], Anya (Derby County) [Martin (Derby County), 81]

England: Hart (Torino), Walker (Tottenham Hotspur), Bertrand (Southampton), Dier (Tottenham Hotspur), Cahill (Chelsea), Smalling (Manchester United), Rashford (Manchester United) [Oxlade-Chamberlain (Arsenal), 65], Livermore (West Bromwich Albion) [Defoe (Sunderland), 90+2], Kane [C] (Tottenham Hotspur), Alli (Tottenham Hotspur) [Sterling (Manchester City), 84], Lallana (Liverpool)

Referee: Paolo Tagliavento (Italy)

Goals:
Scotland: Griffiths (87, 90)
England: Oxlade-Chamberlain (70), Kane (90+3)

SCOTLAND HAD gone into the game with a 1-0 win over Slovenia in March, thanks to a late Chris Martin goal. The qualifying campaign had been unimpressive up to that point with a 5-1 win over Malta the only high spot. But after 3-0 away defeats to both Slovenia and England, the home victory over Slovenia had allowed Scotland to remain in contention for a qualifying place.

The game was largely unremarkable until the last 20 minutes. Even then, it looked like a routine win for England. 'The only word to describe it is bedlam,' Daniel Taylor wrote of the closing moments, in *The Guardian*.

England hadn't lost in Scotland since 1985, and very few people would have expected that statistic to change on a sunny day in June 2017. England also hadn't lost in a World Cup qualifying fixture since 2009.

Alexander Oxlade-Chamberlain, whose father Mark had played against Scotland in 1984, had come on as a substitute in the 65th minute for Marcus Rashford, who Kieran Tierney had effectively nullified. Five minutes later he cut past Brown and, running across the penalty area from right to left, hit a left-footed shot which put England into the lead.

With three minutes remaining, a foul by Gary Cahill gave Scotland a free kick around 30 yards out. With Joe Hart leaving space to his left, Leigh Griffiths put the ball powerfully to that side. Hart was grasping thin air, Griffiths had his first goal for his country, and Hampden went wild.

Three minutes later, it was Jake Livermore who gave away a free kick within shooting distance. Hart positioned himself more to the centre of his goal. Griffiths put the ball over the wall to the keeper's right this time. Hart flailed once more, and it was 2-1 to Scotland.

In the third minute of added time, with all of Hampden anticipating a famous Scottish win, Craig Gordon pushed Eric Dier's free kick out, Kyle Walker won the ball and played it out to Raheem Sterling, who sent a cross to the back post for Harry Kane to volley past Gordon to give England a draw and sink the crowd.

Manager Gordon Strachan commented, 'To do what my players did was phenomenal. You cannot do any more than they did. It was like a middleweight fighting a heavyweight. For Leigh Griffiths to score two goals after the huge amount of work he put in is taking drive to a new level.'

On the receiving end, Hart said, 'As a goalkeeper you set your wall up and sometimes there's nothing you can do. He's produced two bits of quality. They weren't curlers, they were heavy. He put it over the wall and then picked up pace, and you've got to say well done sometimes. To do it twice in a few minutes after not really having a sniff the whole game was a big moment for him.'

The result was followed up by good wins over Lithuania, Malta and Slovakia, with the final group game being a 2-2 draw with Slovenia. Scotland would finish third in the group, narrowly missing out on the play-offs after ending up level with Slovakia on 18 points but with a goal difference of plus five compared to Slovakia's plus ten.

Griffiths reflected on the day when speaking with *The Scotsman* in 2020, 'But for one moment in stoppage time, we would have won. It was just one of those things, but I don't want to be that guy who is just remembered for the one game when it comes to Scotland.'

96

Women's World Cup – 2019

GOING INTO the final day of qualifying, Scotland had to beat Albania in Shkodër and hope that Switzerland failed to win in Poland. Kim Little put Scotland in front after nine minutes, only for Megi Doçi to equalise on the stroke of half-time.

With Switzerland and Poland still goalless it was a nervy second half. In the 68th minute, Jane Ross scored what would prove the winner, and when news came in that Switzerland had drawn 0-0 it meant that Scotland would be making their debut at the Women's World Cup finals.

Scotland were in pot three for the draw. They came out with England, Argentina and Japan. England had been quarter-finalists in 2011 and third placed at the previous tournament in 2015, while Japan had been winners in 2011 and runners-up in 2015. Argentina hadn't qualified since 2007.

The 2019 Women's World Cup was using VAR and its new interpretation of the laws of the game, which had only been introduced on 1 June, one week before the start of the tournament. 'I know these rules apply across the global game,' Chelsea manager Emma Hayes wrote in *The Times*, 'but this is the Women's World Cup – which is by far the most high-profile tournament, the pinnacle of the summer. It is no place for experiments, or to treat the women as guinea pigs.'

Scotland lost 2-1 to both England and Japan, so going into the last group game they had to beat Argentina to have any chance of qualifying as one of the best third-placed teams.

Referee Ri Hyang-ok from North Korea was a former player who had represented her country at the World Cups of 1999 and 2003.

For the first 20 minutes, Argentina put Scotland under pressure. But then things changed.

From an Erin Cuthbert cut-back, Little put Scotland ahead on 19 minutes. Four minutes into the second half Caroline Weir whipped in a cross, and Jen Beattie's header made it 2-0, then with 68 minutes on the clock Erin Cuthbert scored to put Scotland 3-0 up. 'No other goal I've ever scored comes close to what it felt like running towards thousands of celebrating Scotland fans,' Cuthbert said to Steven Lawther for his book *Arrival*. Finally, it looked like a Scotland team would make it out of the group stage at a World Cup finals.

'The atmosphere in that game was probably the best atmosphere I have ever played in,' Weir told Lawther. 'Everything was going so well for us.'

But late in the match, it all went horribly wrong. 'I can't even describe anything that went on,' Lana Clelland said. 'To start with, it was a blur; it was, "What just happened?" Then obviously just all the chaos at the end.'

Milagros Menéndez scored with 17 minutes remaining, although Scotland complained they should have had a free kick in the build-up. Then Florencia Bonsegundo hit a shot which came down off the crossbar and hit goalkeeper Lee Alexander and went in. It was now 3-2, and Scotland, only five minutes earlier in control, were struggling.

Five minutes from time Fiona Brown came on as a substitute, but the referee allowed Argentina to take a free kick before she could take up her position on the pitch. As the ball was sent into the box, Sophie Howard, just on as a substitute herself, brought down Aldana Cometti. 'My only chance was to slide tackle, otherwise she would score,' Howard said. Ri waved play on but soon she stopped the game, indicating that the VAR official had spoken to her.

Consulting the video footage, it took Ri four minutes to decide to award Argentina a penalty, the game now in injury time.

Bonsegundo struck her kick firmly, only for Alexander to make a brilliant save. The Sporting Huelva midfielder followed up on the rebound but Alexander again blocked her shot. The ball was hoofed clear, and Scotland had survived.

But VAR intervened. The new interpretations of the laws were particularly harsh on goalkeepers at penalties; Alexander was ruled not to have had at least part of one foot on the goal line. A retake was awarded and this time Bonsegundo slammed the ball home. From the penalty being awarded to play being restarted with the successful kick, around ten minutes had elapsed. Ri had signalled only four additional minutes to be played. She sounded the final whistle two minutes later.

'I think the referee was just overwhelmed with the whole situation,' Howard said to Lawther, 'and the whole game, and therefore pretty much had a mentality of "get me out of here".'

Fiona Brown said to the *Daily Record*, 'In terms of VAR, I can't sit and say it's a terrible idea because I think the concept is good. However, I think we fell victim to it not being used consistently or accurately. The decisions made by the referee in the last stages of our game were ridiculous, and I hope it is looked at and improved for the future of the women's game.'

It was a devastating end to the tournament for Scotland. 'We've all had disappointments in the past,' said manager Shelley Kerr, 'but this was on a different level.'

97

Andy Robertson

64 caps, 3 goals (2014–present)

'ANDY WAS a tenacious wee player,' Martin Miller, who ran Celtic's junior academy when Robertson was there, told The Athletic, 'a hungry and competitive player with good technique. He was a match for any other player. His hunger to enhance his game and develop his skill always shone.'

Robertson was released by Celtic at under-14 level, and Queen's Park gave him a chance to continue his development and eventually move into the first team. 'He was always very good technically,' David McCallum, head of youth development at Queen's Park, said to the *Hull Daily Mail* in 2014. 'He played with his head up and looked to get on the ball all the time, but he was smaller than a lot of the boys in his age group. It was his willingness to learn that made all the difference. He was always asking questions if he didn't know the answers. He wanted to improve at every opportunity, and that was the key.'

Robertson's Scotland debut came as a Dundee United player in a 1-0 friendly win against Poland under Gordon Strachan in March 2014. He quickly established himself as a regular in the team. By the time of his third cap against Georgia in October, he had signed for Hull City in England's Premier League.

Dundee United's first-team coach, former Scotland international Darren Jackson, said to *The Scotsman* at the time, 'If you are asking who will be the Scotland left-back for the next ten to 15 years, I believe it will be Andy Robertson. The kid is that good.'

His first Scotland goal came in the 3-1 friendly defeat to England at Celtic Park on 18 November. It made Robertson the first Scot to score at home against England since Richard Gough in 1985. 'It's a tough one,' he said to *The Express* after the match. 'A normal person would probably have been delighted to score against England to get their first goal for Scotland. But I've already forgotten about it. We were beaten 3-1, and that's the most annoying thing for me.'

Despite Hull's relegation at the end of 2014/15, Robertson was still a regular for his country. Hull went back up to the Premier League through the play-offs in 2016, but when they were relegated again in 2017 Robertson made a £10m switch to Liverpool.

The move to Anfield allowed Robertson to develop more of an attacking threat to his game. 'When I was playing for Hull in the Premier League, we had to be more defensive-minded because teams pinned us back,' he told The Athletic in 2020. 'I didn't get forward as much. I might only get into decent crossing positions once or twice over 90 minutes. Now I might be in positions like that ten or 11 times in a game with the amount of possession [Liverpool] get.' In December 2022 Robertson became the defender with the most assists in Premier League history, taking his tally to 54.

Alex McLeish took the decision to appoint Robertson as Scotland's captain in 2018. 'Andy has been the epitome of never say die and never give up, which is a kind of Scottish trait,' McLeish told the Associated Press news agency. 'He kept going, he persevered and became the player that he is, but he also carries himself well in the dressing room. He talks well, assertively, and the players look up to him.'

In May 2019, Robertson won the Champions League with Liverpool; the following week, he was looking forward to an international double-header against Cyprus and Belgium. 'Playing for your country is still the biggest honour,' he told *The Guardian*. 'It's irrelevant what we've won and what we've done. It's still a huge honour for me to lead the team out and walk out and play these important games.'

Robertson would only play against Cyprus, scoring Scotland's first goal in a 2-1 win.

'The last 18 months or so have been amazing, really,' Robertson said to *The Guardian* before Scotland faced Ukraine in a European Championship play-off semi-final in June 2020. 'You felt the mood in the camp change. The lads and staff have really come together. We didn't want to be a one-hit wonder team, qualify for the Euros, and that's it done. We wanted that to be the catalyst for more, and now we have a chance to make that the case.'

Unfortunately it wasn't to be, as Ukraine won 3-1 to end Scotland's hopes of reaching the Covid-delayed finals.

Robertson was full of praise for Steve Clarke, appointed Scotland's manager in May 2019, saying to *The Scotsman* in 2023, 'He's set us up in a way that the players and the fans can have a relationship again. Before he came in, the relationship was broken. I don't think there were many people excited to come to Hampden. That was proved with the attendances we've had.'

Robertson cited the full houses Scotland were now getting as evidence the fans were fully behind the team, 'As a player, that makes a huge difference. Playing in front of a full Scotland crowd, knowing the pubs up and down the country will be full of people wanting to watch us. It just shows that the feel-good factor is back.'

98

John McGinn

56 caps, 16 goals (2016–present)

BEGINNING HIS career with St Mirren, playing at left-back, there were fears that John McGinn was too small to make a success of himself.

McGinn comes from a football family. His grandfather, Jack, was Celtic chairman and, for six years, president of the Scottish Football Association. His older brother Stephen had been at St Mirren before joining Watford, while his other brother Paul began at Queen's Park.

John began to show promise, playing as a box-to-box midfielder, and broke into the first team in late 2012. His manager at the time, Danny Lennon, told *The Telegraph*, 'I'll maybe see the pass I think is the right one, but he sees something better.'

McGinn was part of the St Mirren team that won the 2013 League Cup, moving on to Hibernian in 2015 where, despite playing in Scotland's second tier, he was soon in the international squad. Gordon Strachan gave him his debut in March 2016 in a 1-0 friendly win against Denmark.

He helped Hibernian win the Scottish Cup in 2016, the Championship in 2017, and qualify for the Europa League with a fourth-placed finish in 2018. While at Easter Road, McGinn worked to improve his technique and his stamina, becoming stronger and more resilient.

Then came the move to English Championship club Aston Villa, who signed him for £2.75m in the summer of 2018. 'He won the Villa supporters over straight away when he crashed into a tackle and sprayed a 50-yard pass and had a shot in the first few minutes,' said the man who signed him, Steve Bruce.

In his first season, McGinn played 45 times in all competitions, scoring the winner in the play-off final at Wembley that saw Villa go up to the Premier League.

McGinn developed too as a Scotland player, with Alex McLeish taking over from Strachan. 'He got caught out for the opening goal in a 4-0 defeat to Belgium, where he had his pocket picked on the edge of the area, and they scored,' McLeish said to The Athletic. 'But he never hid away after that. He was always showing for the ball and desperate to win it back.'

When Steve Clarke took over as Scotland's manager in 2019, McGinn began to play a more advanced role for his country, getting on the ball in the opponents' half more than his own, becoming almost a second striker.

His first goals for Scotland came that year: his first in a 2-1 loss to Russia in September, then a hat-trick against San Marino in October, the winner against Cyprus in November and a brace in a 3-1 win over Kazakhstan in November.

McGinn is a proponent of a Scottish art not seen since the days of Kenny Dalglish: the use of the bum. As Dalglish did, McGinn uses his posterior to give himself a little bit more time on the ball and create a fraction more space. 'I always say if I didn't have my backside, I'd be at Yeovil,' McGinn said after scoring in the 3-0 win over Ukraine in September 2022.

Yaya Touré, writing for The Athletic, noticed McGinn's particular skills in the Euro 2020 finals match against England. 'What impressed me in that game was how disciplined John McGinn was in midfield,' Touré wrote, 'taking the ball from the defence and protecting it from England players before making the pass. McGinn … has very powerful legs and hips, and there were times where you could see him get the ball with his back to an England player, smell the danger was coming and then use his bum to shield the ball from them.'

The 0-0 draw with England was a battling performance from McGinn and Scotland although, ultimately, a 3-1 defeat to Croatia saw Scotland eliminated from the tournament. 'The bravery and the determination is our Scottish identity,' McGinn said after the Wembley match.

In the summer of 2022, manager Steven Gerrard made McGinn Aston Villa's captain, while he has also captained Scotland, to date, on seven occasions.

'It's been a mental journey,' McGinn said in 2023 of his increasing success with club and country.

99

Serbia 1 Scotland 1 (AET; Scotland Win 5-4 on Penalties) – 2020

12 November 2020
Rajko Mitic Stadium, Belgrade
European Championship play-off
Attendance: Played behind closed doors

Serbia: Rajković (Stade de Reims), Milenković (Fiorentina), S. Mitrović (RC Strasbourg) [Spajic (Feyenoord), 108], Gudelj (Sevilla), Lazović (Hellas Verona), Kostić (Eintracht Frankfurt) [Mladenović (Legia Warsaw), 59], Maksimović (Getafe) [Jović (Real Madrid), 70], Lukić (Torino), Milinković-Savić (Lazio) [Katai (Red Star Belgrade), 70], Tadić [C] (Ajax), A. Mitrović (Fulham)

Scotland: Marshall (Derby County), O'Donnell (Motherwell) [Griffiths (Celtic), 116], Robertson (Liverpool), McTominay (Manchester United), Gallagher (Motherwell), Tierney (Arsenal), McGinn (Aston Villa) [McLean (Norwich City), 82], Jack (Rangers), McGregor (Celtic), Christie (Celtic) [Paterson (Sheffield Wednesday), 87], Dykes (Queens Park Rangers) [McBurnie (Sheffield United), 82]

Referee: Antonio Mateu Lahoz (Spain)

Goals:
Scotland – Christie (52)
Serbia – Jović (90)

THE EURO 2020 finals tournament had been held over by a year due to the Covid-19 pandemic. Scotland's play-off semi-final with Israel set for March 2020 had been delayed until October 2020 and was played behind closed doors at Hampden. A 0-0 draw was settled by a 5-3 win on penalties to set up a final against Serbia at the home of Red Star Belgrade.

Before the players went out to the pitch, manager Steve Clarke told them, 'Don't play with the fear of failure, try to play with the anticipation of success.'

Clarke employed a back three with Motherwell's Declan Gallagher in the centre tasked with subduing Aleksandar Mitrović. 'I knew I couldn't let my concentration drop for a second with Mitrović,' Gallagher told Andy Bargh for his book *A Nation Again*. 'If he won a header, I had to be doing enough to put him off; kick him, tug his jersey, a sly arm round him, whatever I could to unsettle him. Neither of us are blessed with pace, and I was doing a good job of getting to the ball first when he tried to hold it up.' Gallagher knew he had Mitrović beaten after one passage of play when he barged the striker to the ground in a race for the ball, 'He started to get huffy, was too lazy to stay onside and doing his own thing. I tried to wind him up in case he lost his temper because he's that type of guy. I had him in the palm of my hand.'

Instead of playing a rope-a-dope game and absorbing pressure like several pundits thought they would, Scotland took the game to Serbia and were in charge for the first half, although the game was goalless at the interval.

In the 51st minute Lyndon Dykes held the ball up perfectly and, with precision timing, laid it into the path of Andy Robertson, who fired over the bar from 15 yards.

Only a minute later, Callum McGregor stole the ball and passed into Ryan Christie, who swivelled and feinted as if about to complete a one-two as team-mates distracted the defence with decoy runs. Instead he sent a left-footed shot through a heavily congested penalty area. The ball flew into the net off the post.

Serbia began to have more of the ball and more chances as the Scots sweated on the final whistle sounding.

In the 90th minute, Filip Mladenović delivered a corner. Real Madrid's £50m striker Luka Jović rose and connected with a header. It went into the ground, bounced up and beat David Marshall. Serbia had equalised. 'A horrendous moment,' Marshall said to Bargh. 'I thought I was getting it, but gravity was too quick for me, and I was inches away.'

Scotland were so close, but now the match went into extra time. Clarke told the *High Performance Podcast* that he didn't do much to motivate his players. They were doing it themselves. He said, 'That's when you start to hear Robertson, McGinn, Kenny McLean, Ryan Jack, Callum McGregor: "We're still in the competition, we can still get through." That desire was still there, so as a coach, I'm thinking that we're all right because I didn't have to say too much. They did it.'

In the ninth minute of extra time, Marshall made an outstanding save from Sevilla's Nemanja Gudelj, tipping the ball around the post at full stretch. 'That save was so good,' Shay Given, goalkeeping coach at Marshall's club, Derby County, said to The Athletic. 'People might not understand the goalkeeping position, but he's seen it very, very late, and it's actually going away from his body all the time.'

With four minutes remaining, Leigh Griffiths came on for his first cap since September 2018.

But no one could break the deadlock and the match went to penalties. Scotland had won their last play-off match against Israel on penalties, scoring all five, so although they'd drawn the final from a winning position there was no fear going into the contest.

The first nine penalties were scored with Griffiths, McGregor, McTominay, McBurnie and McLean netting for Scotland. Now Mitrović stepped up, needing to score to keep Serbia in the tie. Marshall regularly stayed behind after training to practise penalties with Derby team-mates Wayne Rooney, Martyn Waghorn and Graeme Shinnie, so was confident of saving at least one.

'I won't ever stare at a penalty taker,' Marshall said to Bargh. 'I'll read their body language and combine it with my research, which is more important. Mitrović usually goes to the keeper's left or down the middle and missed his last one for Fulham by going down the middle, so I felt he'd revert back to his favoured side.'

Mitrović hit the ball right-footed as Marshall flew to his left and got a strong hand to it to keep it out.

The abiding image for Scots fans was of Marshall looking to the referee to confirm that his positioning on the line was good and the kick wouldn't be retaken before he would allow himself to celebrate. 'The referee had told me there would be a VAR check, so don't celebrate,' Marshall told the BBC's *Football Focus*. 'I didn't look relatively calm, but it was because I knew that was taking place.' The referee confirmed all was good, and Marshall was met by his delighted team-mates, who swarmed over him in jubilation.

'It's been a very difficult time for everyone,' Clarke said, referring primarily to the Covid pandemic. 'We spoke about trying to make the nation smile; hopefully, we've done our bit.'

Ryan Christie's passionate post-match interview was the toast of social media as he broke down in tears. 'From the start we believed, we picked up so much belief from each other. Conceding that late equaliser, we still dug in then penalties away from home ... unbelievable. Oh, God ... it's been a horrible year for everyone, we knew that coming into the game, and I hope everyone back home is having a party tonight because of everything we've been through over the years.'

Scotland's win gave them a place in Group D of the finals alongside England, Croatia and the Czech Republic.

100

'Yes Sir, I Can Boogie'

SOMETIMES, THE songs that become associated with the Scottish national team can take the Tartan Army by surprise. The tune that was embraced by players and fans in 2021 was a Euro disco song from the 1970s called 'Yes Sir, I Can Boogie'. The song was written by composer Frank Dostal and lyricist Rolf Soja and released as a single by Baccara, a Spanish female duo.

It entered the UK charts in September 1977 at number 50, climbing gradually, and after spending two weeks at number three in mid-October it got to number one at the end of the month. In total it stayed in the charts for 17 weeks, being certified Gold. It was also a hit all over Europe, reaching number one in West Germany, Sweden and Belgium, among other countries.

How it came to be an anthem for the Scottish team goes back to 2015. Aberdeen defender Andrew Considine sang the song with his friends at his stag party, filming a fun music video where he dressed up in drag.

Considine made his Scotland debut at the age of 33 against Slovakia in October 2020. Scotland won 1-0, and three days later he was in the side when the Czech Republic were also beaten 1-0.

When Scotland qualified for the delayed Euro 2020 tournament by defeating Serbia on penalties in November 2020, the players celebrated by singing the song, with unused substitute Considine at the centre. The video of the players' antics was soon a viral hit on Twitter.

Scotland's fans were soon embracing the song, and Baccara's version went back into the charts that month, but this time only spent two weeks there, peaking at number 57.

Baccara singer Maria Mendiola spoke to the BBC, 'With this pandemic, I have been sitting at home and this has uplifted me in a way you cannot imagine. I will always thank the Scottish team and especially Andy Considine for making me so happy after 43 years. I saw all the articles and everyone was calling me. I was delighted. I thanked the Scotland team and spoke with Andy over Instagram. He had such nice words.'

Scotland fans sang 'Yes Sir, I Can Boogie' in the streets, on buses, planes and trains ahead of the Euro 2020 match with England at Wembley, as it cemented its place in the Tartan Army songbook.

101

Scotland 2 Spain 0 – 2023

28 March 2023
Hampden Park
European Championship qualifying Group A
Attendance: 47,976

Scotland: Gunn (Norwich City), Porteous (Watford), Hanley (Norwich City), Tierney (Arsenal) [Cooper (Leeds United), 76], Hickey (Brentford) [Patterson (Everton), 82], McTominay (Manchester United), McGregor (Celtic), Robertson [C] (Liverpool), McGinn (Aston Villa) [Ferguson (Bologna), 83], Dykes (Queens Park Rangers) [Shankland (Hearts), 89], Christie (AFC Bournemouth) [McLean (Norwich City), 75]

Spain: Arrizabalaga (Chelsea), Porro (Tottenham Hotspur) [Carvajal (Real Madrid), 45], Garcia (Osasuna), Martínez (Athletic Bilbao), Gayá (Valencia), Merino (Real Sociedad) [Aspas (Celta Vigo), 57], Rodri [C] (Manchester City), Ceballos (Real Madrid) [Gavi (Barcelona), 79], Pino (Villareal), Joselu (Espanyol), [Iglesias Quintas (Real Betis), 66], Oyarzabal (Real Sociedad) [Williams (Athletic Bilbao), 45]

Referee: Sandro Schärer (Switzerland) (Replaced by Lukas Fähndrich (Switzerland) at half-time)

Goals:
McTominay (7, 51)

IN SCOTLAND'S opening match in the group two days earlier, Scott McTominay had come on as a substitute and scored twice as Cyprus were beaten 3-0, earning him a starting place for the visit of Spain. Scotland hadn't beaten Spain since 1984, a run of five matches, with the last two games, in 2010 and 2011, being European Championship qualifying defeats.

On seven minutes Scotland took the lead. Ryan Porteous played a ball up to Lyndon Dykes; he moved it on to Christie, who slipped a pass down the inside left for Robertson. Captaining Scotland for the 40th time, Robertson looked to have been beaten to it by Porro, but the Spaniard slipped and Robertson cut the ball back from the byline for McTominay, who, from 12 yards out, opened up his body and slotted in.

Dykes had a glorious opportunity to double the lead late on in the first half. John McGinn intercepted a ball inside the Scots' penalty box then Kieran Tierney fired it upfield for Dykes to chase and latch on to. As Kepa backpedalled into his goal, the QPR forward raced in on goal ahead of Garcia, but the Osasuna player managed to get close on Scotland's number nine, who fired over the bar.

'There's so much happening out there,' journalist Tom English said on *Sportsound*. 'The fans are really engaged with it. It's a fantastic, fantastic madcap game of football.'

For the second half, Lukas Fähndrich replaced Sandro Schärer as the referee, with Schärer suffering a pulled muscle and taking over as fourth official.

In the 51st minute Tierney went flying down the left wing, having too much strength for Dani Carvajal. He fired over a cross which was half cleared by Garcia's thigh. The ball fell to the in-rushing McTominay, who rattled the ball low into the Spanish net for 2-0. 'Flower of Scotland' soon echoed around Hampden Park.

Two minutes later, McGinn attempted to catch out Kepa, whipping a free kick towards the keeper's top right, but the ball cannoned off the crossbar and Spain cleared.

As the second half wore on, Scotland began to tire and the match became more and more physical. Scotland battled to hold their shape as Spain assaulted their goal late on. McGregor took the ball for a run down the right in the sixth minute of injury time, leaving Gavi in his wake and putting a ball across the goal for Lawrence Shankland, who had taken on the lone striker role from Dykes. The Hearts striker shot but the ball bobbled straight at Kepa, who gathered. McTominay picked up an odd caution by cuddling Kepa to prevent him from releasing the ball.

The performance was vintage; Scotland had discovered the form to achieve a win of the kind they hadn't delivered in decades.

Analysing the match on television, Ally McCoist said, 'I'm buzzing. That was nothing short of fantastic, and do you know what, we weren't really in any danger.'

According to UEFA's stats, Scotland had 32 per cent possession to Spain's 68 per cent. Scotland completed 149 passes to Spain's 585, but Scotland recovered 37 balls to Spain's 30, and 34 clearances were attempted to Spain's 13. It was only the 2008 and 2012 winners' second defeat in 39 European Championship qualifiers.

Angus Gunn had now kept two clean sheets from his first two caps, and the win put Scotland top of the group with maximum points from two games.

There's nothing fans like better in modern football than the opposition whining, and Spanish captain Rodri made the win even sweeter with his post-match complaints. 'It's the way they play – for me, it's a bit rubbish,' the Manchester City midfielder said. 'It's always wasting time, they provoke you, they always fall. For me, this is not football. The referee has to take a part in this, but he said nothing. It's a bit frustrating because we want to win, and it's difficult because they waste time, waste time. It is what it is.'

Andy Robertson spoke to broadcaster Viaplay after the match, 'Loved it … we knew we had to get off to a good start, put them under pressure and get the fans with it … the second half was a really professional performance and shows you how far we've come. It's a joy to be captain of these lads … we've got so many leaders and young lads that will become leaders.'

Matchwinner McTominay was delighted. 'We knew they'd have a lot of the ball … the manager said we needed to be clinical when we had our opportunities, and we had more than enough tonight to really hurt them and score some goals. Look at this place; it's incredible. These are the nights that people will remember in 20, 30 years.'

The result and, more importantly the performance gives Scotland fans much hope that the current crop of players will go on to match or even better the achievements of the greats that have gone before them.

Bibliography

Books:

Aird, Alistair, *Ally McCoist: Portrait of a Hero* (London: John Blake, 2009)

Alcock, Charles W, *The Classic Guide to Football* (Stroud: Amberley, 2014)

Allan, John, *The Story of the Rangers: Fifty Years of Football, 1873–1923* (Westcliff-on-Sea: Desert Island Books, 1996)

Bale, Bernard, *Bremner! The Legend of Billy Bremner* (London: Andre Deutsch Limited, 1998)

Banks, Gordon, *Banks of England* (London: Arthur Barker Ltd, 1980)

Banks, Gordon, *Banksy: The Autobiography* (London: Penguin Books, 2003)

Bargh, Andy, *A Nation Again: The Inside Story of Scotland's Journey to the European Championship* (Worthing: Pitch Publishing, 2023)

Barnes, John, *The Autobiography* (London: Headline, 1999)

Barton, Leon, *Brian Flynn: Little Wonde*r (Cardiff: St David's Press, 2017)

Bass, Howard, *Glorious Wembley: The Official History of Britain's Foremost Entertainment Centre* (Guinness Superlatives Ltd, 1982)

Bleasdale, John, *Scotland's Swedish Adventure – The Story of Scotland's European Championship Debut* (Worthing: Pitch Publishing, 2022)

Bowler, Dave, *Shanks: The Authorised Biography of Bill Shankly* (London: Orion, 1996)

Bremner, Billy, *You Get Nowt for Being Second* (London: Souvenir Press, 1969)

Brogan, Tom, *We Made Them Angry – The Story of Scotland at the World Cup Spain 1982* (Worthing: Pitch Publishing, 2022)

Brown, Craig & Bale, Bernard, *Craig Brown: The Autobiography* (London: Virgin Books, 1998)

Browne, Ronnie, *That Guy Fae the Corries* (Dingwall: Sandstone Press, 2015)

Burns, Jimmy, *Maradona: The Hand of God* (London: Bloomsbury, 2010)

Busby, Matt, *Soccer at the Top: My Life in Football* (London: Weidenfeld & Nicolson, 1973)

Charlton, Bobby & Ponting, Ivan, *My Life in Football* (London: Headline, 2009)

Connor, Jeff (ed.), *Fanatical About Football: You Must Remember This…* (Edinburgh: Mainstream, 2003)

Crerand, Paddy, *Never Turn the Other Cheek* (London: Harper Sport, 2007)

Dalglish, Kenny & Gallacher, Ken, *King Kenny* (London: Stanley Paul, 1982)

Dalglish, Kenny & Winter, Henry, *Dalglish: My Autobiography* (London: Hodder & Stoughton, 1996)

Darby, Tom, *Talking Shankly: The Man, The Genius, The Legend* (Edinburgh: Mainstream, 2001)

Davies, Pete, *All Played Out: The Full Story of Italia 90* (London: Mandarin, 1991)

Docherty, Tommy, *The Doc: My Story: Hallowed Be Thy Game* (London: Headline, 2006)

Donaldson, Aidan, *Playing for the Hoops: The George McCluskey Story* (Edinburgh: Luath Press Ltd, 2016)

Donovan, Mike, *Dave Mackay: Football's Braveheart: The Authorised Biography* (Worthing: Pitch Publishing, 2021)

Endeacott, Robert & Cocker, Dave, *Cocker Hoop: The Biography of Les Cocker, Key Man for Ramsey and Revie* (Worthing: Pitch Publishing, 2022)

English, Tom, *The Grudge Scotland vs England, 1990* (London: Yellow Jersey Press, 2010)

Ferguson, Alex & McIlvanney, Hugh, *Managing my Life: The Autobiography* (London: Hodder & Stoughton, 1999)

Ferguson, Barry & King, Iain, *Blue: The Life and Times of Barry Ferguson* (Edinburgh: Mainstream, 2007)

Ferrier, Bob & McElroy, Robert, *Rangers Player by Player* (London: Hamlyn, 1998)

Finney, Tom, *My Autobiography* (Headline, 2003)

Gallacher, Don & Gallacher, Colin, *Get Off My Pitch* (Self-published, 2022)

Gallacher, Ken, *Slim Jim Baxter: The Definitive Biography* (London: Virgin Books, 2002)

Gardner, James, *Johnny Haynes: Portrait of a Football Genius* (Worthing: Pitch Publishing, 2017)

Gemmell, Tommy, *The Big Shot* (London: Stanley Paul, 1968)

Gemmell, Tommy & McColl, Graham, *Lion Heart* (London: Virgin, 2012)

Gemmill, Archie & Price, Will, *Both Sides of the Border: My Autobiography* (London: Hodder & Stoughton, 2005)

Giller, Norman, *Billy Wright: A Hero for All Seasons* (London: Chrysalis, 2002)

Giller, Norman, *Jimmy Greaves The One and Only* (Worthing: Pitch Publishing, 2022)

Glennie, Jay, *The Making of Trainspotting* (Coattail Publications, 2021)

Gordon, Alex, *Denis Law King and Country* (Edinburgh: Arena, 2013)

Gough, Richard & Gallacher, Ken, *Field of Dreams: My Ibrox Years* (Edinburgh: Mainstream, 1993)

Grant, Michael & Robertson, Rob, *The Management: Scotland's Great Football Bosses* (Edinburgh: Birlinn, 2011)

Greaves, Jimmy & Giller, Norman, *Football's Great Heroes and Entertainers* (London: Hodder Paperbacks, 2008)

Greaves, Jimmy & Giller, Norman, *Greavsie's Greatest* (Christchurch: A1 Sporting Books, 2010)

Hansen, Alan & Tomas, Jason, *A Matter of Opinion* (London: Partridge, 1999)

Harding, John, *Alex James: Life of a Football Legend* (London: Robson Books, 1988)

Hart, Simon, *World In Motion* (Liverpool: deCoubertin Books, 2018)

Hay, Davie & Gordon, Alex, *The Quiet Assassin: The Davie Hay Story* (Edinburgh: Black and White, 2009)

Hayward, Paul, *England Football: The Biography The Story of The Three Lions 1872-2022* (London: Simon & Schuster, 2022)

Herron, Lindsay, *Rangers Hall of Fame* (London: Hachette Scotland, 2009)

Hill, Jimmy, *The Jimmy Hill Story – My Autobiography* (London: Hodder & Stoughton, 1998)

Hutchison, Tommy & Shannon, Kevin, *Hutch Hard Work and Belief* (Worthing: Pitch Publishing, 2022)

Imlach, Gary, *My Father and Other Working-Class Football Heroes* (London: Yellow Jersey, 2006)

Jardine, Sandy & Aitken, Michael, *Score and More: The Sandy Jardine Story* (Edinburgh: Mainstream, 1987)

Joannou, Paul, *Wembley Wizards :The Story of a Legend* (Edinburgh: Mainstream, 1990)

Jones, Ben & Thomas, Gareth, *Football's 50 Most Important Moments* (Worthing: Pitch Publishing, 2020)

Jordan, Joe & Lawton, James, *Behind the Dream: My Autobiography* (London: Hodder and Stoughton, 2004)

Keevins, Hugh, *100 Cups: The Story of the Scottish Cup* (Edinburgh: Mainstream in conjunction with Scottish Brewers, 1985)

Kelly, Graham, *Terrace Heroes: The Life and Times of the 1930s Professional Footballer* (London: Routledge, 2005)

Kuper, Simon (ed.), *Perfect Pitch. 2) Foreign Field* (London: Headline, 1998)

Kuper, Simon, *The Football Men: Up Close with the Giants of the Modern Game* (London: Simon & Schuster, 2011)

Lamming, Douglas, *A Scottish Soccer Internationalists' Who's Who 1872–1986* (Beverley: Hutton, 1987)

Law, Denis & Wheeler, Kenneth, *Living For Kicks* (London: Stanley Paul, 1963)

Law, Denis & Gubba, Ron, *Denis Law: An Autobiography* (London: Queen Anne Press, 1979)

Law, Denis & Bale, Bernard, *The Lawman: An Autobiography* (London: Andre Deutsch Limited, 1999)

Lawther, Steven, *Arrival: How Scotland's Women Took Their Place on the World Stage and Inspired a Generation* (Worthing: Pitch Publishing, 2021)

Lawton, Tommy, *My Twenty Years of Soccer* (Heirloom Modern World Library, 1955)

Lee, Chris, *Origin Stories: The Pioneers Who Took Football to the World* (Worthing: Pitch Publishing, 2021)

Lee, Chris, *The Defiant: A History of Football Against Fascism* (Worthing: Pitch Publishing, 2022)

Leighton, Jim & Robertson, Ken, *In the Firing Line: The Jim Leighton Story* (Edinburgh: Mainstream, 2000)

Leslie, Colin, *Shades: The Short Life and Tragic Death of Erich Schaedler* (Edinburgh: Black and White, 2013)

Liddell, Billy, *My Soccer Story* (London: Stanley Paul, 1960)

Macari, Lou, *Football, My Life* (London: Bantam, 2008)

Macpherson, Archie, *Action Replays* (Chapmans, 1991)

MacLeod, Ally, *The Ally MacLeod Story: An Autobiography* (London: Stanley Paul, 1979)

Maradona, Diego Armando, Arcucci, Daniel & Bialo, Ernesto Cherquis, *Maradona: The Autobiography of Soccer's Greatest and Most Controversial Star* (New York: Skyhorse Pub., 2007)

Matthews, Stanley, *The Stanley Matthews Story* (London: Oldbourne, 1960)

McCoist, Ally & Brankin, Crawford, *Ally McCoist: My Story* (Edinburgh: Mainstream, 1992)

McGarvey, Frank & Esplin, Ronnie, *Totally Frank: My Story* (Edinburgh: Mainstream, 2008)

McKinstry, Leo, *Rosebery: Statesman in Turmoil* (London: John Murray, 2005)

McLintock, Frank & McNeill, Terry, *That's the Way the Ball Bounces* (London: Pelham Books, 1969)

Menary, Steve & Montague, James, *The Away Leg: XI Football Stories From on the Road* (Worthing: Pitch Publishing, 2021)

Mitchell, Andy, *How International Football Started: Scotland v England 1872* (The New Curiosity Shop, 2013)

Morgan, James, *In Search of Alan Gilzean* (Back Page Press, 2010)

Morse, Graham, *Sir Walter Winterbottom: The Father of Modern English Football* (London: John Blake, 2013)

Mortimer, Gavin, *A History of Football in 100 Objects* (London: Serpent's Tail, 2012)

Moynihan, John, *Football Fever* (London: Quartet Books, 1974)

Moynihan, John, *The Soccer Syndrome* (St Albans, Floodlit Dreams Ltd, 2015)

Miller, Willie & Macdonald, Alastair, *The Miller's Tale: An Autobiography* (Edinburgh: Mainstream, 1989)

Miller, Willie & Robertson, Rob, *The Don* (Edinburgh: Birlinn, 2007)

Nicol, Stevie & Donaldson, Mark, *My Autobiography 5 League Titles and a Packet of Crisps* (Liverpool: Trinity Mirror Sports Media, 2016)

Nixon, Alan & Tremayne, Charlie, *Banned!: An Investigation into the SFA and a Look at Scottish Football* (Glasgow: Strathclyde Student Press, 1976)

Pattullo, Alan, *In Search of Duncan Ferguson: The Life and Crimes of a Footballing Enigma* (Edinburgh: Mainstream Publishing, 2014)

Potter, David & Rowan, Marie, *125 Years of Competitive Matches* (Glasgow: Celtic FC Ltd, 2012)

Powell, Jeff, *Bobby Moore: The Life and Times of a Sporting Hero* (London: The Robson, 1993)

Puskás, Ferenc & de Major, Aranka (Trans.), *Captain of Hungary An Autobiography* (Stroud: Stadia, 2007)

Quiniou, Joël & Etcheverry, Gérard, *Libre Arbitre* (France: TFI Editions, 1996)

Rafferty, John, *One Hundred Years of Scottish Football* (London: Pan Books, 1973)

Randi, James, *The Magic of Uri Geller* (New York: Ballantine Books, 1975)

Reilly, Lawrie & Brack, Ted, *The Life and Times of Last Minute Reilly: The Autobiography* (Edinburgh: Black and White, 2010)

Robinson, Richard, *Queen's Park Football Club* (London: George W. May, 1924)

Robson, Bobby & Hayward, Paul, *Farewell but Not Goodbye My Autobiography* (London: Hodder & Stoughton, 2005)

Saffer, David, *Bobby Collins: The Wee Barra* (Stroud: Tempus, 2004)

Seaman, David, *Safe Hands: My Autobiography* (London: Orion, 2000)

Smith, Paul, *Cult Heroes Rangers FC* (Know the Score, 2007)

Sole, David & Douglas, Derek, *Heart and Sole: A Rugby Life* (London: Headline, 1992)

Stead, Phil, *Red Dragons: The Story of Welsh Football* (Talybont: Y Lolfa, 2012)

Strachan, Gordon & Gallacher, Ken, *Strachan Style: A Life in Football* (Edinburgh: Mainstream, 1991)
St John, Ian & Lawton, James, *The Saint My Autobiography* (London: Hodder & Stoughton, 2005)
Sutcliffe, Richard, *Bremner: The Real King Billy* (Ilkley: Great Northern Books, 2011)
Swan, Peter & Johnson, Nick, *Setting the Record Straight* (Stroud: Stadia, 2006)
Taylor, Hugh (ed.), *The Scottish Football Book No. 7* (London: Stanley Paul, 1961)
Ure, Ian, *Ure's Truly* (London: Pelham, 1968)
Ward, Andrew, *Scotland The Team* (Derby: Breedon Books, 1987)
Ward, Andrew & Williams, John, *Football Nation: Sixty Years of the Beautiful Game* (London: Bloomsbury, 2009)
Whitehead, Richard (ed.), *The Times 50 Greatest Football Matches* (Stroud: The History Press, 2019)
Williams, Jean, *The History of Women's Football* (Barnsley: Pen and Sword, 2021)
Wilson, Jonathan, *The Anatomy of England: A History in Ten Matches* (London: Orion, 2010)
Wilson, Jonathan, *The Outsider: A History of the Goalkeeper* (London: Orion Books, 2012)
Wilson, Mike, *Don't Cry For Me Argentina: Scotland's 1978 World Cup Adventure* (Edinburgh: Mainstream, 1998)
Wolstenholme, Kenneth, *The Pro's* (London: Frewin, 1968)
Young, George, *George Young Talks Football* (London: Stanley Paul, 1958)

Newspapers:

Baltimore Sun (USA)
*Bergens Arbeiderblad (*Norway)
Birmingham Daily Post
Birmingham Mail
Boston Globe (USA)
The Californian (USA)
Clydebank Press
Daily Mail
Daily Record

Daily Telegraph
Daily Telegraph and Morning Post
Derby Daily Telegraph
Devizes and Wilts Advertiser
Dundee Evening Telegraph
Edinburgh Evening News
Edmonton Journal (Canada)
Evening Chronicle
Evening Dispatch
Evening Standard
Evening Times
The Football Post
The Guardian
Hartlepool Northern Daily Mail
Hereford Times
Huddersfield Daily Examiner
Hull Daily Mail
The Independent
Ireland's Saturday Night
Lancashire Telegraph
Leicester Evening Mail
Lennox Herald
Miami Herald (USA)
New York Times (USA)
The Observer
The People
North Wales Weekly News
Port Glasgow Express
Scottish Referee
South Wales Echo
Sunday Mercury
Sunday Mirror
Sunday People
Sunday Post
Sunday Sun
Sunday Telegraph
The Sunday Times
Vancouver Sun (Canada)

The Weekly News
Western Mail and South Wales News
Yorkshire Post

Websites:

150.scottishfa.co.uk
90min.com
andrewwatsoncorinthian.co.uk
arabarchive.co.uk
bleacherreport.com
britishnewspaperarchive.co.uk
coachesvoice.com
dundeefc.co.uk
enfa.co.uk
englandfootballonline.com
espn.co.uk
eu-football.info
eurosport.com
fifa.com
footballgroundmap.com
gameofthepeople.com
gmfc.net
golfcompendium.com
gov.uk
hampdencollection.com
hansard.com
heartsfc.co.uk
historyofsoccer.info
ibiblio.org
kenaston.org
latimes.com
ldshymnology.wordpress.com
lfchistory.net
londonhearts.com
macearchive.org
nd.no
newspapers.com
nifootball.blogspot.com

nrscotland.gov.uk
playupliverpool.com
prabook.com
premierleague.com
queensparkfc.com
rsssf.org
scottishleague.net/forum
scottishsporthistory.com
theathletic.com
thenationalnews.com
thesefootballtimes.co
thisdayinbaseball.com
timeandtidewatches.com
tv2.no
http://s164210041.websitehome.co.uk/wsb4048253801/projects_labnotation.html

YouTube:

https://www.youtube.com/watch?v=2nRzAzonBjs
https://www.youtube.com/watch?v=OyQUI79WSW4
https://www.youtube.com/watch?v=HGLrfSn4dvc
https://www.youtube.com/watch?v=wWIyi3IMu-0
https://www.youtube.com/watch?v=7bmyb7I3oHA

Periodicals:

Nutmeg
When Saturday Comes
The Blizzard
The Celtic View
The Stage
The Economist
Match Weekly
Charles Buchan's Football Monthly
Scottish Football Today
Goal
Shoot!
FourFourTwo
Scottish Football Association minute books

Match programmes:

Scotland vs England, 27 May 1972
Scotland Under-23s vs Netherlands Under-23s, 24 March 1976
Scotland vs England, 15 May 1976
Scotland vs Czechoslovakia, 21 September 1977
Wales vs Scotland, 12 October 1977
Scotland vs Argentina, 2 June 1979
Scotland vs Austria, 17 October 1979
Scotland vs Belgium, 19 December 1979
Scotland vs Northern Ireland, 25 March 1981
England vs Scotland, 23 May 1981
Scotland vs England, 29 May 1982
Scotland vs Brazil, 26 May 1987
Scotland vs Hungary, 9 September 1987
Scotland vs Colombia, 17 May 1988
England vs Scotland, 21 May 1988
Scotland vs England, 27 May 1989
Scotland vs England (rugby union), 17 March 1990
Scotland vs German Democratic Republic, 25 April 1990
Scotland vs Romania, 12 September 1990
Scotland vs Bulgaria, 27 March 1991
Scotland vs England, 13 November 1999
Scotland vs Czech Republic, 3 September 2011
Scotland vs Macedonia, 11 September 2012
Unidentified Morton FC programme

Film and television:

Jimmy Johnstone: Lord of the Wing (Jamie Doran, 2004)
Only a Game? (BBC, 1986)
Faith, Hope and Calamity (STV, 1994)
Clash of the Titans (BBC, 1996)
Arena: The Football Men (BBC, 1997)
Are You Watching Jimmy Hill? (BBC,1998)
Andrew Watson – Scotland's Lost Captain (BBC, 2003)
The Lost Final (BBC Scotland, 2022)
Billy Connolly Does… (UKTV, 2023)

Radio:

Witness: Flower of Scotland (BBC World Service, 2014)

Podcasts:

Brazilian Shirt Name
The Blizzard – Greatest Games
The High Performance Podcast
Shoot! The Breeze
The 42's Behind the Lines
Fergie Time with Barry Ferguson and Keith Jackson

NOTE: Chapters 44 (England 2 Scotland 3 – 1967) and 68 (The Death of Jock Stein – 1985) are both constructed from quotes found in sources listed in the bibliography.